W9-BII-690

HOW THE CHINESE ECONOMY WORKS

Published titles include:

Shangquan Gao
CHINA'S ECONOMIC REFORM

Xiaoping Xu
CHINA'S FINANCIAL SYSTEM UNDER TRANSITION

Malcolm Warner
THE MANAGEMENT OF HUMAN RESOURCES IN CHINESE
INDUSTRY

Tim Wright (*editor*)
THE CHINESE ECONOMY IN THE EARLY TWENTIETH CENTURY

Yanrui Wu
PRODUCTIVE PERFORMANCE OF CHINESE ENTERPRISES

Haiqun Yang
BANKING AND FINANCIAL CONTROL IN REFORMING PLANNED
ECONOMIES

Shujie Yao
AGRICULTURAL REFORMS AND GRAIN PRODUCTION IN CHINA

Xun-Hai Zhang
ENTERPRISE REFORMS IN A CENTRALLY PLANNED ECONOMY

Ng Sek Hong and Malcolm Warner
CHINA'S TRADE UNIONS AND MANAGEMENT

Studies on the Chinese Economy
Series Standing Order ISBN 0–333–71502–0
(*outside North America only*)

You can receive future titles in this series as they are published by placing a standing order.
Please contact your bookseller or, in case of difficulty, write to us at the address below with
your name and address, the title of the series and the ISBN quoted above.

Customer Services Department, Macmillan Distribution Ltd
Houndmills, Basingstoke, Hampshire RG21 6XS, England

How the Chinese Economy Works

A Multiregional Overview

Rongxing Guo

First published in Great Britain 1999 by
MACMILLAN PRESS LTD
Houndmills, Basingstoke, Hampshire RG21 6XS and London
Companies and representatives throughout the world

A catalogue record for this book is available from the British Library.

ISBN 0–333–72993–5

First published in the United States of America 1999 by
ST. MARTIN'S PRESS, INC.,
Scholarly and Reference Division,
175 Fifth Avenue, New York, N.Y. 10010

ISBN 0–312–21570–3

Library of Congress Cataloging-in-Publication Data
Guo, Rongxing.
How the Chinese economy works : a multiregional overview /
Rongxing Guo.
p.   cm.
Includes bibliographical references and index.
ISBN 0–312–21570–3 (cloth)
1. China—Economic conditions.   2. China—Economic policy—1976–
I. Title.
HC427.92.G86   1998
330.951—DC21   98–17296
                                                          CIP

This book is printed on paper suitable for recycling and made from fully managed and
sustained forest sources.

10   9   8   7   6   5   4   3   2
08   07   06   05   04   03   02   01   00

Printed and bound in Great Britain by
Antony Rowe Ltd, Chippenham, Wiltshire

Contents

List of Tables

List of Figures

Preface

Features of this book

The book is intended to provide information and explanations of the operational mechanisms of the Chinese economy through the multiregional and dynamic dimensions. Brief comparisons with both developed and developing economies are also intended to enhance the understanding of the Chinese economy. A full set of time-series data on the Chinese economy has been collected and reconstructed, where appropriate, so that the multiregional economic comparison has been possible. The statistical information for Taiwan, Hong Kong, Macau and Mainland China is also provided for those concerned with the greater China area. A box is attached to each chapter. These are hoped to extend readers' knowledge of Chinese economics. Except for a few of sections, this book is not technically complicated. Therefore, I hope that it will be read widely, as an introduction, by researchers as well as ordinary students who want to acquire some general knowledge about the Chinese economy.

Acknowledgments

Although the plan of writing a book on the Chinese economy was attempted earlier, the first decision for me to prepare this book was mainly initiated by the DAAD-funded academic program in which I was invited to lecture at University of Trier during October 1997 and March 1998.

Many institutions and individuals have helped me with the manuscript. During the first period of writing, many valuable comments and suggestions on different versions of the draft had been received from Mr Zhao Renwei (Professor of CASS) and Dr Eui-Gak Hwang (Professor of Korea University) to whom I am very grateful. During my visit to Germany, I benefited from many discussions with Professor Thomas Heberer who also kindly arranged my stay at Trier. The grants from the National Science Foundation of China (NSFC) make it possible for me conduct a series of field inspections in China and collect some specific regional data, both of which contributed to the writing of some chapters. I also appreciate the PRC Ministry of Coal Industry for its awarding me as a Cross-Century

Academic Leader which makes it possible for me to independently conduct without financial problems economic researches in China. During my stay at the University of Trier, the Department of Political Science and Department of Chinese Studies also provided necessary office facilities with which I was able to finalize this manuscript.

Among the Macmillan staff contributing to the publication of this book, Mr T. M. Farmiloe (Publishing Director) kept in regular communications with me when the draft was prepared; Mr Sunder Katwala (Editor) suggested to me many valuable ideas in relation to the titles as well as the structural improvement of the book. I am especially grateful to Mr Mervyn Thomas of Linda Auld Associates who helped me to correct and polish many parts of the previous draft. Nevertheless, the remaining errors in this book are the author's sole responsibilities.

Last but not the least, I would like to express my thanks to my wife, who also joins me in expressing gratitude to my parents and parents-in-law for their contributions to my life.

Guo Rongxing
St. Annastr. 108, Trier
January 1998

Abbreviations

CCP	Chinese Communist Party
CCPCC	Chinese Communist Party Central Committee
COEs	collectively-owned enterprises
CPE	centrally planned economy
FCAD	first-class administrative division
FDI	foreign direct investment
FYP	five-year plan
GCR	Great Cultural Revolution
GDP	gross domestic product
GLF	Great Leap Forward
GNP	gross national product
GVAO	gross value of agricultural output
GVIAO	gross value of industrial and agricultural output
GVIO	gross value of industrial output
GVSP	gross value of social product
HRS	household responsibility system
IOEs	individually owned enterprises
MPS	material product system
NI	national income
NIEs	newly industrialized economies
NMP	net material product
NPC	National People's Congress
OOEs	other ownership enterprises, mainly comprising joint-ventures and wholly foreign-owned enterprises
PCS	people's commune system
PPP	purchasing power parity
PRC	People' Republic of China
SAR	special administrative region
SETC	State Economic and Trade Commission
SEZ	special economic zone
SNA	system of national accounts
SOEs	state-owned enterprises
SPC	State Planning Commission
SSB	State Statistical Bureau
TVEs	township and village enterprises

Notes from the Author

1. Unless stated otherwise, we have implied in this research that the geographical scope covers only mainland China and that the statistical data used in this book are from *China Statistical Yearbooks* (all issues) published annually by the State Statistical Bureau of P. R. China.

2. The time domain of this research is mainly fixed for the years from 1949 to 1995, with some exceptions when an analysis of the pre-1949 period is needed.

3. Since 1949, with the changes in general price level, the State Statistical Bureau has nationally unified constant prices five times: the 1952 constant prices for 1949–57, the 1957 constant prices for 1958–70, the 1970 constant prices for 1971–81, the 1980 constant prices for 1981–90, and the 1990 constant prices for 1991–present.

4. The Chinese currency is renminbi (RMB), The official exchange rates of RMB yuan to US dollar during 1981–95 are shown below:

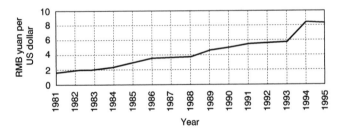

5. Chinese names are customarily written in the order of family name (which is in the single syllable in most cases) followed by given name, while the Western style is usually applied by the Taiwan, Hong Kong and other overseas Chinese.

6. Chinese names and geographical terms in mainland China are written in China's official (*pinyin*) form, while those outside mainland China are in the conventional form.

7. Hainan had been administratively included in Guangdong province before it was established as a new province in 1988.

8. The regional percentages in the tables may not add up to 100 due to rounding errors.

Introduction

China, 'the sleeping giant in Asia' as Napoleon once referred to it, has experienced a series of political, social, and economic transformations since the early twentieth century.[1] During the past century, China's economic development had been interrupted time and again. Nevertheless, in recent decades, the 'sleeping giant' did eventually wake. The Chinese economy was nearly bankrupted at the end of the Civil War in the late 1940s, and seriously damaged in the GLF (1958–60) and GCR (1966–76) movements. However, since the late 1970s when the Chinese government began the gradual transformation of its Stalinesque centrally planned system, the Chinese economy has grown with exceptional rapidity: it has achieved an average GNP annual growth rate of about 10 per cent since the early 1980s (which is among the highest in the world during the same period). Per capita personal consumption in 1978 was 184 yuan, having increased slowly from 76 yuan in 1952. In 1995, it dramatically increased to 2311 yuan which is 30.41 times and 12.56 times of that in 1952 and 1978 respectively.[2]

There have been even more encouraging reports on the Chinese economy. For example, World Bank (1992) issues a range of evidence for why China looks set to become the world's largest economy by the year 2010 and that the Chinese economic area (including mainland China, Taiwan, Hong Kong, Macau, and other Chinese alien areas in Southeast Asia) has been one of the world's 'growth poles'.[3] G. Segal (1994, p. 44) notes that the current figures on Chinese GDP might have been misleading because they do not take into account real PPP rates. According to M. Noland (1994), the Chinese economy is already the second-largest in the world if it is measured by PPP rates instead of standard international prices.[4] What is more important, however, is the trend *per se*, rather than any specific figure. Table I.1 gives more substantial evidence showing that China is approaching the position of number one materials producer in the world.

China has achieved vigorous economic growth since the implementation of market-oriented reform in the late 1970s. The remarkable performance has been accompanied and facilitated by, *inter alia*, historic, geographic, social and cultural factors. Up to now,

1

Table I.1 China's production position in the world, selected years, 1980–95

Item	1980	1985	1990	1995
Grain (10^6 ton)	283.9 (1)	342.6 (2)	398.4 (1)	465.0 (1)
Cotton (10^3 ton)	2710 (1)	4150 (1)	4150 (1)	4500 (1)
Fruits (10^6 ton)	6.8 (8)	11.6 (7)	18.7 (4)	41.9 (1)
Meat (10^6 ton)	12.1 (2)	19.3 (2)	28.6 (2)	50.0 (1)
Aquatic product (10^6 ton)	4.5 (3)	7.1 (3)	12.4 (1)	25.4 (1)
Steel (10^6 ton)	37.1 (5)	46.8 (4)	66.4 (4)	95.4 (1)
Coal (10^6 ton)	62.0 (3)	87.2 (1)	108.0 (1)	124.0 (1)
Oil (10^6 ton)	10.6 (6)	12.5 (5)	13.8 (4)	15.0 (5)
Electricity (10^9 kWh)	30.1 (6)	41.1 (4)	62.1 (4)	100.8 (2)
Cement (10^6 ton)	49.9 (3)	146.0 (1)	209.7 (1)	475.9 (1)
Chemical fertilizer (10^6 ton)	12.3 (3)	13.22 (3)	18.8 (3)	25.6 (1)
Chemical fibres (10^6 ton)	0.45 (6)	0.95 (5)	1.65 (3)	3.50 (1)
TV sets (10^6)	2.49 (7)	16.68 (3)	26.85 (1)	34.96 (1)
Refrigerators (10^3)	50 (–)	1450 (9)	4630 (4)	9185 (1)
Washing machines (10^3)	50 (–)	8870 (1)	6630 (1)	9525 (1)

Note: figures in parentheses are ranks in the word's independent nations.
Sources: (1) *Industrial Statistical Yearbook* and *Monthly Statistics* (UN, various issues); (2) *Statistical Yearbook* (UNFAO, various issues).

the Chinese model has been generally known as the most successful one among former Soviet-type economies according to the measure of economic performance.

However, it should also be noted that China still lags far behind many marketized and industrialized economies. It is only the huge population that causes the Chinese economy to rank at the bottom of the world's economies by the per capita measure. The per capita GNP of China in the early 1990s was only 1 to 2 per cent that of USA, approximately that of South Korea in the early 1970s and that of Japan in the early 1900s respectively.[5]

While China's over-centralized planning system was mainly responsible for those poor socioeconomic performances, there were also historical, social and cultural factors that hindered its socioeconomic development. Indeed, it is not easy to develop a market-system framework within a short period of time in China – a country utilizing the centrally planned system for nearly 30 years and that was, in particular, deeply influenced by long periods of feudalism but rarely by economic democracy. The most problematic phenomenon stems to some extent from a recurring pattern of reform and retrenchment identified by a four-stage cycle: 'decentralization immediately followed by disorder, disorder immediately followed by concentralization, concentralization followed by rigidity, and rigidity followed by decentralization, a cycle of 'decentralization (*fang*) – disorder – concentralization (*shou*) – rigidity'.[6] In his ambitious book entitled *Burying Mao – Chinese Politics in the Age of Deng Xiaoping*, R. Baum (1994, pp. 5–9, 369–76) offers a plausible explanation for the *fang–shou* cycle of Chinese economic reform during 1978–93. According to this explanation the decentralization (*fang*) policy was concentrated on 1978, 1980, 1982, 1984, 1986, 1988, and 1992; while the concentralization (*shou*) policy was concentrated on 1979, 1981, 1983, 1985, 1987, 1989, and 1993.[7]

One of the key initiatives of China's economic reform that started in the late 1970s was the promotion of decentralization in economic operations, that is, transferring economic management and decision-making from central government to provincial and local governments. For example, retail trade which used to be under the control of local government is now determined by collectively and individually owned enterprises. Decentralization and the introduction of market forces together imply that the centres of economic power are moving away from central government to the localities. Since the advent of administrative decentralization, China's national economy had become effectively 'cellularized' into a plethora of semi-autarkic regional enclaves. In order to protect local market and revenue sources, it has become very common in China for provinces to restrict import (export) from (to) other provinces by levying high, if informal, taxes on commodities whose production is seen as important to the province's 'domestic' economy, and also by creating non-tariff barriers. In some provinces, local authorities established, and provided finance for, a variety of schemes that promoted the sales of local products. Enterprises from other provinces, however, often have difficulties in finding office spaces, accommodation or land for their business activities. These protectionist measures, which were often in violation of central directives, were enforced through a patchwork system of roadblocks, cargo seizures, *ad hoc* taxes, commercial surcharges and licensing fees, and in a number of well-publicized cases, illegal highway robberies. Moreover, this competition between provinces could be fierce in the 'battlegrounds' of their border areas, and result in numerous tales of 'trade embargoes' or 'commodity wars' between provinces.[8]

The experiences and lessons from both developed and developing countries during the post World War II period have demonstrated that the success of a nation in promoting its economic development depends to a large extent on a complete legal system and effective management and supervision mechanisms of its own. China's efforts to this end have achieved some progress, but some large-scale changes are still needed. In fact, the 'commodity wars' between provinces and autonomous regions derived from the fact that China does not have any constitutional clauses which specifically prohibit constraints against inter-provincial commerce, even though the central government has been increasingly concerned and many regulations and laws relating to the protection of multiregional cooperation and the removal of local economic blockades have been issued by the State Council (1980a, 1982, 1986 and 1990) and the NPC (1993).

There is no doubt that a well-educated and law-abiding population is an indispensable precondition for China's economic development. The existence of an élite group capable of managing the nation's policies, government and economy is exceptionally important in the transition period. Unfortunately, the Chinese economy is typically characterized by the fact that about 15 per cent of employees have been illiterate or semi-literate and that only about 5 per cent employees in the CCP and government agencies and social organizations have received university level education.[9] Even worse, a few government functionaries are believed to be disqualified in terms of either professional knowledge or occupational ethics. If this governmental illness is not cured properly in China, it will affect seriously the socioeconomic development.[10]

Many provinces, autonomous regions, and municipalities directly under the central government[11] have been informally demarcated in China. As a result, cross-border relations between the relevant FCADs have never been easily coordinated and, sometimes, could become a destabilizing source for social stability and economic development, even though the regulations concerning the resolution of the border disputes have been issued and revised by the State Council (1981 and 1988a). Moreover, there is another geographical characteristic in the Chinese economy: many FCADs' borders are naturally marked by mountains, rivers, and lakes which bless the border regions with abundant natural and environmental resources. Given the cross-border imbroglios between the FCADs, the sustainable exploitation and utilization of natural resources (such as energy, metals, forests, fishery, and so on) as well as environmental protection in the border regions will undoubtedly pose problems and disputes for both central and local governments in China.

Since its People's Republic was founded in 1949, China has achieved a rapid industrial expansion as well as a substantial improvement in the ordinary people's standard of living. However, it has also generated several environmental problems and reduced the non-renewable natural resources. China's agricultural policies have resulted in serious problems of soil erosion, desertification, degradation of fragile ecosystems and loss of biological diversity, and so on. Furthermore, quantities of CO_2, SO_2, NO_x, CH_4, CFCs, and other hazardous waste and toxic materials have dramatically increased as a result of the rapid industrial growth in China. Today air, water and noise pollution, together with the unprocessed refuse are seriously affecting Chinese society. Some evidence suggests that China would become the number one gross national pollutant (gnp) producer before it achieves the largest GNP in the twenty-first century.[12]

In sum, China's current situation poses many crucial challenges to the Chinese reform circle. Many inherent problems in relation to economic development persist. If the Chinese government does not address them properly, its efforts, based on the Chinese-style *laissez-faire* reform, inevitably would be jeopardized.

It should be noted that we are not able to deal with all the issues critical to the Chinese economy. Rather, the main objective of this book is to offer a multiregional analysis of the Chinese economy, providing insights into national and regional economic trends. Against the heterogeneous natural and social conditions, China had uneasily followed a road of autarkic and egalitarian socialism for a long time before economic reform and open-door policies were implemented in the late 1970s. Since then, the Chinese economy has demonstrated an increasing asymmetry between different regions and resulted in a series of regional economic problems which need to be addressed properly by policy makers. The book is composed of eight chapters, which are organized as follows.

Chapter 1 presents a regional topology for the Chinese economy. After having reviewed the historical evolution of China's administrative divisions and the recent literature on Chinese economic regionalization, we outline five topological aspects through which the multiregional analysis of the Chinese economy will be conducted in the following chapters.

Chapter 2 serves to analyse the most important elements for economic development. Natural and human resources are unevenly distributed across China. In short, population and labour force densities are much greater in the eastern belt than in the western belt. The northern part is much richer in deposits of mineral resources than the southern part, except for a few deposits of non-ferrous metals, while, in contrast, the southern part has an advantage for agricultural production and, in particular, dominates most of the nation's rice production. One of the most important implications in Section 2.1 is that the unevenly distributed and coal-dominated energy structure is now the major obstacle to Chinese industrialization and sustainable development. The most noticeable result derived from Section 2.3 reveals that China's education which is irregularly attained among regions is not closely related to its economic development during the reform period.

According to the new institutional economics, system, like other production factors required in economic development, is a special kind of scarce resource and should thus be treated properly in economics. The Chinese government has clearly recognized this point and tried to gradually reform its over-centralized and poorly performing economic system. Since the late 1970s, administrative decentralization and disproportionate economic reforms have been implemented in China, resulting in different regional economic performances. After reviewing the economic reform policy, Chapter 3 compares the Chinese multiregional economic system. More detail will be provided for the analysis of the functional evolution of economic planning, production management, public finance and investment. In addition, we will discuss the differing regional economic performances generated in the transition period.

In Chapter 4, the Chinese economy is compared multiregionally. As mentioned in the previous chapters, most of resources are unevenly distributed in China, resulting in great economic differences between regions. Due to the application of different statistical systems in the pre- and post-reform periods as well as the unavailability of statistical data in some FCADs, a complete multiregional comparison of the Chinese economy is extremely difficult and, to some extent, meaningless. Using the best data and the regression approach, Section 4.2 tries to estimate a set of time-series data on GDP for all FCADs, on which the multiregional economic comparison conducted is based. In Section 4.3, some efforts of consistent economic comparison will be attempted based on the indices of real living standards. Finally, in Section 4.4, the regional inequalities are computed for the years from 1952 to 1995. Not surprisingly, China's economic reform and open-door policies have for the past decades disproportionally aided the coastal FCADs where per capita GDPs are several times higher than in the poor inland FCADs. If this pattern of regional development were to persist, income levels at the end of the 1990s in the coastal area would be similar to – while, in contrast, in the inland area considerably lower than – those currently observed in Southeast Asia.

Despite its long history of civilization, China has lagged far behind the advanced nations in industrial modernization. Generally, the poor industrial performances had to large extent been ascribed to the Chinese socialist construction of 'self-reliance and independence' and the irrational industrial structure in which heavy industry was given priority. In order to make a multiregional comparison of the industrial productivity, we modify the Cobb-Douglas production function based on the data of 500 top enterprises in Section 5.3. The estimated production function suggests that resource-exploiting enterprises have the highest capital productivity in the western belt and that high-technology enterprises have the highest labour productivity in the eastern belt. Section 5.4 discusses Chinese rural industrialization in which the TVEs have played an important role. Finally, Chinese technological progress is reviewed briefly in Section 5.5.

Chapter 6 studies the possibilities and conditions for spatial economic optimization in China. Despite the mutually complementary conditions between different regions, the Chinese economy has been internally affected by the geographical, institutional, and cultural barriers between FCADs. Using five necessary assumptions and then a mathematical model we quantitatively find that the nation's economic optimization has been largely reduced due to the spatial separations in China. As a practical measure to overcome the interregional barriers and to provide a 'bridge' for spatial economic integration, China has established different forms and levels of multiregional economic cooperative zones since the early 1980s. The particular focus of the last part of this chapter will examine briefly the organization and performance of the multiregional economic cooperative zones.

Chapter 7 deals with economic internationalization. The Chinese economy has been transforming from the autarkic to an outward-oriented pattern. The open-door policy was first implemented in the coastal area in the early 1980s, resulting in a rapid economic growth for China and the eastern belt in particular. In the early 1990s, China embarked on another outward-looking policy to promote the cross-border trade and economic development of the inland frontier area. China's efforts on economic internationalization have greatly benefited every sphere of Chinese life. The Chinese government has attempted to adjust further its economic policies so as to meet gradually the needs of the multilateral trading system. By the time China joins in the World Trade Organization (WTO), it is certain that the Chinese economy will become freer and more internationalized.

Finally, Chapter 8 performs extensive analysis of the Chinese economy through a larger geographical scope. Despite their common history and cultural and linguistic homogeneity, the great China area (including Taiwan, Hong Kong, Macau and mainland China) has followed during the past decades divergent political and economic systems, from which different social and economic performances have resulted. Along with mainland China's economic reform and the return of Hong Kong and Macau, from the British and Portuguese governments, to China in 1997 and 1999 respectively, the economic ties between the three parts as a single sovereign nation undoubtedly will be accelerated under the principle of 'one country, two systems' in the twenty-first century. The two sides of the Taiwan strait, however, have been politically separated for almost fifty years due to the mutual distrust and hostile strategies arising from the bloody conflict between the Nationalists and the Communists at the end of World War II. With the Cold War coming to an end and the surging tide of global participation in economic development, more and more Chinese believe that the cross-strait trade and economic cooperation must be *directly* conducted by the two sides, before the national reunification eventually becomes a possibility. Nevertheless, the creation of political harmony and reunification between Taiwan and the mainland may still require both more time and more patience from both parties.

The Chinese economy has experienced drastic changes and a faster development than many other transitional CPEs during the past years. This is certainly determined by both the internal and the external environments. Heading toward the twenty-first century, it can still be seen that China is scheduled to develop its economy according to its own characteristics. But the Chinese government should have a more cautious bearing on this matter. More than two thousand years ago, Confucius (551–475 BC) taught his pupils with the autobiographical story:

I began to study when I was 15 years old and to solely bear responsibilities when I was 30. I was no longer confused at the age of 40 years and knew the futurities when I was 50. I did things better when I was 60. Lastly, at the age of 70 years, I was able to freely do what I wanted while not breaking the laws.[13]

Hopefully, with the approach of the fiftieth year of socialistic construction, the PRC will perhaps have got out of the confused age and know where to go and what to do next, both economically and politically.

1 The Spatial Division of the Chinese Economy

Originally proliferated by Tao,
One gives birth to Two in opposition.
The Two begets Three in triangle under which
everything in the world is ready to be created.
　　　　　　　　Laozi, the founder of Taoism

When referring to the Chinese economy, at least two important points must be noted: first, China's vast territorial size and wide diversity in physical environments and natural resource endowments have inevitably resulted in great regional economic differences; second, with China's population of more than 1.2 billion and 56 nationalities being geographically divided by 30 FCADs, each FCAD is equivalent to a medium-sized country in the rest of the world. In short, the Chinese economy is one of the most complicated and diversified spatial systems that can be found in the world. The only feasible approach one may apply is, therefore, to divide it into smaller geographical elements through which one can have a better insight into the spatial mechanisms and regional characteristics. Usually, the method of regionalization of the Chinese economy may be different depending upon the analytical purposes. In this chapter, we will divide the Chinese economy into (1) administrative divisions, (2) great regions, (3) coastal and inland areas, (4) geographical belts, and (5) southern and northern parts.

1.1 ADMINISTRATIVE DIVISIONS

China had 12 dependent states (*zhou*) in Yao and Shun periods (about 4,000 years ago).[1] Since then, China's FCADs have been named as, *inter alia*, *jun* in Qin dynasty (221–206 BC), *junguo* in Han dynasty (206 BC–220 AD), *zhou* in Wei (220–265 AD), Jin (266–420 AD), and North and South (420–589 AD) dynasties, *dao* in Tang dynasty (618–907 AD), *lu* in North and South Song (960–1279 AD)

10

and Jin (1115–1235 AD) dynasties, *zhongshu-xingsheng* in Yuan dynasty (1279 1368 AD), *xingsheng*[2] in Ming (1368–1644 AD) and Qing (1644–1911 AD) dynasties, and so on.[3] While the formation of most FCADs had taken place far before the PRC was founded, a few others were either incorporated with their neighbouring FCADs or divided into new FCADs during the past decades. In addition, some sub-areas have been administratively transposed between the neighboring FCADs. In this book, unless stated otherwise, we assume that China's FCADs include 22 provinces (*sheng*), five autonomous regions (*zizhiqu*), and three municipalities directly under the central government (*zhixiashi*), as shown in Table 1.1.

It should be noted that, in China, the three kinds of FCADs (*sheng*, *zizhiqu*, and *zhixiashi*) have different functions from each other. For example, some top *zhixiashi* leaders have been appointed as members of the Political Bureau of the CCPCC,[4] while very few *sheng* and *zizhiqu* leaders have. The autonomous regions (*zizhiqu*) are only established in areas where the ethnic minorities consist of the major portion of population. As a result of the cultural differences between the non-Han ethnic minorities and the Han majority, the *zizhiqu* is, at least in form, the most politically and socially autonomous among the three kinds of FCADs. Furthermore, all FCADs are independent from each other in designing local fiscal, tax, labour, and trade policies, and economic development plans which have, *ceteris paribus*, resulted in differing regional economic performances in China.

1.2 GREAT REGIONS

When the People's Republic was founded on 1 October 1949, the Chinese economy was managed through six great administrative regions (i.e., North, Northeast, East, Central South, Southwest and Northwest regions). Except for the North region, which was under the administration of the central government, the other five great regions also had their own governmental bodies in charge of agriculture and forestry, industry, public finance, trade, and so on. In 1954, the six great administrative regions were abolished and, before they were re-organized in 1961, seven cooperative commissions were established in North, Northeast, East, Central, South, Southwest and Northwest regions respectively in 1958. The six great regional administrations were destroyed by the 'Red Guards' during

12 How the Chinese Economy Works

Table 1.1 The political and social conditions for the FCADs, end of 1995

FCAD	Political form	Major ethnic groups[a]	Predominant languages
Anhui (Anhwei)	S	Han, Hui, She	MD
Beijing (Peking)	ZXS	Han, Hui, Man	MD
Fujian (Fukien)	S	Han, She, Hui	MI
Gansu (Kansu)	S	Han, Hui, Tibetan	MD, MG
Guangdong (Kwangtung)	S	Han, Yao, Zhuang	CT, MY
Guangxi (Kwangsi)	ZZQ	Zhuang, Han, Yao	CD, TA
Guizhou (Kweichow)	S	Han, Miao, Buyi	CD, TA
Hainan	S	Han, Li, Miao	CT, TA
Hebei (Hopeh)	S	Han, Hui, Man	MD
Heilongjiang (Heilungkiang)	S	Han, Man, Korean	MD
Henan (Honan)	S	Han, Hui, Mongol	MD
Hubei (Hupeh)	S	Han, Tujia, Hui	CD
Hunan	S	Han, Tujia, Miao	CD, MY
Inner Mongolia	ZZQ	Mongol, Han	MG, MD
Jiangsu (Kiangsu)	S	Han, Hui, Man	CD, WU
Jiangxi (Kiangsi)	S	Han, Hui, Miao	CD
Jilin (Kirin)	S	Han, Korean, Man	MD
Liaoning	S	Han, Man, Mongol	MD
Ningxia (Ningsia)	ZZQ	Hui, Han, Man	MD, MG
Qinghai (Tsinghai)	S	Han, Tibetan, Hui	TB, MG
Shaanxi (Shensi)	S	Han, Hui, Man	MD
Shandong (Shantung)	S	Han, Hui, Man	MD
Shanghai	ZXS	Han	WU
Shanxi (Shansi)	S	Han, Hui, Mongol	MD
Sichuan (Szechwan)	S	Han, Yi, Tibetan	MD, TB
Tianjin (Tientsin)	ZXS	Han, Hui, Korean	MD
Tibet	ZZQ	Tibetan, Han, Menba	TB
Xinjiang (Sinkiang)	ZZQ	Uighur, Han, Kazak	TK, MD
Yunnan (Yunnan)	S	Han, Yi, Bai	MD, TB
Zhejiang (Chekiang)	S	Han, She, Hui	CD

[a] SSB (1996, p. 56).
Notes: (1) S (sheng) = province, ZZQ (zizhiqu) = autonomous region, ZXS (zhixiashi) = municipality directly under the central government; (2) MD = Mandarin, CD = Chinese dialects, CT = Cantonese, TB = Tibetan, MY = Miao-Yao, MG = Mongolian, TK = Turkish dialects, KM = Khmer, TG = Tungus, WU = Wu, TA = Thai, MI = Min; (3) names given in parentheses are in the conventional form.

the GCR period (1966–76). In 1970, the Chinese economy was spatially organized via ten economic cooperative zones (that is, Southwest, Northwest, Centre, South, East, Northeast, North, Shandong, Fujian and Jiangxi, and Xinjiang zones). It is generally believed that this arrangement was based on the centrally planned system and reflected the state's efforts to meet the desperate need for regional self-sufficiency in the high tide of the Cold War era.[5]

Guided by the State Council (1980b), six economic zones were organized in Northeast, North, East, Central South, Southwest and Northwest regions respectively during 1981–85. Notice that Shandong was excluded from the six economic zones; Guangxi was included in both Central South and Southwest economic zones; and eastern Inner Mongolia was included in both North and Northeast economic zones. In 1992 when the Chinese government decided to build up a market-oriented economy, the SPC was authorized to map out plans for the development of the Yangtze River drainage, around the Bohai bay, Southeast coastal, Northeast, Southwest, Central, and Northwest economic regions.[6]

Besides the above definitions, regional scientists and economic geographers have also defined Chinese great regions, with differing numbers and geographical scope, for their own purposes. The following are some examples in which six, seven and ten great regions have been used to divide the Chinese economy respectively.

Six Great Regions

T. Wright (1984, p. 78) roughly divides the Chinese economy into Northeast, North, Northwest, Central East, West and Southwest, and Southeast regions. As an economic geographer, X. Hu (1993, pp. 193–203) defines Northeast region (Liaoning, Jilin and Heilongjiang), North region (Beijing, Tianjin, Hebei, Shanxi, Inner Mongolia, Shandong and Henan), Northwest region (Shaanxi, Gansu, Qinghai, Ningxia and Xinjiang), East Middle region (Shanghai, Jiangsu, Zhejiang, Anhui, Jiangxi, Hubei and Hunan), South region (Guangdong, Fujian, Guangxi and Hainan), and Southwest region (Sichuan, Guizhou, Yunnan and Tibet). Based on the transprovincial commodity flows via the central rail network, K. Yang (1993, p. 270) groups the FCADs into Northeast region (Liaoning, Jilin, Heilongjiang and eastern Inner Mongolia), North region (Beijing, Tianjin, Hebei, central Inner Mongolia, and northeastern, northern and eastern Shandong), Central East region (Shanghai, Jiangsu,

Zhejiang, Anhui, Jiangxi (excluding southern area), Henan, northern Hubei, southern and southwestern Shandong, and Hunan (excluding southwestern area)), South region (Guangdong, Guangxi, Hainan, Fujian, southern Jiangxi, and southern and central Hunan), West region (Shaanxi, Gansu, Qinghai, Ningxia, Xinjiang and Tibet), and Southwest region (Yunnan, Guizhou, Sichuan and southwestern Hubei). In addition, based on the interregional division of labour, Z. Liu (1994, pp. 36–7) frames Northeast region (Liaoning, Jilin, Heilongjiang and eastern Inner Mongolia), North region (Beijing, Tianjin, Hebei, Shanxi, western Inner Mongolia, Shandong, and Henan), Central region (Shanghai, Jiangsu, Zhejiang, Anhui, Jiangxi, Hubei and Hunan), Southeast region (Fujian, Guangdong, Guangxi and Hainan), Southwest region (Sichuan, Yunnan, Guizhou and Tibet), and Northwest region (Shaanxi, Gansu, Qinghai, Ningxia, and Xinjiang).

Seven Great Regions

Using the input–output table developed by the SSB, Li *et al.* (1994, pp. 139–65) analyse the mutually complementary conditions and industrial interdependence between Northeast region (Liaoning, Jilin and Heilongjiang), North region (Beijing, Tianjin, Hebei, Shandong and Inner Mongolia), South region (Fujian, Guangdong and Hainan), Central region (Shanxi, Henan, Anhui, Hubei, Hunan and Jiangxi), Northwest region (Shaanxi, Qinghai, Gansu, Ningxia and Xinjiang), Southwest region (Sichuan, Guizhou, Yunnan, Guangxi and Tibet), and East region (Shanghai, Jiangsu and Zhejiang). In addition, when estimating the Chinese economic disparities, A. Keidel (1995) uses Far Western region (Xinjiang, Tibet, Qinghai, Gansu and Ningxia), Northern Inland region (Heilongjiang, Jilin, Inner Mongolia, Shaanxi and Shanxi), Southern Inland region (Sichuan, Guizhou, Yunnan and Guangxi), Central region (Henan, Anhui, Jiangxi, Hubei and Hunan), Northern Coastal region (Liaoning, Hebei, Beijing, Tianjin and Shandong), Eastern Coastal region (Jiangsu, Shanghai and Zhejiang), and Southern Coastal region (Fujian, Guangdong and Hainan).

Ten Great Regions

Taking into account the spatial characteristics in resource endowment, transport network, and central city, W. Yang (1989, pp. 238–40)

Table 1.2 The six great regions

Great region	Land area (%)	Geographical scope (FCADs)
North	16.3	Beijing, Tianjin, Hebei, Shanxi and Inner Mongolia
Northeast	8.2	Liaoning, Jilin and Heilongjiang
East	8.3	Shanghai, Jiangsu, Zhejiang, Anhui, Fujian, Jiangxi and Shandong
Central South	10.6	Henan, Hubei, Hunan, Guangdong, Guangxi and Hainan
Southwest	24.6	Sichuan, Guizhou, Yunnan and Tibet
Northwest	32.0	Shaanxi, Gansu, Qinghai, Ningxia and Xinjiang

Note: data are based on 1995.

divides the Chinese economy into Northeast, Beijing–Tianjin, Shanxi–Shaanxi, Shandong, Shanghai, Central South, Sichuan, Southeast, Southwest, and Great West zones. In this research, Inner Mongolia is divided into four sub-areas of Northeast, Beijing–Tianjin, Shanxi–Shaanxi, and Great West zones respectively. After clarifying the regional differences in physical environment and cultural identity, S. Yang (1990, pp. 38–40) groups China's provincial economies into Northeast, North, East, Central, South, Southwest, Northwest, Inner Mongolia, Xinjiang and Tibet regions. It can be assumed that the vast land area and clear cultural identity are the main reasons why S. Yang defines each of the three autonomous regions (Inner Mongolia, Xinjiang and Tibet) as a great region. In addition, Z. Liu (1994, p. 36) demarcates the Chinese economy by Northeast, Beijing–Tianjin, Inner Mongolia–Shanxi, Hebei–Shandong–Henan, Shanghai–Jiangsu–Zhejiang, Anhui–Hubei–Jiangxi–Hunan, Fujian–Guangdong, Guangxi–Hainan, Sichuan–Guizhou–Yunnan–Tibet, and Shaanxi–Gansu–Qinghai–Ningxia–Xinjiang zones.

Since the early 1980s, China's official statistical authorities (such as the SSB and other statistical departments and divisions under ministries or administrations) have used six great regions as shown in Table 1.2. The six great regions have been also applied in many scholarly researches.[7]

1.3 COASTAL AND INLAND AREAS

The 12 FCADs surrounded by the Yellow, East China, and South China seas are known as the coastal area, while the remaining 18 FCADs comprise the inland area (see Table 1.3). Generally, the coastal area is more developed than the inland area, as a result of its proximity to the market economies along the western shore of the Pacific ocean as well as the earlier introduction of economic reform and opening up to the outside world.

There have been different definitions of the coastal and inland areas from that in Table 1.3. For example, Z. Mao (1956, p. 286) treats Anhui and eastern Henan provinces as a part of the coastal area according to the principle of geographical proximity to the coastal area, while the State Council (1993) classifies two coastal FCADs of Guangxi and Hainan into the inland area according to the principle of economic similarity to the inland FCADs.

1.4 EASTERN, CENTRAL AND WESTERN BELTS

Even though China's economic divergence has not been so large within the inland area as between the inland and coastal areas, there are still some plausible reasons for why the inland area needs to be further divided into smaller geographical units. As the western part of the inland area has less developed social and economic infrastructures than the eastern part, China's inland area can be classified into two parts – the central belt (next to the coastal area (here it is referred as the eastern belt)) and the western belt.

The eastern, central, and western belts first appeared in the proposal for national economic and social development in the Seventh FYP (1986–90) which was adopted in April 1986 by the NPC.[8] In this FYP, the government advocated that: 'The development of the eastern coastal belt shall be further accelerated and, at the same time, the construction of energy and raw material industries shall be focused on the central belt, while the preparatory works for the further development of the western belt shall be actively conducted.'[9] Generally, the Eastern, Central, and Western belts are geographically defined as in Table 1.3.[10] Nevertheless, there have been different definitions on the tripartite division of the Chinese economy. For instance, Guangxi, a coastal province along the Gulf of Tonkin, is included in the western belt by K. Yang (1989,

Table 1.3 The coastal and inland areas and the eastern, central, and western belts

Area	Belt	Land area (%)	Geographical scope (FCADs)
Coast	East	13.5	Liaoning, Hebei, Beijing, Tianjin, Shandong, Jiangsu, Shanghai, Zhejiang, Fujian, Guangdong, Hainan, and Guangxi
Inland		86.5	
	Centre	29.8	Shanxi, Jilin, Heilongjiang, Anhui, Henan, Hubei, Hunan, Jiangxi and Inner Mongolia
	West	56.7	Sichuan, Guizhou, Yunnan, Shaanxi, Gansu, Qinghai, Tibet, Ningxia, and Xinjiang

Note: data are based on 1995.

pp. 90–6), J. Gu (1995, pp. 45–51) and G. Chen (1994, p. 57). In Gu's analysis, moreover, Jilin and Heilongjiang, two inland provinces in Northeast China, are included in the eastern belt.

1.5 SOUTHERN AND NORTHERN PARTS

The introduction of the 'North and South' concept in this book seems to be necessary for the bi-regional comparison of the Chinese economy. Besides the natural and climatic environments, social and cultural conditions also differ between northern and southern China. Not without good reason, the Chinese are usually identified as Northerners and Southerners in terms of birthplaces and, occasionally, native places when they are introduced to each other. While it is not quite clear when the saying 'South China raises intelligent scholars while marshals mainly come from the North' was aired and whether or not it can be used to spatially characterize China's ethnic nature, many of the international conflicts and wars in Chinese history did take place in the northern part.[11] Naturally, the frequent wars greatly accelerated the emigration of the northern intellectuals to the southern part.

The geographical definition of the southern and northern parts may slightly differ in the research circle. For example, Qinling range and Huaihe river are traditionally used to divide the South and North, while the Yangtze river is sometimes known as the boundary of northern and southern China. In most cases, nevertheless, there are 15 FCADs in each of the northern and southern parts,

Table 1.4 The northern and southern parts

Part	Land area (%)	Geographical scope (FCADs)
North	59.8	Beijing, Tianjin, Hebei, Shanxi, Inner Mongolia, Liaoning, Jilin, Heilongjiang, Shaanxi, Gansu, Qinghai, Ningxia, Xinjiang, Shandong, and Henan
South	40.2	Shanghai, Jiangsu, Zhejiang, Anhui, Fujian, Jiangxi, Sichuan, Guizhou, Yunnan, Tibet, Hubei, Hunan, Guangdong, Guangxi, and Hainan

Note: data are based on 1995.

as shown in Table 1.4. The only difference between the two definitions lies in the fact that Qinling range and Huaihe river are located in Shaanxi, Henan, Anhui and Jiangsu provinces, while the Yangtze river runs through Sichuan, Hubei, Anhui, Jiangsu provinces and Shanghai municipality.

BOX 1

How Many Administrative Divisions Should There Be in China?

At present, there have been three classes of administrative divisions in China – the FCADs (including province, autonomous region, and municipality directly under the central government), the second-class administrative divisions (SCADs) (including prefecture, autonomous prefecture, and municipality under the FCADs), and the third-class administrative divisions (TCADs) (including county, district, and so on under the SCADs). This organizational pattern has generally been known to lack administrative efficiency and therefore a shortened (say, two-class) pattern of administrative divisions has been proposed by scholars. Furthermore, economic geographers and regional scientists have also argued that appropriate size of land area and population may be helpful in improving the economic efficiency of an administrative division. During the past decades, the optimum number of China's FCADs has been suggested, as among others, 58 by F. Hong (1945a and b), 40–3 by H. Hu (1991), and 43 by R. Guo (1993, pp. 153–71).[12]

2 China's Economic Resource Base

When a seed is planted in spring
There are thousands of grains harvested in the fall.
While all land across the country has been cultivated
Why do farmers still die from starvation?

'Linnong' by Li Shen (772–846 AD)

2.1 NATURAL RESOURCES

Natural resources (such as land, climate, biology, water, minerals, energy, and so on) are the basic component among the factors that influence social and economic activities, especially for less-developed economies lacking capital and technology. Theoretically, in a nation whose manufacturing and other high-tech industries are not internationally competitive, one of the most feasible ways to eradicate its poverty and backwardness is to develop the natural resource-based sectors. During recent decades Chinese economic development followed this path. Until recently, the natural resource-based sectors still played the most important role in the less-developed areas of China.

2.1.1 The Overall Situation

With its vast land area, comparable to the USA or Canada, China also possesses an abundance of other natural resources. According to the World Resources Institute (WRI) (1992, pp. 322–3, 262–3), China's cropland (96,615,000 ha)[1] accounts for 6.8 per cent of the world's, and is the fourth largest (after Russia, USA and India); China has 9 per cent of the world's total permanent pasture (only after Australia and Russia), 3.4 per cent of the world's forestland[2] and woodland (after Russia, Brazil, Canada and USA), and 8.39 per cent of the world's reserves of 15 major metals[3] (after Russia, South Africa and USA).

Table 2.1 Major metal reserves of China and the world

Item	Million tons of content[a]			Per capita kg[b]		
	China (1)	World (2)	(1)/(2) (%)	China (3)	World (4)	(3)/(4) (%)
Bauxite	150	21,559	0.70	128.2	3,934.1	3.26
Copper	3.00	321.00	0.93	2.56	58.58	4.37
Iron ore	3,500	64,648	5.41	2,992	11,797	25.36
Lead	6.00	70.44	8.52	5.13	12.85	39.92
Manganese	13.6	812.8	1.67	11.62	148.32	7.83
Molybdenum	0.55	6.10	9.02	0.47	1.11	42.34
Nickel	0.73	48.66	1.50	0.62	8.88	6.98
Tin	1.50	5.93	25.30	1.28	1.08	118.52
Titanium	30.0	288.6	10.40	25.64	52.66	48.68
Tungsten	1.05	2.35	44.68	0.90	0.43	209.30
Vanadium	0.61	4.27	14.29	0.52	0.78	66.67
Zinc	5.00	143.90	3.47	4.27	36.26	16.26

[a] WRI (1992, pp. 322–3);
[b] Figures of population are 1.17 billion for China and 5.48 billion for the world in 1992.

However, if population size is taken into account, China's natural resources are not richer than in the world as a whole. For instance, China's per capita cultivated land area is less than one-third the world's; its per capita forestland and woodland is approximately one-seventh the world's; and, except for tin and tungsten, China's per capita metal reserves are fewer than the world's, as shown in Table 2.1. In addition, natural resources are generally known to be low grade in China. For example, more than 95 per cent of the iron ore reserves are ferriferously poor, and the iron-rich ore that can be directly processed by refineries accounts for only 2.4 per cent of the proven reserves; about two-thirds of the proven copper ore reserves can be refined to only 1 per cent copper products. The phosphoric ore with the composition of phosphorous pentoxide (P_2O_5) at or higher than 30 per cent accounts for only 7.1 per cent – while, in contrast, that at or lower than 12 per cent accounts for 19 per cent – of the proven reserves.[4]

2.1.2 Regional Distribution

The Chinese economy is characterized by heterogeneous and diversified natural conditions: the climate ranges from the tropical zone in the south to the frigid zone in the north and from the arid

Table 2.2 The regional distribution of major mineral resources

Mineral	Major FCADs (in order of reserves)
Argentum (Ag)	Jiangxi, Guangdong, Guangxi, Yunnan, Hunnan
Bauxite	Shanxi, Guizhou, Guangxi, Sichuan
Bismuthum (Bi)	Hunan, Guangdong, Jiangxi, Yunnan, Inner Mongolia
Chromium (Cr)	Tibet, Inner Mongolia, Gansu
Coal	Shanxi, Inner Mongolia, Shaanxi, Guizhou, Ningxia
Collat. (Co)	Gansu, Yunnan, Shandong, Hebei, Shanxi
Copper (Cu)	Jiangxi, Tibet, Yunnan, Gansu, Anhui
Gold (Au)	Shandong, Jiangxi, Heilongjiang, Jilin, Hubei
Hydragyrum (Hg)	Guizhou, Shaanxi, Hunan, Sichuan, Yunnan
Iron (Fe) ore	Liaoning, Sichuan, Hebei, Shanxi, Anhui
Kaolin (Ka)	Hunan, Jiangsu, Fujian, Guangdong, Liaoning
Lead (Pb)	Yunnan, Guangdong, Hunan, Inner Mongolia, Jiangxi
Manganese (Mn)	Guangxi, Hunan, Guizhou, Liaoning, Sichuan
Molybdenum (Mo)	Henan, Jilin, Shaanxi, Shandong, Jiangxi
Natural gas	Sichuan, Liaoning, Henan, Xinjiang, Hebei, Tianjin
Nickel (Ni)	Gansu, Yunnan, Jilin, Sichuan, Hubei
Petroleum	Heilongjiang, Shandong, Liaoning, Hebei, Xinjiang
Platinum (Pt)	Gansu, Yunnan, Sichuan
Silica stone (SiO_2)	Qinghai, Beijing, Liaoning, Gansu, Sichuan
Stibium (Sb)	Hunan, Guangxi, Guizhou, Yunnan
Tantalum (Ta)	Jiangxi, Inner Mongolia, Guangdong, Hunan, Sichuan
Tin (Sn)	Guangxi, Yunnan, Hunan, Guangdong, Jiangxi
Titanium (Ti)	Sichuan, Hebei, Shaanxi, Shanxi
Tungsten (WO_3)	Hunan, Jiangxi, Henan, Fujian, Guangxi
Vanadium (V)	Sichuan, Hunan, Gansu, Hubei, Anhui
Zinc (Zn)	Yunnan, Inner Mongolia, Guangdong, Hunan, Gansu

Source: CISNR (1990, p. 644).

and semi-arid zones in the northwest to the humid and semi-humid zones in the southeast. As a result, in China the regional distribution of natural resources is extremely unequal. In general, the agricultural and biological resources diminish from the south to the north and from the east to the west. Except for hydropower resource which concentrates in Southwest and Central South regions, energy resources are richer in the north than in the south; while metals are mainly distributed in the transitional area (such as Sichuan, Gansu, Hunan, and so on) between the plateau in the west and the mountain and hilly areas in the east. Table 2.2 lists the major mineral resources by FCAD.

One may examine quantitatively the regional distribution of mineral resource in China. Using the total monetary value of 45 major

Table 2.3 A comparison of monetary values of minerals between FCADs

FCAD	Monetary value (billion yuan)[a]	Share to China (%)[b]	Million yuan per km² of land[c]	Thousand yuan per capital[d]
Anhui	1988.45	3.49	15.30	36.98
Beijing	160.07	0.28	9.53	2.98
Fujian	116.09	0.20	0.97	2.16
Gansu	1048.13	1.83	2.69	19.49
Guangdong[e]	546.42	0.95	3.04	10.16
Guangxi	488.35	0.85	2.12	9.08
Guizhou	1736.85	3.03	10.22	32.30
Hebei	2198.26	3.84	11.57	40.88
Heilongjiang	2194.40	3.83	4.77	40.81
Henan	2179.13	3.80	13.62	40.53
Hubei	388.70	0.68	2.16	7.23
Hunan	1249.79	2.18	5.95	23.24
Jiangsu	401.77	0.70	0.37	7.47
Jiangxi	595.58	1.04	5.96	11.08
Jilin	492.13	0.86	3.08	9.15
Liaoning	2436.64	4.25	13.54	45.32
Inner Mongolia	5035.61	8.79	33.57	93.65
Ningxia	802.29	1.40	12.16	14.92
Qinghai	748.18	1.13	1.039	13.91
Shaanxi	144.49	2.52	0.76	2.69
Shandong	2374.53	4.14	15.83	44.16
Shanghai	3.46	0.01	0.60	0.06
Shanxi	11529.22	20.1	76.86	214.42
Sichuan	13239.37	23.1	23.64	246.22
Tianjin	121.59	0.21	11.05	2.26
Xinjiang	1012.33	1.77	0.84	18.83
Tibet	43.57	0.07	0.03	0.81
Yunnan	2648.74	4.62	6.97	49.26
Zhejiang	55.73	0.09	0.56	1.04

[a] J. Sun (1987, pp. 4–8);
[b] the first column divided by the total amount of the first column;
[c] the first column divided by the land area of each FCAD;
[d] the first column divided by the population of each FCAD;
[e] includes Hainan.

minerals, land area and population of each FCAD (shown in Table 2.3),[5] we may estimate that the five richest FCADs are Sichuan, Shanxi, Inner Mongolia, Yunnan and Liaoning and the five poorest FCADs are Shanghai, Tibet, Zhejiang, Fujian, and Tianjin according to the absolute and per-capita values (shown in the second and fifth columns respectively); while the five richest FCADs are

Table 2.4 Energy resources by great region[a] (%)[b]

Great region	Coal	Hydropower[c]	Petroleum[d]	All energy
North	64.0 (98.2)	1.8 (1.3)	14.4 (0.5)	43.9 (100.0)
Northeast	3.1 (54.6)	1.8 (14.2)	48.3 (31.2)	3.8 (100.0)
East	6.5 (72.9)	4.4 (22.5)	18.2 (4.6)	6.0 (100.0)
Central South	3.7 (44.5)	9.5 (51.8)	2.5 (3.7)	5.6 (100.0)
Southwest	10.7 (25.2)	70.0 (74.7)	2.5 (0.1)	28.6 (100.0)
Northwest	12.0 (66.7)	12.5 (31.3)	14.0 (2.0)	12.1 (100.0)
CHINA	100.0 (85.9)	100.0 (13.1)	100.0 (1.0)	100.0 (100.0)

[a] the geographical scopes of the great regions are defined in Table 1.2;
[b] standard coal equivalent conversion rates are as 0.714 t/t for coal, 1.43 t/t for petroleum, 1.33 t/1000m³ for natural gas, 0.143 t/t for oil shale, and 350 g/kWh for hydropower;
[c] the theoretical reserves multiplied by 100 years;
[d] includes natural gas and oil shale.
Note: figures in parentheses are energy structures.
Source: MOE (1991, p. 101).

Shanxi, Inner Mongolia, Sichuan, Shandong, and Anhui, and the five poorest FCADs are Tibet, Jiangsu, Zhejiang, Shanghai, and Shaanxi according to the per-square-kilometre value (shown in the fourth column).

Energy resource is disproportionally distributed in China, as shown in Table 2.4. For example, about 70 per cent of hydropower reserves are concentrated in the Southwest region, while the North, Northeast, and East regions as a whole share only less than 10 per cent; more than 60 per cent of coal reserves are distributed in the North region, with only a small portion, sparsely distributed, in the Northeast, East, and Central South regions; Northeast region accounts for nearly a half of the nation's petroleum and natural gas reserves, while Central South and Southwest regions as a whole only shares a meagre 5 per cent. Nevertheless, Northwest is the only region which is modestly rich in coal, hydropower and petroleum and natural gas. In addition, the energy structure is disproportional among regions. For example, coal nearly monopolizes the North region, while the Southwest and Central South regions are mostly dominated by hydropower. Nevertheless, the East, Northwest and Northeast regions are mainly served by coal rather than by petroleum, hydropower, and natural gas.

The distribution of water is extremely irregular in China. In general, the northern part is poor in surface water, but modestly rich in groundwater in a few FCADs, such as Qinghai, Xinjiang, Inner

Table 2.5   The regional distribution of agricultural products[a]

Product	Major FCADs (in order of output)
Rice	Hunan, Sichuan, Jiangsu, Hubei, Guangdong
Wheat	Henan, Shandong, Jiangsu, Hebei, Sichuan
Maize	Shandong, Jilin, Hebei, Sichuan, Henan
Soybean	Heilongjiang, Henan, Jilin, Shandong, Anhui
Cotton	Shandong, Hebei, Henan, Hubei, Jiangsu
Rapeseed	Shandong, Sichuan, Anhui, Jiangsu, Henan
Tobacco	Henan, Yunnan, Shandong, Guizhou, Hunan
Tea	Zhejiang, Hunan, Sichuan, Anhui, Fujian
Fruit	Shandong, Hebei, Guangdong, Sichuan, Liaoning

[a] based on SSB (1996, pp. 371–3).

Mongolia, and Heilongjiang. The precipitation is more than 1000 mm/yr in the southern part and more than 1600 mm/yr in the southern coastal area; while it ranges from 100 to 800 mm/yr in the northern part. In particular, the Talimu, Tulufan and Chaidamu basins in Northwest region have less than 25 mm of precipitation per annum.[6] As a result of the suitable climate and adequate rainfall, the southern part is the dominant rice producer; wheat is the main foodstuff in the lower Yellow river (such as Henan, Shandong, Hebei, northern Jiangsu and Anhui provinces, and so on) and southern Great Wall areas. Table 2.5 lists the major agricultural FCADs in order of output for the selected products.

Generally, China's resource demand and supply may be geographically identified through four different zones which are labelled as (1) $S_L D_L$ (low supply, low demand), (2) $S_H D_L$ (high supply, low demand), (3) $S_H D_H$ (high supply, high demand), and (4) $S_L D_H$ (low supply, high demand). Obviously, Zones $S_L D_L$ and $S_H D_H$ can reach their respective optimum equilibrium point of social welfare even under the condition that inter-zone trade is not available, as their resource supplies can meet their resource demands. However, under the disequilibrated supply–demand conditions, neither Zone $S_L D_H$ nor Zone $S_H D_L$ can optimize its social welfare. As a matter of fact, as these two Zones' resource supply–demand structures are complementary with each other, the optimization of their social welfare can benefit greatly from their inter-zone trade, more specifically, the import from Zone $S_H D_L$ to Zone $S_L D_H$, or the export to Zone $S_L D_H$ from Zone $S_H D_L$.

The trade-off between Zones $S_H D_L$ and $S_L D_H$ can be further

Figure 2.1 Regional optimum with resource allocation

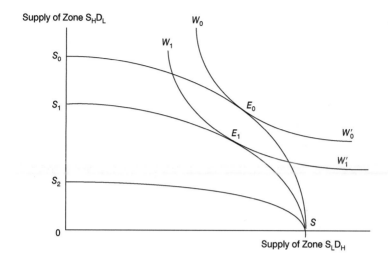

explained by Figure 2.1 in which S_0S illustrates a society's resource supply possibility curve of Zone S_LD_H, W_0W_0' denotes the Zone's social preference curve and OS_0 and OS denote the maximum possibilities of resource supplies of Zones S_HD_L and S_LD_H respectively. Consider the availability of the inter-zone trade and the absence of the resource supplies from other external sources, the optimum allocation of resource between Zones S_HD_L and S_LD_H will be at point E_0 where S_0S and W_0W_0' meet. When a trade embargo rises from Zone S_HD_L, the S_0S curve shifts to the left to, say, S_1S. As a result, Zone S_LD_H will have to end up with more supply of local resources and less social welfare consumption. In this case, the optimum equilibrium will occur at point E_1, which is lower than E_0, indicating a lower social welfare level upon the introduction of trade barriers between Zones S_HD_L and S_LD_H. It must be noted that, the more Zone S_LD_H is committed to the importing of resources in a world of resource constraints, the less is its social welfare consumption, since higher risks and more extra costs will result from the resource imports.[7]

2.2 POPULATION AND LABOUR FORCE

People at present think that five sons are not too many and each son has also five sons, and there are already 25 descendants before the death of the grandfather. Therefore, people are more but wealth is less; they work hard but receive little.

Hanfeizi (280–233 BC)

2.2.1 The Overall Situation

In 1995, mainland China's population surpassed 1.2 billion which accounted for more than one-fifth of the world's; it was nine times that of Japan, five times that of the USA, and three times that of the European Union as a whole. The dynamic mechanism of population growth has greatly influenced China's population policies. When the PRC was founded in 1949, the population of mainland China was about 450 million. Since then China has experienced two major peaks of population growth. From the new Republic's year zero to 1958 when the GLF movement was launched, the birth rate was as high as 3 to 4 per cent while, in contrast, the death rate decreased significantly. This drastic population growth was largely encouraged by the government in line with Mao Zedong's thought 'the more population, the easier are the things to be done'. China's population began to grow rapidly once again after the famine period (1959–61) during which many people died from starvation.[8] The birthrate peaked at 4.3 per cent in 1963 and then decreased gradually but still ran at over 2 per cent until the early 1970s when the government realized the importance of population control. Unfortunately, it was too late for China to control its population which has still been growing at the rate of more than 10 million per annum and will continue to make China be one of the most populous nations in the foreseeable future, as demonstrated in Figure 2.2 and Table 2.6.

When the Chinese government was proud of its achievements which mainly relied upon the 'sea-of-manpower' approach, the population problem raised simultaneously. During the past decades, when the population densities of some developed countries decreased gradually or kept constant, China's population density has drastically increased from 40 persons per square kilometres of land area in 1949 up to 125 persons per square kilometres of land area in 1995, which is more than three times that of the world as a whole. In fact, China's population density is not very high when compared with South Korea

Figure 2.2 Birth, death and natural growth rates, 1949–95

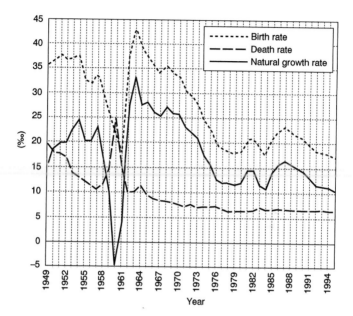

Source: SSB (various issues).

Table 2.6 Population forecasts for selected countries (million persons)

Country	1985	2000	2025
China	1050	1286	1493
India	769	1043	1446
USSR	277	308	351
USA	239	266	301
Indonesia	166	208	263
Brazil	136	179	246
Japan	121	129	129
Pakistan	103	162	267
Bangladesh	101	151	235
Nigeria	95	159	301

Source: United Nations (1988).

(443 persons/km^2), Japan (329 persons/km^2), India (290 persons/ km^2), UK (237 persons/km^2), Germany (226 persons/km^2). However, as much of China's territory consists of mountains, desert and other uninhabitable lands, the number of persons per square kilometres of the *inhabitable* land area is much larger than the nominal population density in China. For instance, as will be discussed later, the population densities of many FCADs in East China are more than 400 persons per square kilometres of land area, much higher than that of most of the most populous nations in the world.

Today, when looking at the poor living conditions in the countryside and the unemployment problem in urban China, one cannot help remembering the ridiculous debate on whether or not the population growth should be controlled effectively. Stimulated by the leftist idea of population equals production, some people believed blindly the link summed up by 'more people→more labour force→more production→faster economic development', which eventually resulted in China's over-population problem.[9]

In fact, confronted with the grim reality of population growth, even Mao Zedong acknowledged the increasing pressure of over-population on the Chinese economy in his late years and began to puzzle about his earlier prediction that 'Of all things in the world, people are the most precious... Even if China's population multiplies many times, she is fully capable of finding a solution'.[10] In the early 1970s, the Chinese government had to implement a birth control policy aiming to encourage late marriages, prolong the time period between births and reduce the number of children in each family. In 1978, the encouragement of birth control first appeared in Article 53 of the PRC's Constitution. Following the implementation of population control policy, the First National Conference on Birth Control (NCBC) was held in Beijing in 1979. The Conference requested: 'that one couple has only one child and at most two children but with a three year interval. Those couples who do not plan to have a second child will be rewarded and those who have a third child will receive economic punishment.'[11]

Since the early 1980s, China has effectively controlled its population growth tendency by establishing a series of strict measures. The population growth rate declined drastically from 3 per cent in the 1960s to 1.055 per cent in 1995. Obviously, without this reduction, China's population would have increased by about 23 million ((0.03−0.01055)×1.2 billion) per annum. In other words, as a result of China's population control effort, the population increase has been reduced by an amount equal to medium-sized nation for every 2 to 3 years. Furthermore, the reduction of population growth also increased China's per capita GNP by approximately 2.0 per cent $(1/(1-(0.03-0.01055))-1)$ in 1995.[12] Despite these successes, some problems still remain.

First, China's population control policy has generated an imbalance between males and females. In poor and remote rural areas, the traditional discrimination against women has still remained very strong. Because there is very little social security in those rural areas, sons are the only hope for parents who are still earning their living by physical labour. This provides a strong incentive for people to have more than one child till they possess son(s). Partly as a result of the birth control policy and partly because of the increasing burden of having an additional child (girl), the inhumane practices of foeticide and infanticide are very common in rural areas where men have a higher social position than women, even though these practices have been prohibited by the Chinese government. In 1995, China's national birth gender proportion (male to female) was 103.67:100, which is much higher than the developed nations'.[13] If taking only the rural area into account, the birth gender difference would be much larger.

Second, a lower birth-rate will eventually result in a higher proportion of aged people. Already this has been a social problem in the advanced nations and will, sooner or later, affect Chinese society. Thanks to the government's efforts in raising women's social position[14] and the strict domicile system for urban citizens, China's only-one-child policy has been successfully implemented in the urban area since the early 1980s. At present, it is very common in urban China for a couple to have only one child. However, the policy is to rigidly transform China's urban family pattern into a reverse pyramid (shown in Figure 2.3) in the coming decades. In 1953, the ratio of the population aged 65 or over was only 4.4 per cent in China. This ratio was further reduced to 3.6 per cent in 1964, but rose again to 4.9 per cent in 1982 and 5.6 per cent in 1990.[15] According to P. Du (1994, p. 88), the percentage of the aged population in China will increase steadily to 6.7 per cent in 2000, 8.1 per cent in 2010, 10.9 per cent in 2020, 14.7 per cent in 2030, 19.8 per cent in 2040, and 20.9 per cent in 2050.

Third, population production has been largely imbalanced between the rural and urban areas of China. In rural and other poor areas, parents who would not receive any subsidies for living from

Figure 2.3 The family pattern under the 'one-child' policy

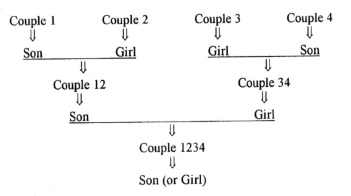

the government after they retire have particularly strong incentives to have more children for whom, however, neither the government nor the parents are able to cover the educational costs. In urban and other relatively rich areas, parents who receive higher education and have lifetime social welfare usually have the trade-off between having more children and improving the living standards and quality of life. Faced with the cramped living space, high cost of education, as well as severe competition for university entrance, urban parents have no incentives to have a second child, not to mention that those who illegally raise more than one child would not receive the subsidies from the government and could be fired from their current posts. As an only child is more protected by its family than one with siblings, the children born in urban areas usually receive better care and education than those born in rural areas. In brief, the fact that the rural and poor people have more children than the urban and well-educated people will reduce the educational level of the Chinese population as a whole.[16]

Labour force is equal to population in the productive age group multiplied by labour force participation rate. The labour force participation rate can be calculated as the ratio of the labour force to the population at certain age or over. The international standard for the productive age is defined as 15 years or over. In a market economy, labour force demand is positively related to gross production output. When labour supply exceeds labour demand unemployment occurs. The Chinese economy has been characterized by a labour surplus problem since the late 1960s – a result of the uncontrolled population growth. In 1995, China had 5.2 million registered urban unemployed persons which accounted for 2.9 per cent of the total urban working population.[17] While China's urban unemployment rate is not as high as the developed nations,[18] there have been more unemployment problems in rural China. In 1952, as many as 87.54 per cent of the Chinese population lived in the countryside and earned their living from the land. Until 1995, this figure decreased gradually to 70.96 per cent. But the total rural population increased from 503.19 million to 859.47 million during the same period.[19] It is inevitable that the situation of a rapidly increasing rural population combined with limited cultivable land will generate a large rural labour surplus, particularly with the increased productivity resulting from the introduction of advanced technologies.

2.2.2 Regional Analysis

As a result of the diverse regional natural and geographic conditions, population is unevenly distributed in China. Generally, the population density is higher in the eastern belt than in the central belt, while the central belt has a higher density than western belt. The most populous FCADs are Shanghai (2440 persons/km^2), Tianjin (856 persons/km^2), Beijing (745 persons/km^2), Jiangsu (707 persons/km^2), Shandong (580 persons/km^2) and Henan (569 persons/km^2). On the other hand, however, Tibet, Qinghai, Xinjiang and Inner Mongolia have only 2, 7, 10 and 21 persons for each square kilometres of land area respectively.[20]

In general, the uneven regional pattern of population growth is mainly determined by two factors: first, there exist large regional economic inequalities in China (as will be discussed in Chapter 4) which with lowering birth and death rates connected to economic development levels largely decided China's regional population pattern; second, China has implemented a more flexible population control policy for the minority groups than the Han majority. This has resulted in higher birth rates in those minority-based FCADs than the Han-based FCADs. Using the data of China's 30 FCADs as shown in SSB (1996, pp. 43, 70), we may obtain two regression equations:

$$BR = 19.09 - 8.06 \times 10^{-4}GDPPC + 3.92D \qquad (2.1)$$
$$ (18.47) \qquad (-5.45) \qquad\qquad (3.58)$$
$$(N = 30, \ R^2 = 0.71, \ SE = 2.47, \ F = 32.58)$$

$$DR = 8.14 - 4.83 \times 10^{-4}GDPPC + 2.43 \times 10^{-8}GDPPC^2 \qquad (2.2)$$
$$(18.80) \quad (3.76) \qquad\qquad\qquad (3.35)$$
$$(N = 30,\ R^2 = 0.35,\ SE = 0.65,\ F = 7.42)$$

where, $GDPPC$ = per capita GDP; BR = birth rate; DR = death rate; D = dummy variable ($D = 1$ for the minority-based FCADs such as Inner Mongolia, Guangxi, Tibet, Ningxia, Xinjiang, Guizhou, Yunnan and Qinghai; $D = 0$ for the remaining FCADs); figures in parentheses below the parameters are the t-statistical values. Obviously, birth rate decreases with respect to $GDPPC$ (shown in Equation 2.1). Death rate shows a diminishing marginal decrease with respect to per capita GDP (that is $-4.83 \times 10^{-4} + 4.86\ 10^{-8}GDPPC$) when $GDPPC$ ranges between 0 and 9938 yuan (shown in Equation 2.2).

2.3 EDUCATION

2.3.1 The Overall Situation

Since Confucianism began to influence Chinese society, people have placed a high value on education in China. However, education has not been successfully achieved in China particularly for the past century. In 1964, when the second national population census was conducted, as high as 56.76 per cent of the total population aged 16 and over were illiterate or semi-literate. Thereafter, the illiterate and semi-literate rate decreased considerably but was still estimated at 31.88 per cent and 20.61 per cent in the third and fourth national population census in 1982 and 1990 respectively.[21] According to UNESCO (1995, tab. 1.3), the literacy rates for China were 87 per cent for males and 68 per cent for females in 1990, which are higher than that of India (62 per cent and 34 per cent), Pakistan (47 per cent and 21 per cent), and many other low-income countries, while still lower than that of Indonesia (88 per cent and 75 per cent), the Philippines (90 per cent and 89 per cent), Thailand (95 per cent and 91 per cent), Malaysia (86 per cent and 70 per cent), and many other low- and upper-middle income countries, and much lower than that of Japan, USA, Germany, and other high income countries.

China's modestly high illiteracy has been decided by both historic and institutional factors. Before 1949, China's education was very backward and had been seriously damaged by the long-lasting wars. For instance, 62 per cent of people born in 1930 and 74 per cent of people born in 1920 were illiterate or semi-literate.[22] During the two peaks of population growth in the 1950s and 1960s, neither the government nor their homes were able to provide an equal education opportunity for each child.[23] During the GCR period (1966–76), China's education system which, to a large extent, had represented Confucianism was effectively reformed. Primary school education was reduced from six years to five years and junior and senior middle school education were each cut by one year. In these cases the textbooks were highly revised and simplified. Even worse, the school teachers who had been highly ranked in traditional Chinese society were the subjects of political discrimination.[24] During this period, the destruction of the higher education system was even more serious because universities were closed during 1966–70 and operated on political merit rather than academic performance during 1971–76. The GCR resulted in a 'breakpoint' of ages for scientists and engineers, which will affect China's socioeconomic development negatively.[25]

Education in China has experienced drastic changes during the post-Mao era. In 1977, the national entrance examinations for higher learning institutes were resumed. One year later, the Chinese government first recognized during the First National Conference on Science and Technology (NCST) that 'science and technology is a productive force' and began to treat intellectuals as 'a branch of the working class'.[26] Since then, education has been the scene of much action. Particularly praiseworthy is the fact that primary education has achieved much progress with the percentage of school-age children enrolled increased from only 49.2 per cent in 1952 to 98.5 per cent in 1995. However, problems still remain in middle school education. For instance, more than a half of the graduates from junior middle schools had not been able to enter senior middle schools in 1995 (see Table 2.7).

A regression of China's educational expenditure with respect to NI reveals that when the per capita NI grew from 250 yuan to 1000 yuan, the ratio of educational expenditure to NI decreased from 6.3 per cent to 2.8 per cent accordingly (T. Hsueh, 1994, pp. 80–1). Obviously, the empirical estimate is inconsistent with the hypothesis that there exists a positive correlation between income level and the ratio of educational expenditure to GNP, as estimated by Chenery and Syrquin (1975, p. 20).[27] Even though the

Table 2.7 School-aged children enrolled and graduates of primary and junior middle schools entering higher level schools, selected years from 1952–95, (%)

Year	School-aged	Primary	Junior middle
1952	49.2	96.0	168.6[a]
1957	61.7	44.2	39.7
1962	56.1	45.3	30.0
1965	84.7	82.5	70.0
1975	96.8	90.6	60.4
1978	95.5	87.7	40.9
1980	93.9	75.9	45.9
1985	96.0	68.4	41.7
1986	96.4	69.5	40.6
1987	97.2	69.1	39.1
1988	97.2	70.4	38.0
1989	97.4	71.5	38.3
1990	97.8	74.6	40.6
1991	97.8	75.7	42.6
1992	97.2	79.7	43.4
1993	97.7	81.8	44.1
1994	98.4	86.6	46.4[b]
1995	98.5	90.8	48.3[b]

[a] the percentage of graduates of junior middle schools entering senior middle schools was higher than 100% as the students graduated from junior middle schools were less than the students enrolled in senior middle schools;
[b] graduates of junior middle school include vocational schools.
Source: SSB (1996, p. 637).

two estimates are based on different statistical definitions, it can still be seen that China's education lagged behind its economic growth. In 1995, China's expenditure on public education was 119.384 billion yuan (about US$14.296 billion). Its per capita expenditure on public education is only US$11.8, much lower than the advanced nations.[28] In 1978, China's expenditure on public education as a percentage of GNP was 2.07 per cent. Thereafter, this ratio increased gradually up to 2.69 per cent in 1986 but then dropped back to 2.08 per cent in 1995 (see Figure 2.4).

The expenditure on public education as a percentage of GNP of China only leads that of a few of poor nations such as Nigeria (0.5%, 1992) but still lags far behind that of the world as a whole (5.1%, 1993) and many other nations such as Canada (7.6%, 1992), Hungary (7.0%, 1992), Bulgaria (5.9%, 1992), Portugal (6.1%, 1990),

Figure 2.4 Government expenditure on education as a percentage of GNP, 1978–95

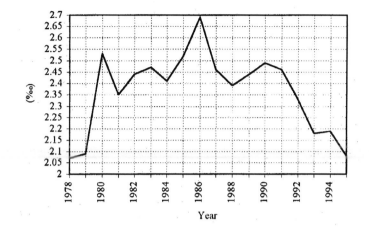

Sources: SSB (1989: p. 670; 1996: pp. 42 and 232).

USA (5.3%, 1990), and Japan (4.7%, 1991).[29] China's position on education can also be shown by the relatively lower wages of the teachers. In 1995, the average wage of formal employees in the education sector was only about three-quarters that in the financial services, insurance, and real estate sectors and approximately 2 per cent and 4 per cent lower than that in government and CCP agencies respectively.[30] After wage reform was introduced in 1985, the wages of senior intellectuals have been generally been lower than that of junior intellectuals. A sample survey of 48 cities conducted by the SSB, for example, reveals that the wage ratios of the junior to senior intellectuals within the universities, research institutes, and hospitals declined considerably from 1:4.1, 1:3.0, 1:3.0, and 1:3.0 prior to the reform to 1:2.1, 1:2.0, 1:2.2, and 1:1.18 after the reform respectively.[31]

2.3.2 Regional Analysis

Education is unevenly provided among the FCADs. For instance, the mean value of education in years is 9.19 in Beijing, almost three times that in Qinghai (see Table 2.8). However, the mean values of education in years are more even in urban area, the reasons

Table 2.8 Mean value of education in years by FCAD

FCAD	Total	Urban	Rural
Anhui	7.09	9.23	4.55
Beijing	9.19	9.90	6.01
Fujian	4.94		4.93
Gansu	7.05	9.26	3.90
Guangdong	8.31	9.55	6.07
Guangxi	5.67		5.67
Guizhou	3.81		3.80
Hainan	6.06		6.04
Hebei	6.40		6.40
Heilongjiang	6.01		6.00
Henan	7.60	9.70	5.13
Hubei	8.18	10.08	5.45
Hunan	6.07		6.07
Inner Mongolia	5.63		5.63
Jiangsu	8.02	9.39	5.48
Jiangxi	5.08		5.08
Jilin	6.43		6.42
Liaoning	8.85	9.29	6.23
Ningxia	4.22		4.22
Qinghai	3.42		3.42
Shaanxi	5.51		5.51
Shandong	5.70		5.70
Shanghai	7.29		7.29
Shanxi	8.70	9.80	6.26
Sichuan	5.46		5.46
Tianjin	6.34		6.32
Yunnan	7.23	9.10	4.05
Zhejiang	5.59		5.59
Standard error[a]	1.47	0.910	0.311

[a] calculated by the author.
Source: Knight and Li (1993, pp. 292–3).

for which may be twofold. First, the central government attempts to equalize educational opportunities among FCADs: the richer FCADs tend to receive less and the poor FCADs more central government funding for education. Second, the assignment of college graduates to employment is done on a national basis. Government gives preferential treatment to the poor FCADs by assigning graduates from colleges in rich FCADs to work in poor FCADs.[32] Nevertheless, the regional differences in educational attainment are greater in rural areas than in urban areas. The mean value of education in years in Qinghai is only 3.42, far less that in Shanghai

(7.29). The standard error of mean values of education in years is 0.910 in rural area, almost three times that in urban area.

2.4 POLICY IMPLICATIONS

The ultimate goal of any economic system is the allocation of scarce resources among competing factions. To accomplish this goal, the economic system must explicitly deal with the supply and demand of goods and services as well as the interaction between the two. There is no exception for the Chinese economy.

The uneven distribution of natural resources in China has heavily influenced the disequilibrated regional structures of exploitation and supply of those resources used as inputs of production to produce desired final goods and services for society. From Section 2.1, we may conclude that China's mineral and energy resources are mainly distributed in the northern and western inland areas, while the largest industrial consumers are located in the eastern and southern coastal areas. Therefore, the long-distance transfers of raw materials and semi-finished products from the northern and western inland areas to the eastern and southern coastal areas should be the only feasible approach by which to efficiently create an equilibrium between supply and demand in the Chinese economy. The Chinese government should recognize this fact and try to deal carefully with the national economic cooperation.[33]

The Chinese economy has been mainly fuelled by coal rather than by petroleum and natural gas as in most industrialized economies. Given its abundance in reserves compared with other energy resources, such as hydropower, petroleum, and natural gas, coal which accounts for 85.9 per cent of China's total energy resources (see Table 2.4) has supplied more than 70 per cent of the nation's total energy supply until recently. Without stressing the low heating conversion rate of coal consumption, the serious environmental damage resulting from the exploitation, transportation, and consumption of coal resources has already posed challenges to the sustainable development of the Chinese economy.

A huge population does not represent an advantage in human resources for economic development, particularly when a country is transformed from an agricultural society that uses mainly traditional methods of production to an industrial society that requires not only advanced sciences and technologies but also qualified workers. A striking problem in the Chinese economy lies in the fact that about 15 per cent of employees have been illiterate or semi-literate and that only about 5 per cent of employees in government agencies, parties and social sectors have received university level education.[34] China's human development index (HDI) was 0.644 which only ranks ninety-fourth in the world. Moreover, the HDI varies greatly among regions, making China one of the nations with the highest regional inequalities of this measure. For instance, the HDI was 0.865 for Shanghai and 0.861 for Beijing (both of which ranked around thirty-first in the world, leading South Korea and Singapore) but only 0.404 for Tibet and 0.550 for Qinghai, making them the one hundred and thirty-first and the one hundred and tenth respectively in the world.[35]

A well-educated and law-abiding population that possesses a strong work ethic is the *sine qua non* of modern economic growth. At present, the development of education is particularly urgent for China – a country with a high proportion of illiteracy and whose educational system had been seriously destroyed in the GCR period (1966–76). At the same time, ways must be found to raise the technical and professional level of the workers already in employment.

BOX 2

Mingong Economics

Since the 1980s, the seasonal movement of tens of millions of rural labourers (*mingong*) between the rural and urban areas has created a special scenario for the Chinese economy. After the Spring Festival – the Chinese New Year which begins at late January or early February and lasts about one month, the rural labourers leave for the urban areas and are employed as industrial workers or self-employed as retailers and servants. During the planting and harvesting seasons in summer and autumn, some of them may return back home for agricultural work. As migration from the countryside to the cities is strictly controlled by the government through a system of registration of urban residents, most of the *mingong* are still treated as 'agricultural residents'.

The *mingong* phenomenon has been changing Chinese society dramatically. First of all, it has met the needs of the workers in urban construction and other labour-intensive sectors. Second, it has become an important source of increases in rural income level and been mainly responsible for the socioeconomic changes in rural China. Third, it provides a competitive mechanism for urban employment and the re-employment of the laid-off workers from the SOEs. The problems that have emerged in the *mingong* tide are, among others, the possible adverse effects on agricultural production as well as urban society.

3 The Economic Systems in Transition

Doctor Bianque went to see King Wu of the state of Qin. The King told the doctor about his health condition and Bianque was ready to give him a treatment. The ministers at the King's sides said to him: 'Your Majesty, the malady is in front of your ears and below your eyes. Even with treatment it might not be cured and very likely you will lose your hearing and sight.' The King passed these messages to Bianque. Bianque was enraged and threw down the stone needle which he used for giving treatment, saying: 'Sire, you discuss your illness with one who knows how to effect a cure but you allow those who know nothing about medicine to spoil the whole thing. If Qin is governed in this way, then a single such mistake on your part is enough to bring down the state.'

Zhanguoce (475–221 BC)[1]

3.1 GENERAL BACKGROUND

The economic system of any nation is the mechanism that brings together natural resources, labour, technology, and the necessary managerial talents. Anticipating and then meeting human needs through the production and distribution of goods and services is the end purpose of every economic system. While the type of economic system applied by a nation is politically decided, it is also to a larger extent the result of historical experience, which over time becomes the national culture. The PRC had uneasily followed its Soviet antecedents for a long time, before it eventually decided to abandon this system and economically open up to the outside world in the late 1970s. Since then, great strides toward the market economic system have been achieved by China. In brief, the institutional evolution in the Chinese economy since 1978 has demonstrated a gradual process and may be outlined by six phases as below:

1. centrally planned economy (before 1978);
2. economy regulated mainly by planning and supplementally by market (1979–84);
3. commodity economy with a plan (1985–87);
4. socialist commodity economy (1988–89);
5. combination of planned and market economy (1989–91);
6. socialist market economy (since 1992).

Before the third Plenum of the eleventh CCPCC was held on 18 December 1978, China had been a CPE.[2] Generally, this system has at least three problems. First of all, it makes almost all productive enterprises subordinate to administrative organs. To a large extent, this neglects the economic independence of the enterprises and thereby leads to the neglect of their material interests and responsibilities, blunting their initiative and enthusiasm. Second, the system involves excessive command planning from above and is too rigid. So long as the enterprises meet their stipulated targets, they are considered to have performed satisfactorily regardless of whether or not its products satisfy the needs of society. Third, the system of unified income and expenditure means that everyone has an 'iron rice bowl' (*tie fanwan*) and 'eats from the same pot' (*daguo fan*), that is, people have guaranteed employment regardless of whether that are productive or not and they can rely on the work of others for their income. Egalitarianism, lack of interest in economic results and a low sense of economic and legal responsibility are all expressions of this mentality.

Guided by the CCPCC (1984), the roles of central planning and market regulation were reversed in the modified system 'commodity economy with a plan'.[3] Generally, Phase 3 was known to be loosely based on the Hungarian model of market socialism. Nevertheless, the state continued to own the bulk of large- and medium-sized enterprises and to regulate production and pricing of a number of strategic commodities, but the market mechanism was permitted to play an increasing role in the pricing and allocation of goods and services and in the allocation and remuneration of labour in some non-strategic sectors. In the ideological struggles between the radical reformers and the conservatives in China's economic reform circle, Phase 4 ('socialist commodity economy')[4] was replaced by Phase 5 ('combination of planned and market economy) after the Tian'anmen Square incident during May–June 1989. Nevertheless, Phase 4 was extremely important in terminology insofar as it legitimated the abolition of traditional mechanisms of the central planning system in favour of an introduction of market regulation.

Even though China's ambitious agenda geared towards transforming the Chinese economy into a market-oriented one was unveiled as early as 1992, when Deng Xiaoping's Southern Speech[5] eventually influenced China's decision-makers, the formal document entitled 'Decision of the CCPCC on Several Issues Concerning the Establishment of a Socialist Market Economic Structure' was finally approved by the Third Plenum of the fourteenth CCPCC on 14 November 1993. According to the decision, the government should withdraw from direct involvement in enterprise management. Instead, 'Government functions in economic management consist mainly of devising and implementing macroeconomic control policies, appropriate construction of infrastructure facilities and the creation of a favourable environment for economic development'.[6] The Plenum also declared that 'the government shall take significant steps in the reform of the system of taxation, financing, investment and planning, and establish a mechanism in which planning, banking and public finance are coordinated and mutually check each other while strengthening the overall coordination of economic operations'.[7]

China's commitment to the creation of a market-oriented economy has been the central plank of its programme of economic reform, and considerable progress towards this end has been achieved since 1978, through the gradual withdrawal of the government from the allocation, pricing, and distribution of goods. In 1977, the extent to which the Chinese economy was market-regulated was only 10 to 15 per cent, while it increased to 40 per cent and was disproportionately distributed by labour (35 per cent), capital (less than 40 per cent), production (55 per cent), and pricing (60 per cent) in 1996.[8]

Reforms introduced since 1978 have so far exhibited remarkable results. Particularly praiseworthy are the facts that the Chinese-type reforms have avoided the output collapse characteristic of transitions in other former CPEs and generated unprecedented increases in the level of living standards across the country. For the last decade, China has successfully implemented a stable economic reform and opening up to the outside world and, in particular, achieved a faster economic growth than any other socialist or former socialist country in the world.

3.2 PLANNING

The economic development in a traditional socialist economy is realized mainly through a plan worked out by the central planning authorities. The plan, however, is a mental construct which may or may not correctly reflect the objective requirements of economic development. If the plan is correct, economic development is smooth; if it is incorrect, not only is it of no help but it may even cause stagnation and decline. This has been obviously proven in China's economic cycle.

When the PRC was founded in 1949, the transformation of private ownership of the means of production into public ownership and the establishment of a powerful socialist sector paved an effective way for planned development of the national economy. During the First FYP period (1953–57), much attention was paid to industrial construction, especially in heavy industry. At the same time, the socialist transformation of agriculture, handicrafts, and capitalist industry and commerce was effectively carried out. In line with these goals, 156 key projects and other items were arranged with the guidance of the Soviet Union. The First FYP was generally known by the PRC's central planners and economists to be very successful because all scheduled targets were fully met during this period: the GVIO grew at 18 per cent annually, higher than the planned rate (14.7 per cent); the annual GVAO growth rate (4.5 per cent) exceeded the planned rate (4.3 per cent).[9] Faced with economic difficulties during the late 1950s and the early 1960s, the CCPCC and the State Council put forward the policy entitled 'readjustment, consolidation, filling-out, and raising standards' (*taiozheng, gonggu, chongshi, tigao*). The production targets for heavy industry were reduced and investment in capital construction was cut back. The accumulation rate which had stood at as high as 39.9 per cent in 1960 was adjusted sharply down to only 10.4 per cent by 1962. The enterprises with high production costs and large losses were closed or switched to other products. With the adjustments, the economy rapidly returned to normal. From 1962 to 1965, the GVIO was growing at an annual rate of 17.9 per cent, GVAO at 11.1 per cent, and NI at 14.5 per cent.[10]

In contrast to the First FYP and the readjustment period (1963–65), the years 1958–60 provided a typical case of errors in planning, resulting in serious economic imbalances. During this period, the GLF movement was effectively launched by setting up a series of high targets within a given period, most of which, however, were impossible to be fulfilled due to the limitation of resources and production capacities.[11] To accomplish its ambitious target for an overnight entrance to the 'communist heaven', large quantities of raw materials and labour force were diverted toward heavy industry while, in contrast, the development of agriculture and light industry received less attention. This situation lasted until 1960 when the serious imbalances between accumulation and consumption and between heavy industry on one hand and agriculture and light industry on the other hand suddenly occurred. Despite this profound lesson, similar problems arose again thereafter.[12]

Since a socialist economy is rigorously directed by state planning, as soon as errors occur in the plan, all economic activities are affected. China bore witness to this point by its experience and lessons. Theoretically, it is essential to make a 'perfect' plan for the healthy operation of the economy. However, it is almost impossible for the state planners to accurately manage a balance between social production and social needs and efficiently distribute the scarce resources even with the use of sophisticated computers. In fact, the central planners could never obtain complete and accurate information on economic activities from which to formulate plans due to information constraints and asymmetries. Furthermore, the centrally planned system also generated many other problems. For example, as wages were fixed, workers had no incentive to work after the output quota of the factory had been reached. Any extra production might have led to the increase of the following year's quota while salaries remained unchanged. Factory managers and government planners frequently bargained over work targets, funds, and material supplies allocated to the factory. Usually, government agencies allocated less than managers requested so managers requested more than they needed; when bargaining over production, managers, however, asked for a smaller quota than they were able to finish, so they were usually set a larger quota than requested.[13]

China's decentralization of its mandatory planning system and introduction of market mechanisms which began at 1978 first focused on a gradual transition from the PCS to the HRS under which farmers were free to decide what and how to produce in their contracted farmlands and, having fulfilled the state's production quotas, could sell their excess products on the free market and be able to pursue some non-agricultural activities. In 1984 when urban reform was implemented, China aimed at regulating industrial production by market forces, in the same way, after fulfilling their output quotas, enterprises could make profits by selling their excess product at free or floating prices. It is worth noting that the above efforts resulted inevitably in dual prices for commodities during the transition period and had both positive and negative effects.[14]

No matter how difficult the transformation of the CPE to a market economy was, mandatory planning in the Chinese economy has been reduced many times. By the end of 1986, the number of key industrial products under direct control of the SPC had decreased from 120 to 60; accordingly, the share of industrial production fell from 40 per cent to 20 per cent; the number of commodities and materials distributed by the state (that is *tongpei wuzhi*) dropped from 250 to 20 and the goods controlled by the Ministry of Commerce (MOC) decreased from 188 to 25; the share of prices which were 'free' or 'floating' increased to about 65 per cent in agriculture and supplementary products, 55 per cent of consumer goods and 40 per cent of production materials.[15] Between 1979 and 1992, the proportion of industrial goods and materials distributed under the central plan system declined from 95 per cent to less than 10 per cent. There was a parallel reduction in the planned allocation of consumer goods: the number of first class goods distributed by the state dropped from 65 to 20 and that of production materials distributed by the state was reduced from 256 to 19 during this period.[16]

Between regions there are some slight differences in the process towards the decentralization of mandatory planning. Roughly speaking, the eastern belt is more marketized than the central belt, while the western belt is the least marketized. Within China, according to Table 3.1, the share of marketized agricultural products ranged between 20.3 per cent (Qinghai) and 43.3 per cent (Jilin) in 1988 and 60 per cent (Henan) and 98.8 per cent (Guangdong) in 1994. It is more interesting to note that some developed FCADs (such as Shanghai, Beijing, Jiangsu, and so on) were not as highly marketized as the poor FCADs (such as Anhui, Guangxi, Hainan, and so on) in 1988. The probable cause of this is the fact that China's agricultural reform was first carried out in Anhui and other poor and agriculture-based FCADs, whereas Shanghai and Beijing – the centrally administered municipalities with strong industrial bases – lagged behind those agriculture-based FCADs. Using the data given in Table 3.1, we can make further analysis for the correlation between the share of marketized agricultural products and the ratio of market-regulated price to state-controlled price:

$$\ln(SMAP94/SMAP88) = 0.9960 + 1.4664\ln RMP \qquad (3.1)$$
$$(33.51)\quad(4.21)$$
$$(N = 23,\ R^2 = 0.46,\ F = 17.73)$$

where, $SMAP$ = share of marketized agricultural products, and RMP = ratio of market-regulated price to state-controlled price. From Equation 3.1, we may find that $SMAP88$ is negatively related to RMP, implying that the higher the market-regulated price to the state-controlled price, the lower the share of marketized agricultural products. This was reasonable and reflected to some extent the government's efforts to stabilize the market, by letting the FCADs with market-regulated price close to or lower than the state-controlled one share a higher proportion of the market-oriented reform in the agricultural sector during the early period of economic reform (1978–88). In 1994, the agricultural marketization was positively related to RMP.

3.3   LABOUR

After the establishment of the new China, the labour market was officially eliminated because according to Marxist theory labour is not a commodity to be bought and sold. From the late 1950s, the system of state allocation for all urban employment was gradually introduced. After 1966, the state became responsible for job allocation for the entire urban labour force. All labour was allocated either to units owned by the states or to large collectives which were essentially the same as state-owned units. In the centrally planned system, labour force was allocated to enterprises by the state and lifetime employment was guaranteed. Wages were also determined by the state in the principle of 'distribution according to working performance' (*anlao fenpei*). There is no doubt that this kind of system eliminated the widespread occurrence of unemployment that had usually existed in the old China and has universally existed in all capitalist countries. It also effectively equalized wages and considerably reduced gaps between the haves and the have-nots.

This rigid system of job allocation, however, has resulted in some disadvantages. Once people were employed in the state sector, their jobs were secure, regardless of the quality of their work. The system thus became known as the 'iron rice bowl' (*tie fanwan*) because of the employment security it implied. Employing units could

Table 3.1 Share of marketized agricultural products by FCAD, 1988 and 1994

| | SMAP (%) | | RMP |
FCAD	1988	1994	1988
Anhui	40.1	81.7	0.822
Beijing	29.6	94.2	1.116
Fujian	32.5	91.0	0.984
Gansu	20.8	85.0	1.119
Guangdong	36.0	98.8	0.887
Guangxi	35.9	81.2	0.940
Guizhou	24.8		1.690
Hainan	34.1		0.887
Hebei	29.3	88.8	0.993
Heilongjiang	29.3	81.2	0.996
Henan	26.4	60.0	1.049
Hubei	27.3	72.7	1.030
Hunan	35.1	79.3	0.970
Inner Mongolia	26.9		0.837
Jiangsu	29.5	77.4	1.015
Jiangxi	31.6	74.7	0.897
Jilin	43.3	85.9	0.957
Liaoning	33.1	90.4	1.042
Ningxia	28.5	81.5	0.961
Qinghai	20.3	77.5	1.215
Shaanxi	31.0	77.2	1.026
Shandong	28.9	73.5	0.953
Shanghai	27.8	91.7	1.024
Shanxi	23.3	80.9	1.005
Tianjin	38.4		1.020
Tibet	23.0		1.008
Yunnan	21.5	67.3	1.164
Zhejiang	33.5	76.5	1.004

Notes: (1) *SMAP* = share of marketized agricultural products; (2) *RMP* = ratio of market price to state-controlled price.
Sources: (1) SSB (1989, p. 130); (2) C. Riskin (1994, p. 350, table 10.11); and (3) PYC (1995, p. 19, table 2).

not freely employ whom they needed and had to provide almost equal pay to those who performed differently. This hindered the improvement of labour productivity. Furthermore, the system did not encourage people to develop their talents and enthusiasm fully since they could not choose the work that best suited them, thus reducing considerably the incentive for them to work harder. Under the equal wage system (namely, 'eating from the same pot', or *daguo fan*) human resources were not allocated in the efficient way and labour productivity growth was not as fast as it might have been.

Realizing the negative effects of this labour system, the government began to carry out a series of reforms in the early 1980s. The earliest effort included the introduction of a contract system – setting up a production quota for each employee. Nevertheless, this system was not so successful in the industrial (mainly state-owned) sector as in the agricultural sector due to the complicated production processes of the former. In July 1986, the NPC announced four laws concerning employment. According to the laws the governmental allocation of workers and lifetime employment were abolished and, at the same time, a contract system (*hetong zhi*) was introduced. In the contract system, all employees were hired as contractual workers (*hetong gong*) and the employed terms varied from less than one year to more than five years. Naturally, when the contract expired, either the worker was laid-off or the contract was renewed. Unfortunately, in practice the contract system has not worked so well in the state sector as in the non-state sector.

Since reform and opening up to the outside world, Chinese employment patterns has been experiencing structural changes, with the decline of the state sector and the growth of the non-state sector (see Figure 3.1). In comparison with the state sector (such as party and government agencies, SOEs, and so on) in which (a) employment is more secure and (b) subsidies on housing, medical care, and so on are provided in most cases, the non-state sector has attracted the job seekers through both a competitive salary and more economic incentives for employees to work hard.[17]

3.4 PRODUCTION MANAGEMENT

3.4.1 Agriculture

After the founding of the PRC, the Chinese government reformed the ownership of land (*tugai*) and proportionally distributed the cultivated land among farmers. As a result, the farmers' incentive to work increased significantly. However, the new leadership only took this land reform as a provisional measure and did not consider it to be proper for a socialist economy. In the second half of the 1950s, China began to transform its private ownership of land. By 1958, the PCS had been adopted as a universal form of

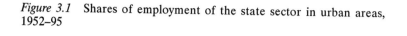

Figure 3.1 Shares of employment of the state sector in urban areas, 1952–95

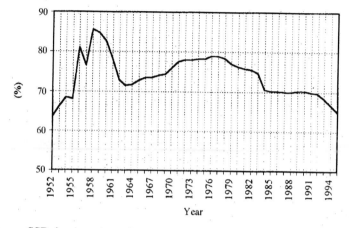

Source: SSB (various issues).

agricultural production throughout mainland China. About 150 million rural households were grouped into five million production teams which in turn were organized nationwide into 50,000 people's communes.[18] Under the PCS, land was owned collectively and the output was distributed to each household according to the work points (*gongfen*). The state purchased a major share of the grain output and distributed it to the non-agricultural population through government agencies. For much of the pre-reform period, the independent accounting unit was the production team. In the GLF and the high tide of the GCR, the production brigade (usually including several production teams) and even the people's commune (usually including several production brigades) were selected as independent accounting units in some 'advanced' areas where peasants were persuaded to have meals with 'big-pot'. Naturally, the PCS generally has been known to provide disincentives for the farmers to work harder.

The PCS lasted for more than 20 years in China before the government began to introduce a household-based and production-related responsibility system (HRS) in the early 1980s. Under the HRS each household may be able to sign a contract with local government to obtain a certain amount of arable land and production equipment depending on the number of rural population in the family and have a production quota. As long as the household completes its quota of product to the state, it can decide freely what to produce and how to sell. Although land is still owned by the state, the HRS and the PCS are definitely different from each other.

3.4.2 Industry

Generally, China's industrial organization experienced a period of concentralization and then a period of decentralization. In much of the pre-reform period, China's industrial organization was implemented via a centrally planned system which offered the advantages of rapid structural transformation through direct and strong government participation and large-scale mobilization of resources and their selective disposition to priority sectors. Such a system enabled the industrial sector to grow at highly creditable rates between 1953 and 1978. The advantages of rapid structural change under a centrally planned system, however, were soon outweighed by the problems of low efficiency, slow technological progress, sectoral disproportion, and sharp annual fluctuations in growth rates.

In general, SOEs were established to serve five important roles in the Chinese economy: (1) they had in many cases led to improved efficiency and increased technological competitiveness; (2) they had generally taken a more socially responsible attitude than the purely private enterprises; (3) they had helped to prevent oligopolistic collusion by refusing to collude; (4) they had helped the government to pursue its regional policy by shifting investment to the poor west of the country; and (5) they had been used by the government as a means of managing aggregate demand to enable it to operate its counter-cyclical policy. Closely copying the Soviet prototype, the SOEs followed a 'unified supply and unified collection' system in which the state supplied all inputs (such as labour, funds, raw material, power supply, and so on) necessary to execute production targets and claimed all output and financial revenues.[19]

The main substantive difference between the COEs and SOEs lies in the extent of government control. The SOEs serve to some extent as the concrete manifestation of the socialist principle of public ownership of the means of production by the whole people. Local governments are responsible for the provision of inputs to the COEs within their jurisdiction and have first if not sole claim on their output and revenues. Usually, the COEs are classified into two parts: urban COEs are directly controlled by local government and subjected to state plans; rural COEs are fully under the jurisdiction of the township and village government units.

Obviously, the IOEs were the freest to decide on investment, labour, output, and pricing and, above all, the most market-oriented. China's IOEs practically ceased to exist from 1958 when the socialist transformation of national capitalist industry was completed to 1979 when the Chinese government began to reform its CPE. During the reform era, the IOEs have experienced a recovery between 1978–88, a short hover between 1989–91, and a mushrooming since 1992. According to the Chinese definition, the IOEs employing up to eight people are officially defined as *getihu* (individual household), and those with eight or more people are officially defined as *shiyingqiye* (privately owned enterprise).[20]

The OOEs mainly comprise joint-ventures and wholly foreign-owned enterprises. Like the IOEs, the OOEs also have grown rapidly since the early 1980s, as a result of dramatic inflows of foreign capitals into China. We will discuss this issue in detail in Chapter 7.

Since 1978, industrial reforms in China have sought to improve enterprise incentive systems, utilize indirect economic levers (price, tax, interest rate, credit, banking, and the rest) to regulate industrial production, endow enterprises with greater relative decision-making autonomy and above all, to compel enterprises to operate according to market regulations. The positive effects of reform on industrial performance are evident from the drastic industrial growth during the reform period (see Chapter 5.2). The dynamism of the industrialization may be attributed to a variety of reform measures. One such measure was the shift in sectoral priorities within industry which allowed a greater share of resources to be diverted away from the input- and capital-intensive producer goods industries towards the more efficient and profitable consumer goods industries. Another measure was the lifting of previous restrictions on the development of the non-state sector and the policy of promoting a diversified ownership structure. This has led to the explosive growth of the non-state sector which is increasingly acting as the engine of industrial development particularly since the early 1990s when China formally tried to transform its economy to a socialist market system. From 1978 to 1995, the shares of industrial output produced by the SOEs, COEs, IOEs, and OOEs changed greatly, with the GVIO growing much slower in the SOEs than in the COEs, IOEs, and OOEs (see Figure 3.2). It can be seen that the SOEs' share in GVIO first began to rank after the COEs' in 1994.

Figure 3.2   Shares of GVIO in different types of industrial enterprises, 1949–95

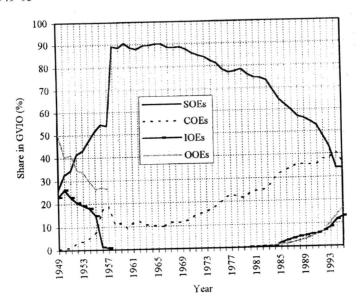

Source: SSB (1996, p. 403; and 1996b, pp. 25–6).

The substantial reform of the state industrial organization started in 1984 with the CCP and government's decision to shift the emphasis of reforms from the agricultural sector to the non-agricultural sector. On 10 May 1984, the State Council issued the 'Provisional Regulations on the Enlargement of Autonomy of State-owned Industrial Enterprises' which outlines ten specific decision-making powers to be enjoyed by enterprises. The 'invigoration' of large- and medium-sized SOEs and the application of indirect means to regulate SOEs were adopted as policy in the State Council's governmental report to the fourth Session of the Sixth NPC on 25 March 1986. In December, the 'Bankruptcy Law Concerning the State Enterprises' was adopted by the NPC. However, the Bankruptcy Law was not effectively applied until the early 1990s due to fears of unemployment and social instability as China does not have a relatively complete social security system.[21]

Following the call for faster economic growth and reform by Deng Xiaoping, the government began to accelerate and intensify market-oriented reforms after 1992. Industrial reform was focused on the issue of property right reform by granting more autonomies for the SOEs. In June 1992, State Commission for Restructuring the Economic Systems (SCRES), SPC, Ministry of Finance (MOF), the People's Bank of China (PBC), and the Production Office of State Council (the former name of SETC) jointly issued the 'Provisional Regulations on Joint-Stock Companies' to govern the formation of shareholding companies. The regulations cover the standardization of joint stock companies, their accounting system, financial management, taxation and auditing, labour and wage system. This was followed by the State Council's 'Regulations on the Transformation of the Operating Mechanisms of State-owned Industrial Enterprises' on 22 July 1992, which codified the independent decision-making powers of the SOEs in 14 key areas (including production, investment, labour, marketing, independent profit and loss accounting, assets, mergers, closures, bankruptcy, and so on).

Since Deng Xiaoping's theory on the construction of a socialist market economy with Chinese characteristics was formally adopted in 1993, there has been rapid and substantial changes in industrial management. One important policy is the importation of a 'modern enterprise system' which in practice follows the modern western-type and market-based corporate system. Besides its critical role in the sustainable improvement of productivity in the industrial sector, industrial reform is also the institutional *sine qua non* of establishing an effectively functioning competitive market system.

Geographically, the transformation from the monotonous industrial system to a multifarious one was unevenly implemented in China, as can be illustrated in Table 3.2. In 1978, the largest share of GVIO derived from the SOEs in all the 30 FCADs with Shanghai sharing the highest ratio (91.7 per cent) and Jiangsu the lowest ratio (61.5 per cent). Since then the GVIO share of the SOEs decreased considerably. In 1995, the GVIO was mainly contributed by the non-state sectors (such as COEs, IOEs, or OOEs) in nine FCADs. Specifically, the output values of the COEs in eight FCADs (Hebei, Jiangsu, Zhejiang, Anhui, Fujian, Shandong, Henan and Guangdong) exceeded that of the SOEs; the output values of the OOEs in three FCADs (Shanghai, Guangdong and Fujian) and the IOEs in Zhejiang province began to lead that of the SOEs.

Table 3.2 Shares of different ownership enterprises in GVIO by FCAD, 1978 and 1995 (%)

FCAD	1978		1995			
	SOEs	COEs	SOEs	COEs	IOEs	OOEs
Anhui	79.9	20.1	31.7	43.1	17.8	7.4
Beijing	82.7	17.3	53.8	20.7	1.0	24.6
Fujian	74.2	25.8	18.0	31.9	15.5	34.7
Gansu	90.9	9.1	66.4	19.2	10.0	4.4
Guangdong	67.8	32.2	17.9	30.8	9.0	42.3
Guangxi	78.8	21.2	40.2	25.2	23.4	11.2
Guizhou	81.0	19.0	67.0	15.1	12.9	5.1
Hainan	82.5	17.5	40.8	9.6	14.8	34.9
Hebei	71.8	28.2	36.2	37.5	16.9	9.4
Heilongjiang	83.1	16.9	66.4	19.1	7.0	7.4
Henan	74.0	26.0	33.9	39.1	20.0	7.0
Hubei	77.3	22.7	38.1	37.0	16.7	8.2
Hunan	75.0	25.0	41.7	30.9	21.8	5.6
Inner Mongolia	77.2	22.8	63.4	18.8	10.9	6.9
Jiangsu	61.5	38.5	21.1	60.0	4.4	14.4
Jiangxi	78.2	21.8	52.8	29.5	11.2	6.6
Jilin	78.9	21.1	62.3	18.1	8.7	10.9
Liaoning	82.5	17.5	44.0	30.2	15.3	10.5
Ningxia	82.8	17.2	68.9	12.9	5.7	12.5
Qinghai	83.5	16.5	84.0	12.0	2.6	1.4
Shaanxi	84.2	15.8	60.8	23.8	8.9	6.4
Shandong	67.6	32.4	30.8	45.7	12.6	10.9
Shanghai	91.7	8.30	39.5	18.5	1.1	40.8
Shanxi	74.4	25.6	45.9	33.1	18.6	2.4
Sichuan	81.4	18.6	40.3	31.4	17.5	10.8
Tianjin	80.7	19.3	33.1	32.2	2.8	32.0
Tibet	76.5	23.5	73.0	17.8	5.7	3.6
Xinjiang	89.1	10.9	73.5	20.9	2.8	2.8
Yunnan	80.5	19.5	69.5	20.9	5.7	4.0
Zhejiang	61.3	38.7	14.1	46.1	27.9	11.9
CHINA	77.6	22.4	34.0	36.6	12.9	16.6

Sources: (1) G. Liu (1994, p. 9, table 5) and (2) SSB (1996, p. 405).

3.5 PUBLIC FINANCE

Public finance decides to a large extent the use of a nation's aggregate resources and, together with monetary and exchange rate policies, influences the macro balance of payments, the accumulation of foreign debt, and the rates of inflation, interest, and so on. However, the degree of impact may differ significantly and depend upon whether the economy is managed under the market-oriented system or centrally planned system. Public finance usually plays an important role in promoting balanced development and equilibrium in both wealth accumulation and distribution for a planned economy in which central government collects and directly dispenses much of its budget for society, while the local budget is collected from and used for local administrative organs, factories, enterprises, and welfare facilities. As the market economy is a private-ownership system, the channels of policy influences are much more indirect and mainly through the *laissez-faire* approach.

Since the late 1970s, public finance, as an important component of the Chinese economic system, has undergone a series of reforms of the central–local relations.[22] The goals of these reforms were to decentralize the fiscal structure and strengthen the incentive for local government to collect more revenue for themselves and for the central government to maintain an egalitarian fiscal redistribution among the FCADs. Briefly, China's efforts towards this end have experienced four different stages, all of which sought to find a rational revenue-raising formula between the central and local governments:

The First Stage (1980–84)

The Chinese government began to implement the fiscal system entitled '*huafen shouzhi, fenji baogan*' (divide revenue and expenditure, set up diversified contract system) in 1980. The main contents of the fiscal reform included (1) the transformation from the traditional system of 'having meals in one pot' (*yizhao chifan*) to that of 'having meals in different pots (*fenzhao chifan*); (2) the transformation of financial redistribution from mainly through sectors directly under the central government to mainly through regions; and (3) the transformation of the divisions of revenue and expenditure and the proportion of revenue sharing between the central and local governments from being fixed annually to being fixed for every five years.

During this period, the basic structure of central–local fiscal relations was framed and amended frequently. In 1980, there were ten FCADs (Inner Mongolia, Fujian, Guangdong, Guangxi, Guizhou, Yunnan, Tibet, Qinghai, Ningxia and Xinjiang) on which the central government taxed a zero marginal rate. Specifically, Guangdong – a coastal province with close proximity to Hong Kong and Macau – was required to pay a lump-sum tax (LT) to the central government; Fujian – another coastal province with close proximity to Taiwan – was able to retain all the revenue it collected plus a lump-sum subsidy (LS) from central government; the other eight poor provinces and ethnic minority-based autonomous regions could retain all the revenue they collected and additionally received a lump-sum but growing subsidy (GS) from the central government. In five FCADs (Beijing, Tianjin, Liaoning, Shanghai and Jiangsu), the total revenue collected was to be shared with the central government in fixed proportions (SOR) which varied from 12 to 90 per cent.[23] In the remaining FCADs, revenue was shared between the central and local governments in more complicated ways and, as a result of considerable and frequent politicing, negotiating and bargaining with central government, the fiscal arrangements were amended and the shares of these provinces were generally raised in 1982 and lowered in 1983 in accordance with central government's revenue requirement (see Table 3.3).

The Second Stage (1985–87)

The fiscal system entitled 'huafen shuizhong, heding shouzhi, fenji baogan' (divide the categories of tax, verify revenue and expenditure, and set up diversified contract system) was introduced from 1985. This system, which was to strengthen the method of 'having meals in different pots', divided revenue into three parts: the centrally fixed revenue, the locally fixed revenue, and the revenue shared by the central and local governments. Among other changes of the central–local fiscal relations, Jilin, Jiangxi, and Gansu provinces moved from DRS to LS, Shaanxi province from SOR to LS, Heilongjiang province from DRS to SOR in 1985 and LT in 1986 respectively. Simultaneously the favourable fiscal policies were still applied in Guangdong and Fujian provinces and other minority-based autonomous regions, as demonstrated in Table 3.3.

Table 3.3 Changes of the central–local fiscal relations, 1980–93

FCAD	1980 –81	1982	1983 –84	1985	1986 –87	1988 –90	1991 –93
Anhui	DR	SOR	SOR	SOR	SOR	SOR	SOR
Beijing	SOR	SOR	SOR	SOR	SOR	STR	STR
Fujian	LS	LS	LS	LS	LS	LS	LS
Gansu	DR	SOR	DRS	LS	LS	LS	LS
Guangdong	LT	LT	LT	LT	LT	GT	GT
Guangxi	GS	GS	GS	GS	GS	GS	LS
Guizhou	GS	GS	GS	GS	GS	GS	LS
Hainan						GT	LS
Hebei	DR	SOR	SOR	SOR	SOR	STR	STR
Heilongjiang	DRS	DRS	DRS	SOR	LT	LT	LT/STR
Henan	DR	SOR	SOR	SOR	SOR	STR	STR
Hubei	DR	SOR	SOR	SOR	ROR	ROR	LT/SGT
Hunan	DR	SOR	SOR	SOR	SOR	GT	GT
Inner Mongolia	GS	GS	GS	GS	GS	GS	LS
Jiangsu	SOR	SOR	SOR	SOR	SOR	STR	STR
Jiangxi	DRS	DRS	DRS	LS	LS	LS	LS
Jilin	DRS	DRS	DRS	LS	LS	LS	LS
Liaoning	SOR	SOR	SOR	SOR	SOR	STR	STR/SGT
Ningxia	GS	GS	GS	GS	GS	GS	LS
Qinghai	GS	GS	GS	GS	GS	GS	LS
Shaanxi	DR	SOR	SOR	LS	LS	LS	LS
Shandong	DR	SOR	SOR	SOR	SOR	LT	LT/SGT
Shanghai	SOR	SOR	SOR	SOR	SOR	LT	LT
Shanxi	DR	DR	SOR	SOR	SOR	SOR	SOR
Sichuan	DR	SOR	SOR	SOR	ROR	ROR	LS/STR
Tianjin	SOR	SOR	SOR	SOR	SOR	SOR	SOR
Tibet	GS	GS	GS	GS	GS	GS	LS
Xinjiang	GS	GS	GS	GS	GS	GS	LS
Yunnan	GS	GS	GS	GS	GS	GS	LS
Zhejiang	DR	SOR	SOR	SOR	SOR	STR	STR

Note: the definition and formulation of the contents are given in Table 3.4.

Sources: World Bank (1990, p. 89), Oksenberg and Tong (1991, pp. 24–5), R. Argarwala (1992, p. 68), W. Wei (1994, p. 298), and Knight and Li (1995, p. 4).

Table 3.4 Definition and formulation of the fiscal policies

Fiscal policy	Definition	Revenue goes to FCAD Gov.	Revenue goes to the central Gov.	Marginal tax rate
DR	dividing revenue	$\Sigma\alpha_i C_i$	$\Sigma(1-\alpha_i)C_i$	$\Sigma(1-\alpha_i)C_i/\Sigma C_i$
DRS	dividing revenue and receiving growing subsidy	$\Sigma\alpha_i C_i + S_0(1+r)^t$	$\Sigma(1-\alpha_i)C_i - S_0(1+r)^t$	$\Sigma(1-\alpha_i)C_i/\Sigma C_i$
GS	receiving lump-sum but growing subsidy	$C + S_0(1+r)^t$	$-S_0(1+r)^t$	0
GT	paying lump-sum but growing tax	$C - T_0(1+r)^t$	$T_0(1+r)^t$	0
LS	receiving lump-sum subsidy	$C + S$	$-S$	0
LT	paying lump-sum tax	$C - T$	T	0
ROR	retaining overall revenue	C	0	0
SGT	sharing overall revenue and paying growing tax	$(1+\alpha)C - T_0(1+r)^t$	$-\alpha C + T_0(1+r)^t$	$-\alpha$
SOR	sharing overall revenue	αC	$(1-\alpha)C$	$1-\alpha$
STR	sharing target revenue but retaining residual revenue	$C - (1-\alpha)C_0(1+r)^t$	$(1-\alpha)C_0(1+r)^t$	0

Notations:

C = revenue collected by FCAD (C_0 denotes C at time zero);

C_i = revenue collected by FCAD from source i (i = 1, 2, and 3 denote revenue from source i goes to central government, to FCAD government, and is shared between them respectively)

S = lump-sum subsidy from central government (S_0 denotes S at time zero);

T = lump-sum tax to central government (T_0 denotes T at time zero);

r = annual growth rate;

α = fixed share of revenue accruing to FCAD ($0 < \alpha < 1$);

α_i = $\alpha_1, \alpha_2, \alpha_3$ (where $\alpha_1 = 0$, $\alpha_2 = 1$, $0 < \alpha_3 < 1$).

The Third Stage (1988–93)

A fiscal responsibility system entitled '*chaizheng baogan*' was introduced through two sub-stages as below.

(a) 1988–90: Seven methods were introduced during this period: (1) STR (*shouru dizheng baogan*); (2) SOR (*zhong'e fencheng*); (3) GT (*shangjie'e dizheng baogan*); (4) LT (*ding'e shangjie*); (5) LS (*ding'e buzhu*); (6) GS (*ding'e buzhu, meinian dizheng*); and (7) ROR (*zhong'e baogan*):

(b) 1991–93: Six methods were introduced during this period:[24] (1) STR: Beijing ($\alpha = 50\%$, $r = 4\%$), Hebei ($\alpha = 70\%$, $r = 4.5\%$), Liaoning ($\alpha = 58.25\%$, $r = 3.5\%$), Jiangsu ($\alpha = 41\%$, $r = 5\%$), Zhejiang ($\alpha = 61.47\%$, $r = 6.5\%$), and Henan ($\alpha = 80\%$, $r = 5\%$)) and Shenyang of Liaoning ($\alpha = 30.29\%$, $r = 4\%$), Harbin of Heilongjiang ($\alpha = 45\%$, $r = 5\%$), Ningbo of Zhejiang ($\alpha = 27.93\%$, $r = 5.3\%$), and Chongqing of Sichuan ($\alpha = 33.5\%$, $r = 4\%$); (2) SOR: Tianjin ($\alpha = 46.5\%$), Shanxi ($\alpha = 87.55\%$), and Anhui ($\alpha = 77.5\%$); (3) GT: Guangdong ($T_0 = ¥1.413$ billion, $r = 9\%$) and Hunan ($T_0 = ¥0.8$ billion, $r = 7\%$); (4) LT: Shanghai ($T_0 = ¥10.5$ billion), Shandong ($T = ¥289$ million), and Heilongjiang ($T = ¥299$ million); (5) LS: Jilin ($S = ¥107$ million), Fujian ($S = ¥50$ million), Jiangxi ($S = ¥45$ million), Shaanxi ($S = ¥120$ million), Gansu ($S = ¥125$ million), Inner Mongolia ($S = ¥1.852$ billion), Guangxi ($S = ¥608$ million), Yunnan ($S = ¥673$ million), Guizhou ($S = ¥742$ million), Qinghai ($S = ¥656$ million), Hainan ($S = ¥138$ million), Hubei ($S = 4.78\%$ of Wuhan's revenue), and Sichuan ($S = 10.7\%$ of Chongqing's revenue); and (6) SGT (*zhong'e fencheng jia zhengzhang fencheng*): Dalian of Liaoning ($\alpha = 27.74\%$, $\alpha' = 27.26\%$), Qingdao of Shandong ($\alpha = 16\%$, $\alpha' = 34\%$), and Wuhan of Hubei ($\alpha = 17\%$, $\alpha' = 25\%$).[25]

The Fourth Stage (1994–)

Since 1994, China has implemented the 'tax-sharing system' (*fenshui zhi*) under which central government collects all shared as central taxes, and local government collects only those designated as local taxes. The fourth stage fiscal reform, by transferring much of the revenue collection function to central government, attempted to tackle the principal–agent problem of the revenue contracting period. The solution was essentially to transpose the principal and agent. It can be seen from Table 3.5 that China's diversified fiscal systems have resulted in differing central–local relations since the early 1980s.

Table 3.5 Shares of central and local revenue and expenditure, 1971–95

Year	Revenue			Expenditure		
	Total (10⁹ yuan)	Central (%)	Local (%)	Total (10⁹ yuan)	Central (%)	Local (%)
1971–75	391.97	14.7	85.3	391.94	54.2	45.8
1976	77.66	12.7	87.3	80.62	46.8	53.2
1977	87.45	13.0	87.0	84.35	46.7	53.3
1978	113.22	15.5	84.5	112.21	47.4	52.6
1979	114.64	20.2	79.8	128.18	51.1	48.9
1980	115.99	24.5	75.5	122.88	54.3	45.7
1981	117.58	26.5	73.5	113.84	55.0	45.0
1982	121.23	28.6	71.4	123.00	53.0	47.0
1983	136.69	35.8	64.2	140.95	53.9	46.1
1984	164.29	40.5	59.5	170.10	52.5	47.5
1985	200.48	38.4	61.6	200.43	39.7	60.3
1986	212.20	36.7	63.3	220.49	37.9	62.1
1987	219.94	33.5	66.5	226.22	37.4	62.6
1988	235.72	32.9	67.1	249.12	33.9	66.1
1989	266.49	30.9	69.1	282.38	31.5	68.5
1990	293.71	33.8	66.2	308.36	32.6	67.4
1991	314.95	29.8	70.2	338.66	32.2	67.8
1992	348.34	28.1	71.9	374.22	31.3	68.7
1993	434.90	22.0	78.0	464.23	28.3	71.7
1994	521.91	55.7	44.3	579.26	21.7	69.7
1995	624.22	52.2	47.8	682.37	29.2	70.8

Notes: (1) 'revenue' excludes borrowing from domestic and abroad, 'expenditure excludes repayment of the principal and payment of interest on borrowing from domestic and abroad; (2) percentages are calculated by the author.
Source: SSB (1996, p. 235).

During 1980–84 when the first stage fiscal reform was implemented, China's share of central revenue to total revenue increased from 24.5 to 40.5 per cent; while its share of central expenditure to total expenditure decreased from 54.3 to 52.5 per cent accordingly. In the following years, both the share of central to total revenue and the share of central to total expenditure had decreased considerably before the 'tax-sharing system' was implemented in 1994.[26]

3.6 INVESTMENT

After three years (1950–52) of recovery, the PRC government began to construct its economy through a centrally planned approach. To overcome effectively the disequilibrated industrial distribution between the coastal and inland areas, the government shifted investment to the inland area from the coastal area. During 1953–78, the basic construction funded by the state was split 35.7 per cent in the coastal area and 55.2 per cent in the inland area (see Table 3.6). As a result, industrial production grew unevenly between the coastal and inland areas. From 1952 to 1978, the inland area's share of GVIO increased from 31.8 per cent to 40.2 per cent, while the coastal area's share of GVIO decreased from 68.2 per cent to 59.8 per cent accordingly.[27] After 1978, when the Chinese government began to realize the importance of reforming its CPE and paying more attention to efficiency rather than regional equality, capital investment was weighted to the coastal area. Between 1979–90, the coastal area accounts for 49.9 per cent of the nation's capital investment, while the inland area's share decreased accordingly to 43.2 per cent, as demonstrated in Table 3.6.

Table 3.6 Regional distribution of capital investment between coastal and inland areas,[a] 1953–90[b]

Period	Coastal (%)	Inland (%)	Coastal/inland
1953–57 (1st FYP)	36.9	46.8	0.788
1958–62 (2nd FYP)	38.4	56.0	0.686
1963–65	34.9	58.3	0.599
1966–70 (3rd FYP)	26.9	64.7	0.416
1971–75 (4th FYP)	35.5	54.4	0.653
1976–80 (5th FYP)	42.2	50.0	0.844
1981–85 (6th FYP)	47.7	46.5	1.026
1986–90 (7th FYP)	51.7	39.9	1.296
1953–78 (pre-reform)	35.7	55.2	0.647
1979–90 (post-reform)	49.9	43.2	1.155
1953–90	45.0	46.8	0.962

[a] the coastal and inland areas are defined in Table 1.3;
[b] the total investment of coastal and inland areas are less than 100.00% due to the exclusion of spatially 'unidentified' investment which includes (1) the trans-FCAD investment in railway, post and telecommunication, electric power, and so on; (2) the unified purchase of airplanes, ships, vehicles, and so on; (3) the investment in national defence.
Sources: (1) SSB (1991, 1992) and (2) Li and Fan (1994, p. 65).

Since the early 1980s, there has been a fundamental change in the investment system, mainly characterized by decentralization and regional autonomy. Concerning decentralization, the responsibilities are proportionally shared between central and local governments: (1) projects which are closely related to the overall structure of the national economy, such as key energy, raw material industry bases, transprovincial communication and transportation networks, key mechanical, electronic, and other high-tech development projects, key agricultural bases, as well as the national defence industry are still financially controlled by the state; (2) the primary industrial and local projects, such as agriculture, forestry and wood, local energy, raw material industries, regional communication and transportation networks, mechanical and light industries, science and technology, education, culture, public health, urban public infrastructure and services, and so on are mainly invested and managed by local government. In the case of regional autonomy, the quotas of industrial construction and technological remoulding items needed to be approved by the SPC increased from 30 million yuan or over to 50 million yuan or over for energy, communication and raw material industries and from 10 million yuan or over to 30 million yuan or over for light and other industries. Production construction items beyond the above limits and non-productive construction items are decided by the FCADs themselves.[28]

3.7   SUMMARY

In China, economic development has been a priority for all FCADs since the late 1970s. Beginning with a common background of ideological system and history, but proceeding with differing paces of economic reform, China has chosen different economic policies and plans by which to develop its FCADs and promote the welfare of their people.

The economic incentives facing the FCADs appeared to improve over time for much of the post-reform period. In 1980, for example, no fewer than 19 FCADs were on some form of revenue sharing or division, whereas in 1985 revenue division had ceased and 15 FCADs shared their respective revenues. In 1988's reform, most of these FCADs were switched to lump sum taxation or the sharing of target revenues, while only three FCADs remained on a revenue sharing formula. In sum, this account of the fiscal relationship between central and local governments highlights four problems: first, the non-uniform treatment of FCADs appeared neither efficient nor equitable; second, the uncertainty associated with changing rules and bargaining had disincentive effects on the revenue collection of the FCAD governments; third, the high marginal tax rates faced by some FCADs could be expected to deter revenue collection; finally, the aim of various efforts to reform the centralized fiscal system was to reduce the share that central government received of the revenue collected by the FCADs.[29]

Inevitably diversified economic systems and other natural and social factors will result in the regional economic differences. A multiregional comparison of the macroeconomic performances of China will be conducted in Chapter 4.

BOX 3

Double-Track Economics

China's economic reform began in the late 1970s, carrying out a double-track system in which the share of production subject to both central and local governments declined continuously. The reform was first implemented in agricultural products and spread slowly to consumer goods and intermediate goods. In each case, a free market in which the price was subject to the market regulations developed in parallel with a controlled market in which the price was kept almost unchanged at an officially fixed level. Because the price was higher in the market-regulated track than in the state-controlled track, supply in the free market grew rapidly, so its share in total output rose steadily. Meanwhile, the planned price was able to raise incrementally until it approached the market price when the gap between supply and demand narrowed. The dual pricing system provided opportunities for people who had access to state-controlled goods and materials to make large profits by buying them at an officially-fixed low price and reselling them at a market-based price, which often led to unequal competition as well as official corruption. Nevertheless, this dual market created various distortions and speculative transactions. But it was at least better than taking no action at all during the process of rationalizing prices.

The double-track system extended through almost every sphere of the Chinese economy, from agriculture, industry, commerce, transportation, post and telecommunications to health care, education, and so on during the transition period from the centrally planned to a market-oriented system in China. By the mid-1990s, the dual pricing system had decontrolled more than 90 per cent of retail prices and 80 to 90 per cent of agricultural and intermediate product prices and removed the mandatory plans of a large number of products including fuel and raw materials.

4 A Multiregional Economic Comparison

To have good fruit you must have a healthy tree; if you have a poor tree, you will have bad fruit.

Matthew 13: 33

As we have seen in Chapter 2, natural and human resources are irregularly distributed in China. Specifically, the eastern belt is blessed with a mild climate and rich soil, while the western belt has a vast territory and sparse population. The northern part is much richer in mineral resources than the southern part, except for a few non-ferrous metals. In contrast, most of the southern part, given its favourable climate and terrain, has an agricultural advantage over most, if not all, of the northern part, the desert North and North-west regions and, in particular, dominates most of the nation's rice production. All the above regional characteristics in the distribution of resources, together with the spatially diversified economic systems and policies discussed in Chapter 3 and other historical and cultural factors, have led to the uneven spatial structure of the Chinese economy. In this chapter, a multiregional economic comparison will be conducted, with the emphases on the macroeconomic indicators, real living standards, and regional inequalities.

4.1 ABOUT THE STATISTICAL DATA

The lack of high-quality and comparable cross-section data is always the major hurdle in the study of multiregional economic issues, particularly in the CPEs. During the pre-reform period, China only published a fragmentary set of data on such indicators as NI, GVSP, GVAO, and GVIO, the reliability of which, however, is not certain. The recent research environment has been increasingly improved, along with the transformation of the Chinese economy from the centrally planned system to a market-oriented system. Since the early 1980s, an increasingly complete set of data on regional

65

Table 4.1 The main sources for China's statistical data

Title	Years	Editor(s)	Publisher
China Statistical Yearbook	1981–	SSB	CSPH
A Compilation of Historical Statistical Materials of China's Provinces, Autonomous Regions and Municipalities (1949–89)	1949–89	SSB (1990) Hsueh et al. (1993)	CSPH WVP
Almanac of China's Economy	1981–		EMP
China Economic Science Yearbook	1986–89 1990–	Xiao et al. Li et al.	ESP CSPH
China Industrial Economic Statistical Yearbook	1988–	SSB	CSPH
China Yearbook for Energy Statistics	1986–92 1993–	SSB SETC	CSPH CSPH
Price Yearbook of China	1990–	ECPYC	CPP

Acronyms: SSB = State Statistical Bureau; CSPH = China Statistical Publishing House; EMP = Economics and Management Press; ESP = Economic Science Press; SETC = State Economic and Trade Commission; ECPYC = editing committee of *Price Yearbook of China*; CPP = China Price Press; WVP = Westview Press.

economic performances have been released, as shown in Table 4.1. Regardless of this progress, many problems, however, still exist when one tries to apply the officially published data to compare the Chinese economy multiregionally.

Since the mid-1980s, China has started compiling national income statistics according to the United Nations' SNA.[1] Many theoretical and practical problems on how to adopt the SNA to Chinese economic accounting, however, still remain unsolved. For instance, the sum of the regional GDPs may not equal the national GDP published by the SSB, the reason for which is that the statistical data compiled by the SSB are derived from the records of the various ministries in charge of their related sectors whereas the regional statistical data are compiled by the regional statistical bureaux.[2]

The compilation of the GDP data left many unpersuaded in China, especially under the dual pricing system. With the exception of the data on the tertiary sector, the transformation of NMP data to the corresponding GDP data were simply devised by the SSB and, therefore, some question whether the GDP data may be arrived at by multiplying the NMP by some conversion factors. In fact, since a socialist accounting system does not take into account output value of the service sector, historical records of this sector were very fragmentary. China has published the GDP indices at constant prices with 1978 being the base year. The GDP data at constant prices are inextricably linked to the real NMP data collected by the old system. Unlike Western countries that derive real GDP using a system of price indices, the basic production units at the lowest level of the statistical reporting system are responsible for computing the real output value based on a catalogue of fixed prices (*bubian jia*) handed down from above. The raw data are then reported to the higher level of the system to be further aggregated. Many analysts argue that problems may arise in this reporting process of the compilation of GDP data.[3]

There is another question: should real or nominal GDP/NMP data be used for a multiregional comparison of the Chinese economy? Ideally, the adjusted GDP/NMP based on the PPP method in the sprit of Wolf (1985) and Summers and Heston (1991, pp. 327–68) should be used in China because of the vast range of natural and social environments and varying price levels and inflation rates across the country. Unfortunately, few such efforts have been made on the measurement of China's regional GDPs using the PPP methodology due to the lack of sufficient and up-to-date information and data. Hsueh (1994a, pp. 22–56) modifies the nominal NMP data of 29 FCADs using the 1980's fixed prices of industrial and agricultural products of which Beijing's relative price index is assumed to be 100 in 1981, while the NIs of the remaining FCADs are converted by their Beijing-based price levels respectively. Hsueh's attempt to estimate China's NMP, although heroic, is surely controversial and will leave many unpersuaded, particularly when the FCADs' industrial structures differ greatly from one another.

Difficulties may arise from the multiregional economic comparison between the pre-reform period during which China was virtually a CPE and the post-reform period during which China has been gradually approaching a market economy. In market economies, GNP is the total value of all final products and services generated and NI is the total of all incomes received by all factors in production during a defined period of time. In the CPEs, however, the NI accounts record only productive activities carried out in their territories, rather than incomes received by their residents. China's NI accounts during the pre-reform period were virtually based on the MPS, whose most important aggregate is NMP. The NMP comprehensively covers value added in the 'material' sectors of production. The sum of the outputs of all separately enumerated production units multiplied by relevant prices of outputs is called gross value of social product (GVSP). As GVSP includes also the values of intermediate products which are simply the material costs for consecutive production units, values of products were counted more than once. Obviously, the use of the GVSP concept might result in a series of negative effects particularly when using it as an indicator to evaluate multiregionally the sizes of the economies, as a part of the GVSP is contributed by intermediate products that are never meaningful to the social welfare no matter how large it is. The NI represents the sum of net product (value added) of all separately enumerated branches of the economy during a given period. In terms of value, it is equivalent to the value of the total social product within the time period minus the value of the means of production consumed during that period; in terms of materials, it is equivalent to the total social product (including means of production and means of consumption) within the given period minus the means of production consumed during that period.[4] The NI was only created in China by material production sectors, such as industry, mining, agriculture, forestry, animal husbandry, building construction, and service trades that were of a productive nature and carried out such activities as assembly, processing and repairs. However, it ignored the contributions from non-productive labours, particularly in such non-material spheres as banking, insurance, science, education, culture, health, administration, military, and so on.

With regard to most official publications that can be taken as they exist, economic data with political implications such as income distribution, inflation, credit rationing, shadow interest rates, use of foreign capital, and military expenditure, and so on are, at least partially, under government control, they had been so particularly before the early 1990s. Furthermore, the decline of professional ability and job ethics of some local officials in charge of the collection and processing of economic data could largely devalue the quality of data. For instance, it is not uncommon for rural industrial enterprises to report nominal output under the rubric of output at constant prices; government cadres and business officers in rural areas whose promotion is partly based on agricultural and industrial growth may falsify the statistical data by enlarging the output valuation.[5] Therefore, some care should be taken in the use of these published time series data.

Due to the diversified natural and social conditions among different regions, China's regional inequalities have had a long history. It is generally admitted that the eastern belt has a relatively higher per capita GNP and, of course, higher living standard than the western belt. It is noticeable that different results have emerged in the estimates of the regional economic inequalities in China. Some researchers believe that China's regional inequalities have definitely increased, reflecting the first stage of the invertedU process in Williamson (1965, pp. 165–204) as well as China's uneven regional development strategy.[6] In contrast, others argue that only the gaps between the eastern, central, and western belts have been widened for the past years while the inter-FCAD gaps have been substantially narrowed since economic reform was introduced in 1978.[7]

With the use of different data and measurements, it seems that there is never a consensus on this issue. For example, P. Zhang (1994, p. 300) uses 27 FCADs (excluding Qinghai and Tibet) for 1980, 28 FCADs (excluding Tibet) for 1981–88 and 28 FCADs (excluding Tibet and Hainan, a new province established in 1988) for 1989–90 and obtains an increasing regional inequality in terms of per capita income in rural China. Based on the multiregional data in which three municipalities directly under the central government are incorporated into their neighbouring provinces (Beijing and Tianjin into Hebei, Shanghai into Jiangsu) and Tibet and Hainan are excluded from the analysis, K. Tsui (1993) shows inter-FCAD inequality declined from the late 1970s to the mid-1980s and a reversed trend preceding the reform era. Jian *et al.* (1996, pp. 1–22) use the data of 28 FCADs (Tibet and Hainan are excluded) and obtain a V-shaped pattern for China's multiregional inequalities from 1978 to 1993. Obviously, the regional inequalities will demonstrate differing patterns if different measurements and regionalizations are employed. In addition, some care should be taken when one uses the official data to estimate China's regional inequalities for the pre- and post-reform periods during which different statistical systems were employed. We will discuss this further aspect later in this chapter.

4.2 MACROECONOMIC INDICATORS

4.2.1 General Situation

Briefly, China's macroeconomy has experienced drastic changes during the past decades (see Figure 4.1), which includes a steady growth in the First FYP (1953–57), a short leap forward followed by a sudden economic disaster between 1958–62, a rapid growth period (1963–65), a chaotic period stemming from the GCR movement (1966–76), a fast growth period (1977–) during the post-reform era with a few exceptions in 1981 and 1989–90. Particularly praiseworthy is that economic growth in China has sustained at an average rate of about 10 per cent annually since 1978 and has been among the highest of the dynamic nations during the same period. It is approximately three times that of the developed nations, more than double that of India, whose conditions are similar to those of China, and even larger than that of the NIEs such as South Korea, Taiwan, Hong Kong, Singapore, and the rest.

In 1995, China's GNP reached 5760 billion yuan (about US$694 billion), which made China the seventh largest in the world, behind the US, Japan, Germany, France, Italy, and the UK. Although China's total GNP is large, its per capita GNP is only US$530 in 1994, which is higher than that of India (US$310), Mongolia (US$340) but much lower than that of South Korea (US$8220), Malaysia (US$3520), Thailand (US$2210) and the Philippines (US$960).[8] According to the *World Bank Atlas 1996*, China had still been grouped as the least developed economy by per capita GNP.

It should be noted that, however, if it is calculated by the PPP rates, China's economic size would be much larger than that measured by the current exchange rate. Table 4.2 gives some different estimates on the per capita GDP in accordance to the PPP and exchange rate conversion methods. Generally, even though they differ greatly, the per capita GDPs adjusted by PPP rates are approximately two to four times that measured by the exchange rate. Of course, the optimistic estimations of Chinese GDP have not been widely accepted, due to incomplete price statistics.[9] Nevertheless, it is unbelievable that the gaps of real living standards between China and the advanced nations are as large as that of the per capita GNPs in US dollars between them. We will discuss this issue later in detail in Section 4.3.1.

Figure 4.1 Economic growth, 1950–77 (NI) and 1978–95 (GNP)

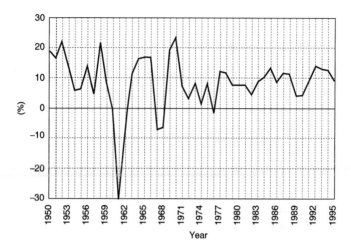

Source: SSB (various issues)

Table 4.2 Different estimates of China's per capita GDP

Year	Conversion method	Per capita GDP (US$)	Conversion ratio[a]	Author(s)
1979	PPP rate	1000	0.41	WB
1986	PPP rate	2440	0.37	HS
1988	PPP rate	2472	0.54	K
1990	PPP rate	1031	1.58	RC
1990	PPP rate	2140	0.76	LS
1991	PPP rate	1680	1.11	BUAA
1992	PPP rate	1600	1.42	IMF
1993	PPP rate	2120	1.36	WB
1993	Exchange rate	485	5.95	WB
1993	Exchange rate	510	5.65	SSB
1994	PPP rate	2510	1.55	WB
1995	Exchange rate	574	8.24	SSB

[a] implied PPP of the US dollar or exchange rate of RMB yuan to US dollar.

Acronyms: HS = Hesiods and Samorse; K = Kravis; RC = Rand McNolly & Company; LS = Lorentz Samoese; BUAA = Beijing University of Aero. & Astro.; IMF = International Monetary Fund; WB = World Bank staff estimates; SSB = State Statistical Bureau.

Sources: (1) World Bank (1996, p. 21) and (2) J. Zheng (1996, p. 1).

4.2.2 Estimation of GNP for the Pre-reform Period

Since the founding the PRC, China has adopted two different concepts (NI/GVSP and GNP/GDP) to measure its national and regional economic performances. As explained earlier, the concept of NI deviates from that of GNP *ex facto*, because the former is based on the traditional MPS used by most CPEs, while the latter is based on the SNA used by the market economies. Therefore, it is useful for us to estimate China's GNP for the pre-reform period during which the MPS was introduced.

Different approaches have been suggested to estimate the GNP for the CPEs. Marea (1985, pp. 15–6, 27–119), for example, presents five alternative approaches. The first approach entails building a more or less complete set of national accounts from disaggregated data, and then computing GNP as the sum of value added in the production sectors. This approach needs production data aggregated according to some sort of labour cost valuation. The second approach is scaling up from NMP to GNP on the basis of an average relationship found to hold for either other CPEs or market economies. Differences in economic systems as well as in qualities and levels of development must be taken into consideration. The third approach relates to scaling up from NMP by adding net value added in the non-material sectors plus depreciation, and otherwise adjusting as necessary to make the GNP estimates for CPEs comparable with those for market economies. The method is subject to estimation errors, and is also time-consuming because of the need for data reconstruction and adjustments. The fourth method is to derive GNP as the sum of the end-use values of all economic units (consumption, investment, government expenditure, and net export). This is an expenditure approach which is widely used in estimating income in market economies. The fifth method is called 'physical indicators approach', which involves GNP directly in dollars by currency exchanges rate conversion or some type of PPP. The essence of this approach is the determination of a regression relationship between a set of physical indicators (such as consumption and the stock of certain assets) of development and the per capita dollar GDP of arbitrarily chosen sample countries. This approach sounds well grounded and practical, but it too encounters the problems of structural and development-level differences between the target country and the reference country.

None of the above methods, as argued by E. Hwang (1993,

p. 108), could be applied to the CPEs with no comprehensive, consistent, and up-to-date statistical information on the NMP or physical aggregation data for direct use. Before the reform, China had been an autarkic CPE, therefore, Marea's approaches could not be applied to estimate the GNP for that period. As China has adopted the SNA since the mid-1980s while at the same time did abandoning the MPS until 1994, it is possible for us to quantitatively estimate the correlation between the MPS and the SNA. Based on the data from 1985 to 1993, we may estimate three linear equations between GNP and GVSP, NI and GVIO:[10]

$$GNP = 0.4837GVSP \quad (1985\text{–}93, R^2 = 0.991, D.W. = 0.343) \quad (4.1)$$
$$(78.456)$$

$$GNP = 1.3259NI \quad (1985\text{–}93, R^2 = 0.993, D.W. = 0.796) \quad (4.2)$$
$$(84.587)$$

$$GNP = 0.5799GVIAO \quad (1985\text{–}93, R^2 = 0.967, D.W. = 0.719) \quad (4.3)$$
$$(39.210)$$

Using Equation 4.2 (as it is the most significantly estimated among the three equations), we can approximately derive China's GNP series from 1952 to 1978. By replacing the NI series into Equation 4.2, the GNP derivation is shown in the second column of Table 4.3. It is worth noting that China's NI/GNP ratio $(1/1.3259 \approx 0.7542)$ estimated in Equation 4.2 is less than North Korea's (0.8) estimated by E. Hwang (1993, p. 118). The causes of the difference between China and North Korea need to be explored in detail.

The differences between the estimated GNP (the second column of Table 4.3) and the SSB's GNP (the fourth column of Table 4.3) may be possibly explained by (1) the estimation errors produced in Equation 4.2 and (2) the official miscalculation arising from the incomplete application of the SNA. If NI had been more accurately stated by SSB than GNP from 1986 to 1993, we may conclude that China's actual GNP had been understated before 1992 and overstated after 1992 by the SSB.[11] On the other hand, however, the Chinese economy could have been underestimated if international statistical standards are applied. For example, according to the evidence released by the SSB, China's actual GDP could have been over 30 per cent larger than the current figure, which is contributed by (1) real estate sector (10 per cent), (2) government, science and technology, education, culture, and health care sectors

Table 4.3 Estimated and officially reported GNPs at current prices, 1952–95

Year	GNP (billion yuan)		Per capita GNP (yuan)	
	Estimated	*Official*	*Estimated*	*Official*
1952	78.1	NA	135.86	NA
1953	94.0	NA	159.89	NA
1954	99.2	NA	164.57	NA
1955	104.5	NA	169.98	NA
1956	116.9	NA	186.13	NA
1957	120.4	NA	185.63	NA
1958	148.2	NA	224.62	NA
1959	162.0	NA	241.08	NA
1960	161.8	NA	244.32	NA
1961	132.1	NA	200.52	NA
1962	122.5	NA	182.05	NA
1963	132.6	NA	191.68	NA
1964	154.6	NA	219.29	NA
1965	183.9	NA	253.53	NA
1966	210.3	NA	282.11	NA
1967	197.2	NA	258.17	NA
1968	187.6	NA	238.90	NA
1969	214.4	NA	265.77	NA
1970	228.9	NA	275.75	NA
1971	275.4	NA	323.12	NA
1972	283.2	NA	324.87	NA
1973	307.3	NA	344.51	NA
1974	311.3	NA	342.64	NA
1975	331.9	NA	359.09	NA
1976	321.8	NA	343.37	NA
1977	350.6	NA	369.12	NA
1978	399.1	358.8	414.61	372.74
1979	444.2	399.8	455.37	409.87
1980	489.0	447.0	495.41	452.86
1981	522.5	477.3	522.16	476.96
1982	564.6	519.3	556.00	511.42
1983	627.9	580.9	612.66	566.76
1984	749.4	696.2	724.23	672.82
1985	933.4	856.8	881.84	809.44
1986	1047.3	972.6	974.17	904.69
1987	1241.2	1195.5	1135.59	1093.78
1988	1560.6	1492.2	1405.62	1344.01
1989	1747.0	1691.8	1550.08	1501.10
1990	1907.2	1859.8	1668.11	1626.65
1991	2195.3	2166.2	1895.39	1870.27
1992	2681.4	2665.2	2288.45	2274.62
1993	3299.1	3456.1	2752.69	2883.69
1994	NA	4653.3	NA	3882.60
1995	NA	5727.7	NA	4728.91

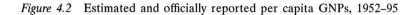

Figure 4.2 Estimated and officially reported per capita GNPs, 1952–95

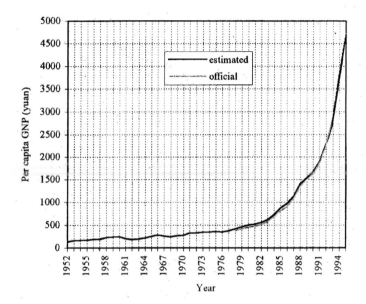

Source: Table 4.3

(4 per cent), (3) self-service within enterprises (3 per cent), (4) rural construction (2.2 per cent) and other rural economic activities (2 per cent), and (5) national defence and underground economic activities[12] (10 per cent).[13]

4.2.3 A Multiregional Comparison

The FCADs' NI statistical data were only reported from 1952 to 1993, while their GDP statistical data have been available since 1978. In order to conduct a consistent multiregional comparison of the Chinese economy across the pre- and post-reform periods, we have to apply the NI data and Equation 4.2 to estimate the GDP indicators for the pre-reform period. As the GDP data were not statistically reported by a few FCADs (such as Liaoning in 1978 and 1979, Qinghai in 1979 and 1981–84, Guangxi in 1979, 1981–85 and 1987, and Tibet in 1978–84) during the early period when the MPS was transferred to the SNA, we have to make some approximations of per capita GDP for these FCADs according to their NI data and Equation 4.2. Finally, there still exists an obstacle in the multiregional comparison of the Chinese economy: Tibet had not officially reported any statistical data before 1980. The only possible method we can use is to estimate Tibet's per capita GDP using other FCADs to which Tibet is the most similar in economic conditions as reference. In 1980, the per capita NI of Tibet was 266 yuan, approximately 1.127 times that of Yunnan. Based on Yunnan's GDP data and a conversion factor of 1.127, we may obtain Tibet's per capita GDP data for the period from 1952 to 1979.[14] The estimated per capita GDP data for the selected years (1952, 1979, 1990 and 1995) are shown in Table 4.4, from which the FCADs that prospered and those stagnated that can be derived.

1952–79

(29 FCADs are included): 15 FCADs (Beijing, Hebei, Shanxi, Liaoning, Jilin, Jiangsu, Zhejiang, Shandong, Henan, Hubei, Sichuan, Yunnan, Tibet, Shaanxi and Qinghai) ranked higher than before, ten FCADs (Tianjin, Inner Mongolia, Heilongjiang, Anhui, Fujian, Jiangxi, Hunan, Guangxi, Ningxia and Xinjiang) ranked lower than before, and four FCADs (Shanghai, Guangdong, Guizhou and Gansu) remained unchanged.

1979–90

(29 FCADs are included): ten FCADs (Jiangsu, Zhejiang, Anhui, Fujian, Shandong, Hubei, Guangdong, Yunnan, Tibet and Xinjiang) ranked higher than before, 11 FCADs (Hebei, Shanxi, Inner Mongolia, Jilin, Heilongjiang, Guangxi, Sichuan, Guizhou, Shaanxi, Gansu and Qinghai) ranked lower than before, and eight FCADs (Beijing, Tianjin, Liaoning, Shanghai, Jiangxi, Henan, Yunnan and Ningxia) remained unchanged.

1990–95

(30 FCADs are included): 11 FCADs (Hebei, Inner Mongolia, Jiangsu, Zhejiang, Anhui, Fujian, Shandong, Henan, Guangxi, Hainan and Sichuan) ranked higher than before, 12 FCADs (Shanxi, Liaoning, Jilin, Heilongjiang, Jiangxi, Hubei, Tibet, Shaanxi, Gansu, Qinghai, Ningxia and Xinjiang) ranked lower than before, and seven FCADs (Beijing, Tianjin, Shanghai, Hunan, Guangdong, Guizhou and Yunnan) remained unchanged.

Table 4.4   Per capita GDP (yuan)[a] by FCAD, 1952, 1979, 1990 and 1995[b]

FCAD	1952[c]	1979	1990	1995
Anhui	102(22)	170(27)	1090(24)	3332(21)
Beijing	330(3)	2234(2)	4881(2)	11150(2)
Fujian	126(14)	265(20)	1551(12)	6674(8)
Gansu	124(16)	299(16)	1059(27)	2270(29)
Guangdong	117(18)	274(18)	2395(5)	7836(5)
Guangxi	81(27)	169(28)	933(29)	3535(18)
Guizhou	73(29)	136(29)	794(30)	1796(30)
Hainan	–(NA)	–(NA)	1473(15)	5030(11)
Hebei	145(9)	383(7)	1367(17)	4427(13)
Heilongjiang	276(4)	485(5)	1901(8)	5443(10)
Henan	101(23)	262(21)	1045(28)	3300(23)
Hubei	110(20)	277(17)	1493(13)	4143(15)
Hunan	102(21)	261(22)	1159(20)	3435(20)
Inner Mongolia	198(7)	338(14)	1328(18)	3647(16)
Jiangsu	126(13)	375(10)	1953(7)	7296(6)
Jiangxi	137(11)	254(24)	1118(23)	2966(26)
Jilin	189(8)	389(6)	1617(10)	4356(14)
Liaoning	257(5)	870[c](4)	2452(4)	6826(7)
Ningxia	138(10)	266(19)	1320(19)	3309(22)
Qinghai	125(15)	378(9)	1478(14)	3437(19)
Shaanxi	100(24)	343(12)	1148(21)	2846(27)
Shandong	112(19)	340(13)	1599(11)	5747(9)
Shanghai	774(1)	3792(1)	5818(1)	17403(1)
Shanxi	124(17)	303(15)	1423(16)	3550(17)
Sichuan	76(28)	198(26)	1064(26)	3121(24)
Tianjin	347(2)	1447(3)	3620(3)	9768(3)
Tibet	94[d](25)	255[d](23)	1127(22)	2333(28)
Xinjiang	208(6)	371(11)	1688(9)	5025(12)
Yunnan	83(26)	206(25)	1074(25)	3024(25)
Zhejiang	135(12)	382(8)	1978(6)	8161(4)

[a] at current prices;
[b] from SSB (1986, 1990, 1991 and 1996) except for ([c]) and ([d]);
[c] estimated based on the data of NI (SSB, 1990b) and Equation 4.2;
[d] estimated by the author.
Note: figures in parentheses are ranks.

4.3   REAL LIVING STANDARDS

4.3.1   General Situation

The standard of living improved significantly in China during the First FYP (1953–57) but suffered a sudden decline thereafter due to the failure of the GLF (1958–60). It did not start to improve significantly until the end of the GCR (1966–76) during which people were largely encouraged to be rich in 'sprit' but *not* 'material'. Since the early 1980s, the Chinese living standard has improved steadily. Table 4.5 shows that among China's eight FYPs the Eighth FYP is the best one in which the per capita personal consumption growth rate is the highest for China as a whole, while the Sixth FYP is the best one in which the per capita personal consumption growth rate is the highest for the agricultural households. This was not only because of economic growth but also because of continuous reduction in population growth. In 1995, China's per capita personal consumption at current prices was estimated at 2311 yuan, which is 12.56 and 30.41 times that of 1978 and 1952 respectively (see Table 4.6).

If China's per capita personal consumption is measured in US dollars, the figure is still quite small. However, China's commodity prices are very low. If the Chinese standard of living were measured by purchasing power, it would definitely increase. For instance, after having calculated personal consumption in China and Japan using exchange rate, Mizoguchi *et al.* (1989, p. 28) find that China's per capita personal consumption expenditure is only 3.1 per cent of Japan's. However, when per capita personal consumption expenditure is recomputed using purchasing power, China's figure is 21.5 per cent of Japan's when Japan's consumption structure is used for weighting and 15.7 per cent when China's consumption structure is used for weighting. Nevertheless, after having compared eight consumer durables between China, Japan, the UK and Russia (see Table 4.7), we find that, except for TV sets, the numbers of consumer durables per 100 households of China are much smaller than that of the advanced nations, even though they have increased drastically since the early 1980s.

China's data on people's livelihood (such as employment, disposable income and expenditure of residents, level of consumption, housing condition, quantity of consumer goods owned, and so on) have been compiled annually by the SSB based on surveys

Table 4.5 Growth rates of per capita personal consumption in eight FYPs, %

Period	China	Agricultural residents	Non-agricultural residents
1st FYP (1953–57)	4.2	3.2	4.8
2nd FYP (1958–62)	–3.3	–3.3	–5.2
1963–65[a]	8.6	8.2	12.3
3rd FYP (1966–70)	2.2	2.5	2.1
4th FYP (1970–75)	2.1	1.3	4.2
5th FYP (1976–80)	4.8	4.1	4.9
6th FYP (1981–85)	8.6	10.1	4.9
7th FYP (1986–90)	3.6	2.2	5.4
8th FYP (1991–95)	8.9	7.7	8.6

[a] 'adjustment period'.
Sources: SSB (1993, p. 281; 1996, p. 280).

Table 4.6 Per capita personal consumption (yuan/person), 1952–95

Year	China (1)	Agricultural residents (2)	Non-agricultural residents (3)	(3)/(2) = (4)
1952	76	62	148	2.39
1957	102	79	205	2.59
1960	102	68	214	3.15
1978	184	138	405	2.93
1980	227	173	468	2.71
1981	249	194	487	2.51
1982	267	212	500	2.36
1983	290	235	523	2.23
1984	330	268	592	2.21
1985	407	324	754	2.33
1986	452	352	865	2.46
1987	550	417	1089	2.61
1988	693	508	1431	2.82
1989	762	553	1568	2.84
1990	803	571	1686	2.95
1991	896	621	1925	3.10
1992	1070	718	2356	3.28
1993	1331	855	3027	3.54
1994	1781	1138	3979	3.50
1995	2311	1479	5044	3.41

Sources: SSB (1986, p. 646; 1987, p. 670; 1993, p. 281; 1996, p. 280).

Table 4.7 A comparison of selected consumer durables per 100 households between China, Japan, the UK and Russia

Item	China		Japan	UK	Russia
	(1978)[a]	*(1995)*[b]	*(1990)*[c]	*(1990)*[c]	*(1991)*[c]
Sewing machines	15.89	64.99	80.6	NA	60
Bicycles	34.96	164.13	81.7	NA	55
Electric fans	4.54	117.34	NA	NA	NA
Washing machines	0.00	43.00	99.4	86.3	78
Refrigerators	0.00	27.26	98.9	98.1	95
TV sets	1.36	94.14	99.3	98.1	112
Recorders	0.91	44.70	75.5	NA	59
Cameras	2.23	11.97	86.9[d]	NA	36

[a] SSB (1991c, p. 93);
[b] SSB (1996, pp. 282–3, 300, 309);
[c] SSB (1994b, pp. 422–4);
[d] 1988.

of different samples. Some questions and ambiguities remain when different samples and measurements are chosen. For instance, the SSB makes no allowance for the rental value of housing. Furthermore, the SSB coverage of income in kind and subsidies also appears to be much less comprehensive than it is. Under the joint direction of Zhao and Griffin, the economists, statisticians, and computer specialists from China, the United States and the United Kingdom launched research on Chinese income distribution in which the definition of income differs considerably from that used by the SSB.[15] This research shows that the real per capita rural income is 760 yuan, about 39 per cent higher than the SSB estimate of 545 yuan and per capita disposable urban household income is 1842 yuan, about 55 per cent higher than the 1988 SSB estimate of 1119 yuan (1989, p. 719). Moreover, Khan *et al.* (1993, pp. 34–7) explain in detail why their estimates are different from the SSB's: the difference in the case of the rural sample is almost certainly due to differences in the definition of income and the method of estimation rather than difference in sampling method or in measurement errors; for the urban area, as the sample is much more weakly related to the SSB sample, the difference between the two estimates could therefore be due in part to differences in sampling and to measurement errors. If we can assume that their calculations are more accurate than the SSB's, we may thus conclude that the NI under China's macroeconomic accounting was underestimated during the 1980s, which is consistent with our hypothesis in Section 4.2.2.

Finally, when comparing China's living standards with other countries, one should remember that China has a very comprehensive social welfare system (even if it is not available to all Chinese citizens). Ma and Sun (1981, p. 568), for example, estimate that total work-related insurance and other types of social welfare expenditure might have been as high as 526.7 yuan per year for each worker, or 81.7 per cent of the average wage before 1980. In addition, urban residents have also access to low-cost housing. According to the urban surveys conducted by the SSB, the per capita expenditure for residence in most urban area is only 32.23 yuan in 1985 and 250.18 yuan in 1995, which accounts for approximately only 4.3 per cent and 5.8 per cent of the total per capita incomes respectively, far lower than that of the market economies.[16]

4.3.2 Rural–Urban Disparity

China's rural-urban gap experienced differing patterns during the past decades. As demonstrated in Table 4.8, the urban–rural ratio of per capita income was much higher in 1995 than in the mid–1980s and in much of the pre-reform period, even though it has slightly decreased recently.[17] Before starting our in-depth analysis for the causes, some issues relating to the definition of the rural and urban income should be clarified. The estimates of China's rural and urban incomes conducted by the SSB and World Bank as well are based on the conventional definition of income which excludes several items such as subsidies and payments in kind and undervalues others (production for self-consumption). The understatement of income sources will of course artificially decrease both rural and urban true incomes and may miscalculate the income gap between the two.

Before the reform, the distribution of income between rural and urban areas was rather uneven. In 1957 when the Chinese economy was the most prosperous, per capita personal income in urban area was 3.48 times that in rural area. As shown in Table 4.8, the income gap between the rural and urban areas continued to decrease until 1983, but after 1985 the gap began to widen again and by 1994 the rural–urban inequalities were even greater than in the mid-1960s and 1970s. How can one explain these changes in the relative incomes of the rural and urban populations in China?

Table 4.8　Per capita income by rural and urban area, 1957–95

Year	Rural area	Urban area	Urban/rural
1957	73	235	3.22
1964	102	243	2.38
1978	134	316	2.36
1980	191	439	2.30
1981	223	458	2.05
1982	270	500	1.85
1983	310	526	1.71
1984	355	608	1.72
1985	398	685	1.72
1986	424	828	1.95
1987	463	916	1.98
1988	545	1119	2.05
1989	602	1261	2.09
1990	686	1387	2.02
1991	709	1544	2.18
1992	784	1826	2.33
1993	922	2337	2.53
1994	1221	3179	2.60
1995	1578	3893	2.47

Sources: SSB (1986, pp. 667, 673; 1996, p. 281).

R. Zhao (1993, pp. 82–3) argues that China's income differentials between rural and urban areas have resulted largely from government policy. For example, in the pre-reform era, it was the policy to keep agricultural prices low in order to accumulate funds for industrialization. Migration of labour from the low-income countryside to the high-income cities was strictly controlled by the government through a system of registration of urban residents. The consequence of these policies, however, was to aggravate rural–urban inequalities. Since the reform, income differentials between urban and rural China have experienced different patterns. In the early period of economic reform which was concentrated on the introduction of HRS to the agricultural sector, rural income increased very rapidly and the gap between rural and urban areas narrowed until 1985. Since then, the rural–urban gap has begun to increase again as a result of the diminishing marginal returns of the agricultural sector on the one hand and urban industrial reform on the other hand. As demonstrated in Table 4.8, the ratio of urban to rural per capita income fell from 2.36 in 1978 to 1.70 in 1983. It then rose steadily to 2.60 in 1994.

Table 4.9 Indicators of economic lives by rural and urban areas, 1978 and 1995

	Urban		Rural		Urban/Rural	
	1978	*1995*	*1978*	*1995*	*1978*	*1995*
Per capita income (yuan)	316	3893	134	1578	2.36	2.47
Per capita personal consumption (yuan)	405	3538	138	1310	2.93	2.70
Engel coefficient (%)	58.7[a]	49.9	67.7	58.6	0.87	0.85
Per capita saving (yuan)	9.0	667.2	0.7	72.1	12.83	9.25
Per capita living space (km^2)	3.6	8.1	8.1	21.0	0.44	0.39
Durables per 100 households						
Bicycles	23.3	194.3	30.7	147.0	0.76	1.32
Sewing machines	8.6	63.7	19.8	65.7	0.43	0.97
Washing machines	–	89.0	–	16.9	–	5.26
Refrigerators	–	66.2	–	5.2	–	12.86
Electric fans	–	167.4	–	89.0	–	1.88
TV sets[b]	1.3	117.8	0.1	80.7	13.00	1.46
where, color TV sets	–	89.8	–	16.9	–	5.31
Cameras	–	30.6	–	1.4	–	21.52

[a] 1982;
[b] including color and black and white TV sets;
Sources: SSB (1983, p. 501; 1985, p. 563; 1996, pp. 69, 279–82, 287, 300, 304, 309).

Table 4.9 compares the urban and rural economic lives in 1978 and 1995 respectively. The per capita income in urban areas was 2.47 times higher than that in rural areas in 1995, up from 2.36 times higher than that in rural area in 1978.[18] Meanwhile, the per capita personal consumption in urban areas decreased from 2.93 times that in rural areas in 1978 to 2.70 times that in rural areas in 1995. Per capita saving in the urban areas was still 9.25 times that in the rural areas in 1995, even though it had decreased since 1978 when the urban–rural ratio of per capita saving was as high as 12.83. In 1978, few households were in possession of consumer durables such as washing machines, refrigerators, electric fans, and colour TV sets in both rural and urban areas. Since the early 1980s, consumer durables per 100 households have increased rapidly in China, especially in the urban areas whose possession of major consumer durables (such as TV sets, electric fans, washing machines, and so on) reached the level of the middle-income nations in 1995. While, in contrast, the possession of consumer durables in the rural area has still been very low, even though it increased dramatically from

1978 to 1995. In 1995, washing machines, refrigerators and cameras per 100 households in urban areas were 5.26, 12.86, and 21.52 times that in rural areas respectively. Nevertheless, the urban–rural gap of TV sets narrowed considerably from 1978 to 1995, as demonstrated in Table 4.9.[19] Taking all indicators into account, we may roughly conclude that the gap of living standards between rural and urban areas has been still very high.

4.3.3 A Multiregional Comparison

The vast size of, and diversified natural conditions, in China generate many regional differences in terms of climate, geography, soil fertility and other resource endowments, which in turn make the living standard vary from region to region. In particular, South and East regions have natural advantages for agriculture over the Northwest region. Mineral and energy resources are much richer in the North than in the South. In other aspects, the eastern coastal area, due to its geographical proximity to the market economies, may introduce more easily the *laissez-faire* approach than the central and the western inland areas. All these factors have inevitably resulted in great economic disparities among regions, as demonstrated in Table 4.10.

A brief look at the Chinese composition of personal consumption shows that the proportion of total expenditure going on food and beverages has dropped in both rural and urban areas since the reform, reflecting Engel's Law (see Table 4.9); while demand for housing, furniture and utensils, clothing, health care, education, and others is seen to be more income-elastic, as the Law suggests. However, economic transformation in China has raised some problems in relation to the application of the Law. For instance, when estimating the Engel coefficients with respect to the per capita net incomes, we obtain a significant regression for the rural area and an insignificant regression for the urban area:

$$REC = 69.47 - 5.87 \times 10^{-5}RNI$$
$$(-5.06)$$

$$(N = 30, \ R^2 = 0.48, \ F = 25.64) \tag{4.4}$$

$$UEC = 50.20 + 9.75 \times 10^{-5}UNI$$
$$(0.15)$$

$$(N = 29, \ R^2 = 0.001, \ F = 0.02) \tag{4.5}$$

Table 4.10 Rural and urban differences of living standards by FCAD, 1995

FCAD	Net income (yuan/person)		Engel coefficient (%)	
	Rural	Urban	Rural	Urban
Anhui	1302.82	3796.93	58.4	53.7
Beijing	3223.65	6237.91	50.7	48.5
Fujian	2048.59	4510.53	61.0	62.7
Gansu	880.34	3155.78	70.9	51.7
Guangdong	2699.24	7445.10	54.5	48.0
Guangxi	1446.14	4809.43	63.2	51.0
Guizhou	1086.62	3935.46	71.1	53.8
Hainan	1519.71	4803.36	68.2	59.3
Hebei	1668.73	3923.15	56.8	45.3
Heilongjiang	1766.27	3377.24	55.0	48.2
Henan	1231.97	3302.14	58.6	50.1
Hubei	1511.22	4031.90	60.6	48.9
Hunan	1425.16	4705.21	60.3	48.8
Inner Mongolia	1208.38	2873.94	59.7	48.4
Jiangsu	2456.86	4647.33	54.8	51.9
Jiangxi	1537.36	3380.92	61.7	54.4
Jilin	1609.60	3176.33	56.3	51.2
Liaoning	1756.50	3707.53	60.3	51.9
Ningxia	998.75	3386.79	58.1	46.4
Qinghai	1029.77	3319.86	65.0	52.5
Shaanxi	962.89	3311.11	59.3	47.2
Shandong	1715.09	4265.35	55.9	45.2
Shanghai	4245.61	7196.42	44.0	53.2
Shanxi	1208.30	3306.66	63.2	48.0
Sichuan	1158.29	4004.79	65.7	51.3
Tianjin	2406.38	4931.41	58.9	52.1
Tibet	1200.31	NA	74.4	NA
Xinjiang	1136.45	4183.81	50.1	44.8
Yunnan	1010.97	4113.19	61.5	52.5
Zhejiang	2966.19	6224.62	50.4	47.0

Sources: SSB (1996, pp. 288–9, 303, 305, 310–11).

where, *RNI* and *UNI* are the per capita rural and urban net incomes listed in the second and third columns of Table 4.10; *REC* and *UEC* are the rural and urban Engel coefficients listed in the fourth and fifth columns of Table 4.10. Equation 4.4 demonstrates a negative correlation between the rural Engel coefficient (*REC*) and per capita net income (*RNI*), which is consistent with the Engel's Law. It should be noted that the insignificant and positive correlation between *UEC* and *UNI*, with far smaller t-statistical values in parentheses, R^2 and F-values in Equation 4.5, does not mean that

Engel's Law has been overthrown by the Chinese urban data, rather, it implies that the Chinese data need to be further clarified in detail. Briefly, two major factors may have miscalculated and perhaps enlarged the Engel coefficients for the Chinese urban areas: first, subsidies coming from the government usually ascribe to the personal consumption in housing and health care; second, the Chinese meals are more complex and therefore more costly to prepare than Western style food.

The vast territory size, together with a less-developed transport system and rigid spatial economic barriers (as will be discussed in Chapter 6.1) differentiates regional purchasing powers, that is, the same monetary income level may result in different real living standards in different regions. Theoretically, if the price indices and consumption structures are known, the personal consumption expenditure can be recomputed for different regions of China based on the purchasing power. Due to the difficulties in collecting the comparable regional data, we have to leave this ambitious task. Nevertheless, one is still able to witness the regional differences of purchasing power based on the retail prices of consumers goods at free markets. On 25 December, 1995, for instance, the price tags of some foodstuff demonstrate that 1 kg of rice costs only ¥2.8 in Xi'an and Chengdu but ¥4.2 in Guangzhou; 1 kg of oil costs ¥7.8 in Zhengzhou and Shanghai but ¥12.2 in Guangzhou; 1 kg of chicken costs ¥8.8 in Yinchuan but ¥20.0 in Chengdu; 1 kg of fish costs ¥4.4 in Hefei but ¥11.0 in Chengdu, Guiyang, Tianjin and Beijing; 1 kg of eggs costs ¥6.2 in Harbin but ¥9.4 in Guiyang; 1 kg of apples costs only ¥3.0 in Taiyuan, Kunming and Lhasa but ¥7.0 in Beijing, Tianjin and Hohhot.[20]

4.4 REGIONAL INEQUALITIES

4.4.1 About the Measurement

The simplest measurement for regional inequalities is standard error (SR).[21] SR is a statistical approach by which regional disparities are measured in absolute terms, while other approaches, such as Gini coefficient, coefficient of variation (CV), weighed mean error (M_W), and so on may be used to derive the regional disparities in relative terms.[22] Usually, the results of regional inequalities derived from CV and Gini approaches are consistent with each other, while in some cases, an inconsistency of measurements may be generated by the two approaches.[23] Unlike Gini and CV approaches, generalized entropy (GE) is a family of measures depending on a parameter (c). Users may adjust the value of the parameter to suit their ethical preferences. As described in Shorrocks and Foster (1987, pp. 485–97), the parameter (c) determines the relative sensitivity of distribution: when c is less than two, the corresponding GE is sensitive in the sense that composite progressive-cum-regressive income transfers of the same magnitude at the upper and lower tails of the income distribution lead to an increase in inequality. In two special cases – when $c = 0$ and 1 – the GE family becomes two versions of Theil's entropy (TE) measure.[24]

It must be noted that SR, CV, Gini and M_W approaches can only deal with the measurement of regional inequalities in terms of a single index. However, it is necessary sometimes for one to analyse jointly regional disparities according to different indices, particularly when these indices are contradictory with each other. For instance, Nolan and Sender (1992, pp. 1279–303) and A. Sen (1992, pp. 1305–12) argue that China has paid more attention to economic growth rather than education, health care, and other service sectors since the early 1980s. Thus, when evaluating the regional inequalities in China, one should take different indices into account.[25]

4.4.2 Regional Inequalities (1952–95)

Let us first look at the poorest and richest FCADs in China. In 1952, the per capita NI of Shanghai was estimated at 584.15 yuan which is 10.67 times that of Guizhou (54.77 yuan). In 1979, Shanghai's per capita NI rose to 2860.92 yuan, 27.85 times of Guizhou's (102.72 yuan).[26] Obviously, during the pre-reform period, the economic gap between the richest and poorest FCADs widened rapidly. How large is this gap during the post-reform period? Briefly, the economic gap has experienced two different patterns if we take into account the per capita GDP (see Table 4.4). Shanghai's per capita GDP was 27.88 times of Guizhou's in 1979 and 7.34 times of Guizhou's in 1990, which implies that the per capita GDP ratio of Shanghai to Guizhou decreased greatly during the above period. From 1990 to 1995, however, the per capita GDP ratio of Shanghai to Guizhou increased once again to 9.70. Until now, we may conclude that the economic gap between the richest and the poorest regions has been very high in China.

Figure 4.3 Changes of regional inequalities, 1952–95

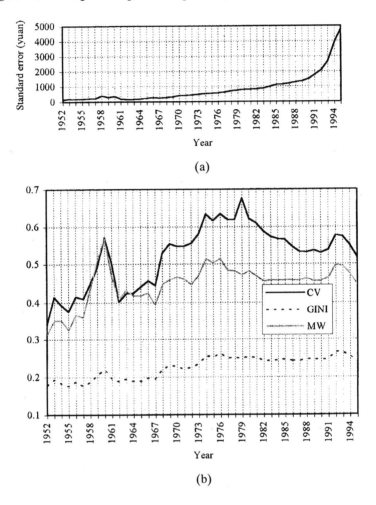

(a)

(b)

Note: 29 FCADs are considered from 1952 to 1988 (during which Hainan is included in Guangdong province) while 30 FCADs are considered from 1989 to 1995.
Sources: (1) estimation by the author for 1952–78 and (2) SSB (various issues) for 1979–95 with some exceptions of the FCADs whose GDPs are estimated by the author (more details may be found in Section 4.2.2).

How about China's regional inequalities when all FCADs are taken into account? Using the FCADs' per capita GDP data which have been officially reported by the SSB for the years from 1978 to 1995[27] and estimated in Section 4.2.2 for the years from 1952 to 1977, we may calculate the coefficients of SR, Gini, CV, and M_W for the years from 1952 to 1995 (see Figure 4.3).

Regional inequalities in absolute terms (SR) jumped from 136.57 yuan in 1952 up to 4753.84 yuan in 1995 (see Figure 4.3(a)), while the regional inequalities in relative terms (Gini, CV, and M_W) fluctuated frequently during the above period (see Figure 4.3(b)). Except for a few years (such as 1954–55, 1957, 1961–62 and 1967), China's regional inequalities increased from the early 1950s to the late 1970s. For instance, the Gini, CV, and M_W coefficients were 0.178, 0.339, and 0.312 in 1952; in 1980, however, they increased significantly to 0.253, 0.621, and 0.483 respectively. Obviously, China's egalitarian policy did not bring about any economic equalities among the FCADs during this period. Since the early 1980s, except for a few years in the early 1990s, regional inequalities have decreased among the FCADs, although the SR increased steadily. For instance, the Gini, CV, and M_W coefficients were 0.238, 0.517, and 0.446 in 1995, down by 5.93 per cent, 16.78 per cent, and 7.77 per cent from 1980 respectively.

By contrast, a glance at the year-to-year per capita GDPs of the Eastern, Central and Western belts simply reveals that the regional inequalities have increased significantly, as demonstrated in Figure 4.4. For instance, the per capita GDP in the Eastern belt was 87 per cent higher than that in the Western belt in 1978; in 1995, however, it was 124 per cent higher (see Table 4.11).

4.5 CONCLUDING REMARKS

When addressing the Chinese economy multiregionally, at least two issues should be noted. First, China's rural–urban inequalities are very high compared with other developing countries. For example, in Indonesia the ratio of urban to rural income was 1.66 in 1987. In Bangladesh the highest observed ratio during the 1980s was 1.85 whereas the typical ratio was close to 1.5.[28] Admittedly the household surveys on which these estimates are based make a less than full accounting of subsidies and incomes in kind. But these components in Indonesia and Bangladesh are tiny compared to that in

Table 4.11 Per capita GDPs of the Eastern, Central and Western belts,[a] 1978–95, yuan

Year	Eastern	Central	Western	E/C	E/W	C/W
1978	467	312	250	1.50	1.87	1.25
1979	517	356	289	1.45	1.79	1.23
1980	572	389	316	1.47	1.81	1.23
1981	617	421	332	1.47	1.86	1.27
1982	672	457	370	1.47	1.82	1.24
1983	733	514	408	1.43	1.80	1.26
1984	869	599	478	1.45	1.82	1.25
1985	1045	704	571	1.48	1.83	1.23
1986	1158	775	619	1.49	1.87	1.25
1987	1358	927	713	1.46	1.90	1.30
1988	1692	1087	885	1.56	1.91	1.23
1989	1890	1193	972	1.58	1.94	1.23
1990	2008	1272	1104	1.58	1.82	1.15
1991	2281	1362	1226	1.67	1.86	1.11
1992	2870	1601	1418	1.79	2.02	1.13
1993	4148	2022	1898	2.05	2.19	1.07
1994	5493	2867	2469	1.92	2.22	1.16
1995	6777	4310	3019	1.57	2.24	1.43

[a] the eastern, central and western belts are defined in Table 1.3.
Sources: calculated by the author based on SSB (various issues).

China. Second, even though not taking into account its two SARs (Hong Kong and Macau) and Taiwan,[29] China still had a per capita GDP ratio of 9.70 for the richest to the poorest FCAD in 1995, which is only lower than Indonesia (20.8, 1983), but much higher than many other countries, such as former Yugoslavia (7.8, 1988), India (3.26, 1980), the Netherlands (2.69, 1988), Italy (2.34, 1988), Canada (2.30, 1988), Spain (2.23, 1988), France (2.15, 1988), West Germany (1.93, 1988), Greece (1.63, 1988), UK (1.63, 1988), South Korea (1.53, 1985), Japan (1.47, 1981), USA (1.43, 1983), and Australia (1.13, 1978).[30]

How large will China's regional inequalities be and how will they eventually affect the Chinese economy and society? We are watching with open eyes.

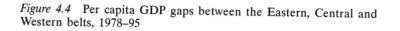

Figure 4.4 Per capita GDP gaps between the Eastern, Central and Western belts, 1978–95

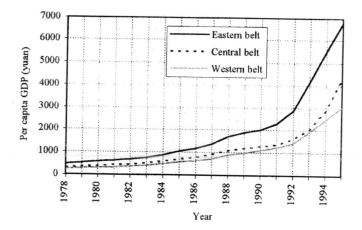

Source: Table 4.11.

BOX 4

Delta Economics

In the *Longman Dictionary of Contemporary English*, 'delta' is defined as 'an area of land shaped like a Δ where a river divides into branches towards the sea'. The famous deltas are Nile River delta in northern Egypt, Niger River delta in southern Nigeria, Rio Orinoco delta in Venezuela, Mahanadi River delta in India, Irrawaddy River delta in southern Myanmar, Yangtze River delta in eastern China, and so on. Despite the above precise definition, 'delta' is usually in practice treated as a larger economic area. Due to their favourable conditions in terrain and irrigation and access to water transportation, many deltas have advantages for agricultural development and foreign trade over other areas with which they share similar natural and social conditions.

Located in southern Guangdong province and bordering on Hong Kong and Macau, the Pearl River delta has a land area of 41,596 square kilometres and a population of 20 million, excluding an itinerant population of some 8.5 million.[31] The delta was the first area in China to introduce reform and open-door policies. Since the late 1970s, the delta's annual GDP growth has represented a rate of 18 per cent, which surpassed the levels of South Korea, Taiwan, Singapore and Hong Kong during their respective upsurges. In 1995, its per capita GDP of 18,000 yuan was 3.8 times the national average. According to Guangdong's development plan, the delta's GDP is expected to grow by an average rate of 16 per cent annually by the year 2000 and will maintain an annual rate at or above 8 per cent during the first decade of the coming century, with all related indices reaching those of medium-developed economies.

5 Industrialization and Technological Progress

A man of the state of Song was worried about his seedling growing too slowly. He pulled up the seedlings one by one and came home exhausted, saying to his family 'I am tired out today by helping the seedlings to grow'. His son hurried to the fields and found that all the seedlings had shrivelled up.

Mencius (372–289 BC)

5.1 CHINA's EFFORTS ON INDUSTRIALIZATION

China had been a typical agrarian society with more than 90 per cent of its population living in rural areas before the PRC was founded in 1949. Thereafter, the Chinese government abandoned the old political and economic systems through socialist transformation of the capitalist industry and commerce. Between 1949 and 1956, some 123,000 capitalist enterprises were transformed into 87,900 industrial units under joint state–private ownership and, at the same time, many small workshops run by individual labourers were re-organized as collectives.[1]

During the early period of the PRC, the development of modern and comprehensive industry had always been given priority. With the direct involvement of central and local government, the targets of the First FYP (1953–57) were fully completed.[2] During this period, the NI increased annually by 8.9 per cent and the annual GVIO growth rate was 18.0 per cent (see Table 5.1). As the First FYP was nearing completion, Mao Zedong pointed out at an enlarged meeting of the Political Bureau of the CCPCC held on 25 April 1956: 'The emphasis in our country's construction is on heavy industry. The production of the means of production must be given priority, that's settled. But it definitely does not follow that the production of the means of subsistence, especially grain, can be neglected.'[3] In the subsequent years, however, the construction of heavy industry was overheated.

Table 5.1 Major economic indicators, 1950–78

Item	1950 –52	1953 –57	1958 –62	1963 –65	1966 –70	1971 –75	1976	1977	1978
1 *Annual growth rate*									
1.1 NI (%)	19.3	8.9	–3.1	14.5	8.4	5.6	–2.7	7.8	12.3
1.2 GVAO (%)	14.1	4.5	–4.3	11.1	3.9	4.0	2.5	1.7	9.0
1.3 GVIO (%)	34.8	18.0	3.8	17.9	11.7	9.1	1.3	14.3	13.5
(1) heavy industry	48.8	25.4	6.6	14.9	14.7	10.2	0.5	14.3	15.6
(2) light industry	29.0	12.9	1.1	21.2	8.4	7.7	2.4	14.3	10.8
2 Accumulation/NI (%)		24.2	30.8	22.7	26.3	33.0	30.9	32.3	36.5
3 NI/100 yuan investment	35	1	57	26	16	–10		26	34
4 *Distribution of capital construction*									
4.1 Agriculture (%)		7.8	12.3	18.8	11.8	11.3			
4.2 Light industry (%)		5.9	5.2	3.9	4.0	5.4			
4.3 Heavy industry (%)		46.5	56.1	49.8	57.4	54.8			

Sources: W. Liang (1982, p. 63, table 4); F. Dong (1982, pp. 88–9, table 9).

Guided by Mao's general line of building socialism with 'greater, faster, better and more economical results' (*duo kuai hao sheng*), the GLF movement was launched by the Chinese government, calling for a doubling of output within one year.[4] In 1958, the target for steel production was raised from the planned output of 6.3 million ton to 10.7 million ton, amounting to a doubling of the real output of the previous year.[5] Obviously, achievement of this target was impossible due to the limitations of production capacity and resource bases. Nevertheless, the fulfilment was stubbornly insisted upon and consequently tens of millions of people had to be mobilized for steel production. The scale of capital construction grew dramatically so that the rate of accumulation suddenly rose from 24.9 per cent in 1957 to 33.9 per cent in 1958.[6]

Stimulated by the arbitrary directions given by the central authorities, many heavy industrial enterprises were set up blindly during the GLF period (1958–60), without any consideration given to their sources of raw materials and their technological requirements. Quality was low and many unwanted and unusable goods were produced, resulting in great losses. Even worse, as large quantities of materials and labour were diverted towards heavy industry, the development of agriculture and light industry received accordingly less attention.[7] This situation lasted until 1960, resulting in serious imbalances between accumulation and consumption and between heavy industry and agriculture and light industry. Consequently, from 1959 onwards, agricultural production dropped spectacularly. The GVAO in 1961 was 26.3 per cent below that in 1958; compared with the preceding year, industrial production dropped by an incredible 38.2 per cent in 1961 and 16.6 per cent in 1962. The productivity of industrial labour was 5.4 per cent lower in 1962 than in 1957, while NI declined by 14.4 per cent over the same period.[8] Although natural disasters and the deterioration of the Sino–Soviet ties played some role in these setbacks, the major cause should ascribe to China's overheated industrial policy.

In the following period, economic readjustment was attempted so as to correct some of the previous errors. Factories were either closed, suspended, merged or switched to other lines of production. The construction of some large-sized plants was cancelled or delayed. Many industrial workers were redeployed to the countryside (*xiafang*). During the readjustment period (1963–65), some sound progress towards industrial construction was made. The launching of the GCR in 1966 and the ten years of social chaos that followed, however, disrupted this process. Similar errors of blind and subjective leadership of industrialization were committed. Many large-scale industrial enterprises were built without adequate sources of raw materials and with no consideration of transport availability and social needs.

From the early 1960s to the late 1970s, China spatially divided its economy into three fronts according to the principle of 'preparing for wars': (1) the eastern (coastal) FCADs were defined as the front line due to their proximity to the capitalist world; (2) a number of inland FCADs (such as Sichuan, Guizhou, Shaanxi, Gansu, Qinghai, Ningxia, Yunnan, the western parts of Hubei, Hunan, Henan, Shanxi and Hebei, the northern part of Guangdong, and the northwest part of Guangxi) – most of which are covered by mountains – were treated as the third-front; (3) the remaining FCADs were treated as the second-front. During the GCR period (1966–76), the development of the third-front area was given priority in Chinese industrialization as it was believed that World War III would occur very soon and that the front-line area could inevitably become the battlefield. As a result of governmental involvement, the third-front area's share of China's capital investment sharply increased from 30.60 per cent in the First FYP (1953–57) to 52.70 per cent in the Third FYP (1966–70) and the per capita GVIO increased from 22.04 yuan in 1952 to 373.97 yuan in 1983, while the coastal area increased from 93.77 yuan to 871.3 yuan during the same period.[9] Promoted by the third-front development strategy, many large and key enter-prises (mainly in military, aeronautic and astronautic, electronic, and other high-tech industries), universities, and research institutions were transferred from the coastal (urban) area (the front line) to the mountainous, remote, and, usually, rural inland area (the third-front).[10]

The third-front area development policy quickly industrialized some areas of China's inland FCADs (see Table 5.2) and provided a peculiar pattern for developing countries to avoid the 'polariza-tion' between rich and poor areas. During 1953 and 1978, the an-nual GVIO growth rates of Shaanxi, Qinghai, Shanxi, Guizhou, and Sichuan provinces reached 20.1, 16.3, 12.0, 11.2, and 11.8 per cent respectively, which were much higher than that of the coastal FCADs.[11] However, it has not been known as a successful approach to modernize the Chinese economy as a whole. This can be dem-onstrated by the fact that the average annual capital output coeffi-cient (that is, output/investment ratio) of the third-front area was only 0.256, far less than that of the coastal area (0.973) during 1953–79.[12] In addition, K. Yang (1989, p. 76) estimates that there would have been a net increase of 1434 billion yuan GVIO (in other words, approximately 45 per cent of China's total GVIO in 1975), had the investment been distributed in the coastal area rather than the third-front area during that period.

After the death of Mao Zedong in September 1976, the Chinese government once again tried to speed up economic development by setting up targets that were much higher than maximum capa-bilities. These impetuous and unrealistic plans started in 1978 and resembled, in many ways, those of the GLF started in 1958. Pro-posals were made enthusiastically by the post-Mao leadership to produce 400 million ton of grain, 60 million ton of steel, 250 mil-lion ton of oil, and to develop 120 large- and medium-sized projects, including ten major oil fields, ten major steel plants, and ten ma-jor coal mines, and to import large amounts of modern equipment and technology by the end of the Sixth FYP (1981–85).[13] It was not until the Third Plenum of the eleventh CCPCC in December 1978 that the Chinese government began to shift its main focus of national task from the 'class struggle' to the realization of socialist economic construction, calling on the entire people to strive to achieve the four modernizations of industry, agriculture, national defence and science and technology at the end of the twentieth century. However, many economic problems had been cyclically generated by the previous political struggles and could not be solved

Table 5.2   Industrial outputs of the third-front area as percentage of China, 1952, 1965, and 1978, %

Item	1952	1965	1978
GVIO	17.9	22.3	25.7
Steel	13.9	19.4	27.9
Coal	33.0	40.9	47.6
Electricity	10.5	25.2	33.5
Machine tools	2.2	15.7	27.3
Cars	–	–	12.1
Tractors	–	77.4	30.6
Cement	14.1	13.6	37.0
Clothing	15.9	27.9	30.7
Paper	7.1	14.5	23.0
Cigarettes	28.6	34.5	42.0

Source: Z. Liu (1983).

immediately. In late 1979, China decided to temporarily halt industrial expansion and carried out a policy entitled 'readjustment, reform, consolidation and improvement' (*tiaozheng, gaige, gonggu, tigao*) in order to tackle properly the existing structural imbalances of the Chinese economy. This policy lasted for three years and many industrialization programmes did not start to work until 1984.

During the pre-reform period, China's industrialization was mainly implemented via a centrally planned system. Direct and strong government participation and large-scale mobilization of resources and their selective disposition to priority sectors enabled the industrial sector to grow at an average rate of over 10 per cent annually (with a few exceptions in 1961–62, 1967–68 and 1974), resulting in a drastic increase of its share in NI from 19.5 per cent in 1953 to 49.4 per cent in 1978 (see Table 5.1 and Figure 5.1). The shares of agricultural, light and heavy industrial outputs in GVIAO structurally changed from 56.9, 27.8 and 15.3 per cent in 1952 to 24.6, 35.4 and 40.0 per cent respectively in 1980.[14] The advantages of rapid industrial expansion from a centrally planned mechanism, however, were soon outweighed by problems of low efficiency, disequilibriated industrial structure dominated by heavy industry, slow technological progress, sectoral disproportions, and sharp annual fluctuations in growth rates. In addition, the self-reliant and inward-looking policies that had been implemented by the Chinese government for most of the pre-reform period also bore responsibility for these poor industrial performances.

Figure 5.1 Industrial growth during the pre-reform period (1949–78)

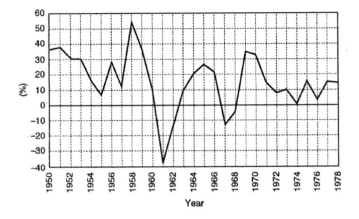

Sources: SSB (1996b, p. 23 and 1996, p. 403).

5.2   POST-REFORM INDUSTRIALIZATION

Industrialization contributes directly to economic development through an increase in income levels, job opportunities, exports and the availability of foreign capital and technology, and so on. In the NIEs, industrialization served as the key engine in the early period of economic takeoff. Therefore, most developing nations (especially poor and agrarian nations) have placed great emphasis upon it. China's industrialization had been affected to a large extent by political movements during the pre-reform period. Since the end of the GCR, industrial fluctuations have been significantly reduced. At the beginning of economic reform, the industrial output increased annually by over 10 per cent, but declined to a meager 5 per cent in 1981. The industrial growth rate rose by over 20 per cent in 1985, followed again by less than 10 per cent during 1989–90 as a result of the conservative and tight monetary policy employed by the government. Since the early 1990s, China's industrial output has achieved the longest and fastest growth in the post-reform period (see Figure 5.2).

Economic development, on the other hand, decides the industrial structure of a country. Increases in per capita income usually lead to increased consumption, which in turn shifts the industrial

Figure 5.2 Industrial growth during the pre-reform period (1978–95)

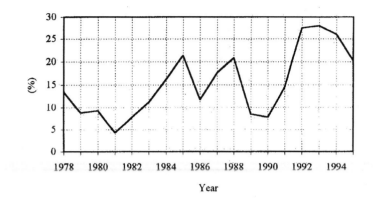

Sources: SSB (1996b, p. 23 and 1996, p. 403).

structure away from agriculture towards manufacturing and service sectors. This also determines the distribution of labour force among industries. From 1952 to 1995, China's sectoral employment shares had changed from 83.5 to 52.9 per cent for primary industry, 7.4 to 23.0 per cent for secondary industry, and 9.1 to 24.1 per cent for tertiary industry (shown in Table 5.3 and Figure 5.3). Regardless of the increasing transference towards secondary and tertiary industries, Chinese employment has still been dominated by primary industry, especially in Tibet (77.2 per cent), Yunnan (75.8 per cent), Guizhou (73.7 per cent), Guangxi (66.4 per cent), with the exception of a few FCADs whose employment is dominated by secondary industry (such as Shanghai, Tianjin and Liaoning) and by tertiary industry (such as Beijing) in 1995.[15]

'Industry' refers to the material production sector engaging in extraction of natural resources and processing of natural resources and agricultural products and reprocessing. With regard to light and heavy industry, there exist differing definitions in different countries. In China, 'light' refers to an industry that produces consumer goods and tools. It consists of two categories: (1) using farm products as raw materials, and (2) using non-farm products as raw materials. Heavy industry refers to general products used by other manufacturers. According to the purpose of production or use of products, heavy industry comprises three branches: (1) extraction of petroleum, coal, metal, and non-metal ores and timber felling,

Table 5.3(a) Industrial structure under the MPS, selected years, 1952–80

Year	National income (%)			Labour force (%)		
	A	M	S	A	M	S
1952	57.7	23.1	19.2	83.5	7.4	9.1
1955	52.9	26.5	20.6	83.8	8.6	8.1
1960	27.2	52.8	20.0	65.8	15.9	18.4
1965	46.2	40.2	13.6	81.6	8.4	10.0
1970	40.4	45.1	14.5	80.8	10.2	9.0
1975	37.8	50.5	11.7	77.2	13.5	9.3
1980	36.0	53.9	10.1	68.9	18.3	12.8

Notations: A = agriculture, forestry, and fishery; M = mining, electric power, and rural industry; and S = transportation and commerce.
Source: SSB (1989, pp. 32, 105).

Table 5.3(b) Industrial structure under the SNA, selected years, 1978–95

Year	Gross national product (%)			Labour force (%)		
	P	S	T	P	S	T
1978	28.1	48.2	23.7	70.5	17.4	12.1
1980	30.1	48.5	21.4	68.7	18.3	13.0
1985	28.3	43.0	28.4	62.4	20.9	16.7
1986	27.1	44.0	28.9	60.9	21.9	17.2
1987	26.8	43.9	29.3	59.9	22.3	17.8
1988	25.7	44.1	30.2	59.3	22.4	18.3
1989	25.0	43.0	31.9	60.0	21.7	18.3
1990	27.0	41.5	31.3	60.0	21.4	18.6
1991	24.4	42.0	33.4	59.7	21.4	18.9
1992	21.8	43.9	34.3	58.5	21.7	19.8
1993	19.9	47.5	32.8	56.4	22.4	21.2
1994	20.3	48.1	31.8	54.3	22.7	23.0
1995	20.9	49.2	31.6	52.9	23.0	24.1

Notations: P = primary industry; S = secdonary industry; and T = tetiary industry.
Source: SSB (1996, pp. 42, 88).

Figure 5.3 Employment by type of industry 1952–95

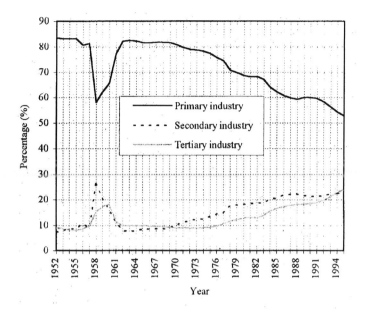

Sources: SSB (1989, p. 105; 1996, p. 88).

(2) smelting and processing of metals, coke making and coke chemistry, chemical materials and building materials such as cement, plywood and power, petroleum and coal processing, and (3) machine-building industry which equips sectors of the national economy, metal structure industry and cement works, industry producing the means of agricultural production, and the chemical fertilizers and pesticides industry.[16]

Between the early 1950s and the end of the GCR, China devoted much of its energy to heavy industrialization at the expense of agriculture and light and service sectors (see the last rows of Table 5.1). Since the early 1980s, the Chinese government has effectively shifted the emphasis away from heavy industry to industries more directly connected with people's lives. This is a correct approach for China to undertake not only because those industries can meet people's demands but also because they are *labour-intensive* and therefore more appropriate for China – a country with the advantage of a cheap and surplus labour supply.

The economic performances of light and heavy industry differed

Table 5.4 Indicators of industrial enterprises under independent accounting system by light and heavy industry, 1988 and 1995

| | Light industry | | Heavy industry | |
Item	1988	1995	1988	1995
Employees (thousand person) (L)	19550	26340	44750	39750
Fixed assets (billion yuan) (K)	193.9	1179.6	685.7	2664.8
Newly-added output (billion yuan) (O)	462.8	2349.1	680.9	3145.6
Pre-tax profits (billion yuan) (P)	74.9	191.8	102.6	313.3
Capital/labour (yuan/person) (K/L)	9918	44784	15320	67039
Output/capital (O/K)	2.39	1.99	0.99	1.18
Labour productivity (yuan/person) (O/L)	23677	89184	15217	79135
Income/capital share (%) (P/O)	16.18	8.16	15.07	9.96
Profit/capital share (%) (P/K)	38.63	16.26	14.96	11.76

Sources: SSB (1989, pp. 324–5, 331, 333; 1996, pp. 414–17).

in China during the post-reform period. As shown in Table 5.4, the capital/labour ratio (K/L) of heavy industry was much higher than that of light industry, which implies that heavy industry was more capital-intensive and labour-saving than light industry. The output/capital ratio (O/K) of light industry was higher than that of heavy industry, which implies that light industry was more efficient than heavy industry. Nevertheless, the K/L and O/K differences between light and heavy industry were reduced from 1988 to 1995. On the other hand, labour productivity was far higher in light industry than in heavy industry, which can be demonstrated by the high K/L and O/L ratios for light industry compared with the low K/L and O/L ratios for heavy industry. The differences for the relative pre-tax profit shares of output (P/O) and capital (P/K) still existed between light and heavy industry, even though they decreased from 1988 to 1995 considerably. This result is simply due to the fact that most heavy industrial products were controlled by the government and their prices were officially fixed very low during the earlier stage of industrial reform, in addition to the use of outdated equipment and poor management in this industry.

In order to compare China's industrial performances during the post-reform period internationally, one may simply employ the results by T. Hsueh (1994b, pp. 74–99) for China and the results by Chenery and Syrquin (1975, pp. 20–1) for the international case. Both data use the same specification as below:

$$X = \alpha + \beta_1 \ln Y + \beta_2 (\ln Y)^2 + \gamma_1 \ln N + \gamma_2 (\ln N)^2 + \Sigma(\delta_i T_i) \qquad (5.1)$$

Table 5.5 China's industrialization at different values of per capita NI, with an international comparison

Variable	International case[a]			Chinese case[b]		
	US$100 (1)	US$400 (2)	(2)–(1) (3)	¥250 (4)	¥1000 (5)	(5)–(4) (6)
Va	0.452	0.228	–0.224	0.513	0.196	–0.317
Vm	0.149	0.276	0.127	0.276	0.584	0.308
Vl				0.118	0.282	0.164
Vh				0.164	0.303	0.139
Lp	0.658	0.438	–0.220	0.892	0.462	–0.431
Lm	0.091	0.135	0.144	0.041	0.323	0.282
Ls	0.251	0.327	0.076	0.067	0.215	0.149

[a] Chenery and Syrquin (1975, pp. 20–1);
[b] Hsueh (1994b, p. 80).

Variables: Va = ratio of value-added agricultural output in NI; Vm = ratio of value-added industrial output in NI; Vl = ratio of value-added light industrial output in NI; Vh = ratio of value-added heavy industrial output in NI; Lp = ratio of labour of primary sector in total social labour; Lm = ratio of labour of manufacturing sector in total social labour; and Ls = ratio of labour of service sector in total social labour.

where, X denotes each of the variables shown in the first column of Table 5.5; Y is the per capita NI (RMB yuan) at the constant price of 1980 for the Chinese case and per capita GNP (US dollar) for the international case; N is the population size (million persons); and T_i denotes the time period. In Hsueh's analysis, two periods (1980–84 and 1985–89) were selected. Arguably this is reasonable, because the year 1985 was generally known as the watershed for China's HRS-based agricultural reform and urban industrial reform, while it was the latter that significantly influenced industrialization. For most FCADs, per capita NI ranged between RMB250 to 1000 yuan during the 1980s, which can be approximately converted to the per capita GNP of US$100 to 400 for the international case during the 1950 to 1970 period in Chenery and Syrquin (1975).

From Table 5.5, we find that the Chinese industrial structure was similar to the international version. For both versions, the ratios of value-added agricultural output were declining, while that of industrial output were increasing. However, the only difference is that China had larger marginal changes in industrial structure with respect to economic growth than the international version. For example, when the per capita GNP ranged from US$100 to US$400, the changes of the ratio of value-added agricultural output and the ratio of value-added industrial output in GNP were -0.224 and 0.127 respectively for the international case; while the changes of the ratio of value-added agricultural output and the ratio of value-added industrial output in NI for the Chinese case were -0.317 and 0.308 respectively during the approximately same development stage. Furthermore, when the per capita NI increased from 250 yuan to 1000 yuan, the ratio of value-added light industrial output and the ratio of value-added heavy industrial output in NI increased by 0.164 and 0.139 respectively, implying that light industry served as a stronger engine on the Chinese economy than heavy industry. In Table 5.5, when the per capita NI increased from 250 yuan to 1000 yuan, the ratio of value-added agricultural output in NI decreased from 0.513 to 0.196, and the ratio of labour of primary sector in total social labour decreased from 0.892 to 0.462 accordingly; in contrast, when the per capita NI increased from 250 yuan to 1000 yuan, the ratio of value-added industrial output in NI increased from 0.276 to 0.584, while the ratio of labour of industrial sector in total social labour increased from 0.041 to 0.323 accordingly.

5.3 A MULTIREGIONAL ANALYSIS

Chinese industrialization differs greatly from region to region, as demonstrated in Table 5.6. For instance, the Eastern belt, with only 12 FCADs and 13.5 per cent of the land area, has 244,183 industrial enterprises under independent accounting system, 10.5 per cent more than that of the Central and Western belts as a whole (18 FCADs) which account for 86.5 per cent of the land area. Regional industrial differences can be further explored in detail. In 1994, the number of employees and fixed assets in the Eastern belt were 62.6 per cent and 105.9 per cent higher than that in the Central belt, and 249.2 per cent and 292.6 per cent higher than that in the Western belt respectively; while the GVIO, newly-added output, and pre-tax profit in the Eastern belt were 185.7, 136.4 and 134.0 per cent higher than that in the Central belt, and 536.5, 397.6 and 325.9 per cent higher than that in the western belt respectively. From Table 5.6, we find that the relative industrial indicators of the Eastern belt were the best among the three belts. A glance at the Central and Western belts reveals that, except for the output/capital ratio (O/K), all other relative industrial indicators

Table 5.6 Major industrial indicators[a] of the Eastern, Central, and Western belts, 1994

Item	Eastern	Central	Western
Number of enterprises (N)	244183	156075	64981
Employees (thousand persons) (L)	44770	27527	12822
Fixed assets (billion yuan) (K)	1921.51	933.25	489.39
GVIO (billion yuan)	3407.3	1192.7	535.3
Newly added output (billion yuan) (O)	905.15	382.93	181.92
Pre-tax profits (billion yuan) (P)	296.93	126.88	69.72
Average (million yuan) (K/N)	7.87	5.98	7.53
size (persons) (L/N)	183.3	176.4	197.3
Capital/labour (yuan/person) (K/L)	429196	339031	381680
Output/capital ratio (O/K)	0.47	0.41	0.37
Labour productivity (yuan/person) (O/L)	202178	139111	141881
Income/output share (%) (P/O)	32.80	33.13	38.32
Profit/capital share (%) (P/K)	15.45	13.60	14.25

[a] for industrial enterprises under independent accounting system only.
Source: calculated by the author based on SSB (1996b, pp. 79–81).

were better in the Western belt than in the Central belt, which is inconsistent with the results in Table 4.11.

In order to conduct an in-depth comparison of industrial performances between different regions, we may build a multiregional production function. The general form of a Cobb–Douglas function can be written as $Y = e^{\lambda}K^{\alpha}L^{\beta}e^{u}$, where, Y = output, K = capital, L = labour, α = elastic coefficient of capital, β = elastic coefficient of labour, λ = factor of technological progress, and μ = system error. If we use a regional variable, D_1 (where, $D_1 = -1$ denotes the Western belt, $D_1 = 0$ denotes the Central belt, and $D_1 = 1$ denotes the Eastern belt) and a sectoral variable, D_2 where $D_2 = -1$ denotes the resource-exploiting enterprises, $D_2 = 0$ denotes the resource-processing enterprises, and $D_2 = 1$ denotes the high-tech enterprises), the modified Cobb–Douglas production function may be written as

$$Y = e^{\lambda_0}K^{(\alpha_0 + \alpha_1 D_1 + \alpha_2 D_2)} L^{(\beta_0 + \beta_1 D_1 + \beta_2 D_2)}e^{u} \tag{5.2}$$

where, λ_0, α_0, α_1, α_2, β_0, β_1, β_2 are constants to be estimated. Using the data of 500 top industrial enterprises compiled by CEEC (China Enterprise Evaluation Centre, 1990), we obtain a log-form regression equation as below:[17]

$$\ln Y = 6.87 + (0.50 - 0.02D_1 - 0.17D_2)\ln K +$$
$$(10.11)\ (-4.53)\ (-2.40)$$

$$(-0.10 + 0.03D_1 + 0.09D_2)\ln L \qquad (5.3)$$
$$(-17.0)\ \ \ (4.94)\ \ \ \ (2.51)$$

$$(N = 500,\ R^2 = 0.76,\ F = 194.98)$$

where, ln represents a natural logarithm, R^2 is a multiple correlation coefficient, F is the F-statistic and the figures in the parentheses under the parameters are the t statistics. Using Equation 5.3, we may obtain the elasticities of capital (K) and labour (L) on production for each geographical belt and industrial sector (see Table 5.7).

From the perspective of the three belts, we may find that (1) the capital elasticity of the Western belt is larger than that of the Central belt, and the latter is larger than that of the Eastern belt, which suggests that the Western belt has the highest efficiency for capital input in large-sized enterprises; (2) the labour elasticity of the Eastern belt is larger than that of the Central belt, and the latter is larger than that of the Western belt, which suggests that the Eastern belt has the highest efficiency for labour input in the large-sized enterprises.

From the perspective of the three sectors, we may find that (1) the capital elasticity of the resource-exploiting enterprises is larger than that of the resource-processing enterprises, and the latter is larger than that of the high-tech enterprises, which suggests that the resource-exploiting enterprises have the highest efficiency for capital input in the large-sized enterprises; (2) the labour elasticity of the high-tech enterprises is larger than that of the resource-processing enterprises, and the latter is larger than that of the resource-exploiting enterprises, which suggests that the high-tech enterprises have the highest efficiency for labour input in the large-sized enterprises.

In addition, it is rather surprising that the labour elasticity is negative for all enterprises, except for high-tech enterprises in the Eastern belt of China, implying that there must have existed some problems in relation to labour productivity in China's large-sized enterprises.

Table 5.7 The elasticities of K and L on industrial production[a]

Sector	Western belt ($D_1 = -1$)		Central belt ($D_1 = 0$)		Eastern belt ($D_1 = 1$)	
	K	L	K	L	K	L
Resource-exploiting ($D_2 = -1$)	0.68	−0.32	0.66	−0.30	0.64	−0.23
Resource-processing ($D_2 = 0$)	0.51	−0.13	0.50	−0.10	0.48	−0.07
High-tech ($D_2 = 1$)	0.35	−0.04	0.33	−0.01	0.31	0.02

[a] derived from Equation 5.3.

5.4   RURAL INDUSTRIALIZATION

In 1978, more than 80 per cent of the population in China still lived in rural areas. In the following years, the rural population as a percentage of total population in China experienced a substantial reduction as a result of industrial expansion. However, it has still been higher than that in many countries, such as USA (3.9 per cent), Japan (10.7 per cent), UK (2.6 per cent), West Germany (4.9 per cent), South Korea (33.5 per cent), and India (66.2 per cent).[18] This resulted to a large extent from the long-standing government policy that strictly controlled rural–urban migration. With little prospect for expanding cultivated land and a large and still growing population, the Chinese government began to recognize the urgency of shifting the rural labour force from farming to more productive non-agricultural sectors. However, the government also remained convinced that this occupational shift must be achieved without significantly enlarging the urban population through rural–urban migration. Accordingly, the policy entitled '*litu bu lixiang, jinchang bu jincheng*' (leave the soil but not the countryside, enter the factory but not the city) has been implemented since the late 1970s.

The growth of the rural industrial sector has been extremely rapid and is largely responsible for the drastic increases in income level in rural China. Almost overnight, a huge number of new industrial activities emerged and millions of IOEs and COEs were established in the countryside. Of particular importance is the rapid growth of enterprises that are collectively owned and operated by the townships and villages. The proliferation of TVEs has had far-reaching consequences, because millions of rural workers have shifted from farming to industrial activities and in the process helped to transform the economic structure of rural China. For example, in 1978, the rural non-agricultural workers accounted for only 7.12 per cent of the total rural workers. In 1995, however, the share of rural non-agricultural workers in the total rural labour had nearly quadrupled to 28.21 per cent.[19]

The growth of the TVEs is extraordinary. In 1978, there were only 1,524 thousand TVEs in rural areas, while the number of TVEs increased drastically to 22,027 thousand in 1995. Output has grown by over 30 per cent per annum since 1978. The share of value-added output in GDP rose from about 10 per cent in the early 1980s to over 30 per cent in 1995.[20] So far, the TVEs have created more than 120 million jobs for the surplus rural workers during the past years and is becoming a more and more important component of the Chinese economy. Total factor productivity in the TVEs is much higher than in the state sector and is growing by 5 per cent a year, more than twice the rate in the SOEs.[21]

The proliferation of industrial activities in rural China stemming from rural reform have created more economic opportunities for China's rural population. The rural residents have seized these opportunities aggressively and shifted vast amounts of resources from agricultural to more profitable non-agricultural activities. It appears that large amounts of 'surplus labour' existing in China has facilitated the rapid rural industrial development. The problems that have emerged in the process of rural industrialization are, *inter alia*, the occupation of farm land by TVEs, possible adverse effects of rural industrial production on agriculture, waste of energy by TVEs, and environmental pollution.[22]

5.5 TECHNOLOGICAL PROGRESS

The four great Chinese inventions (paper-making, gun powder, movable-type printing and the compass) have greatly contributed to the world's civilization. In recent centuries, however, China lagged far behind the Western nations.[23] After the PRC was founded in 1949, China began to import technology from the Soviet Union. Unfortunately, this process was halted abruptly when Sino-Soviet relations worsened diplomatically in the late 1950s. Following its *rapprochement* with the United States and Japan, China gradually began to import advanced technology from the capitalist nations. But economic relations between China and the technologically advanced nations did not improved significantly until the late 1970s when the new CCP and the state leaders tried to abandon the 'leftist' ideology (that is, self-reliance and independence). By the early 1980s, China's production technology in the iron and steel industry was still that of the advanced nations in the 1950s; the scientific and technological level of the electronic industry was approximately 15 to 20 years behind advanced international standards.[24] According to the national industrial census conducted in 1985, 23 per cent of the machines and equipment used by 8285 large- and medium-sized companies were produced during the period from 1949 to 1970.[25]

It must be mentioned that some important progresses in science and technology had been achieved during the pre-reform period. Particularly praiseworthy is the development of atomic bomb in 1964 and artificial satellite in 1970, which granted China a political seat in the superpowers. However, as this kind of technology has been controlled by the Science and Technology Commission for National Defence (STCND) and guided by the State Council and the Military Commission of the CCPCC, the transfer of military technology to social and economic uses is to some extent limited. In other aspects, China's metallurgical, coal, machine-building, oil, chemical, power, electric and precision instrument industries had acquired a stock of relatively advanced equipment. This provided the foundation for industrial modernization. Taken as a whole, however, the level of productivity still remained very low, as did the level of labour productivity.

For a long period, China followed an extensive development pattern and paid more attention to the construction of new industrial projects rather than the reconstruction of the old ones. It is often reported that outdated machinery and equipment is still used by many Chinese factories. Technologically outdated machinery and equipment implies low labour productivity and high energy consumption. In Table 5.8, the labour productivity in the Chinese steel, electricity and petrochemical industries is only 3 to 25 per cent that of the advanced nations; while the energy consumption level of China is 16 to 100 per cent higher than that of the advanced nations. The technologically outdated machinery and equipment also lead to poor quality products. According to the sample survey conducted by the State Technological Supervision Bureau (STSB) in 1995, only 86.8 per cent, 75.1 per cent, and 24.2 per cent of the commodities produced by the SOEs, TVEs, and IOEs respectively met the national standards.[26]

Table 5.8 A comparison of industrial production between China and the advanced nations

Item	Advanced nations (1)	China (2)	(2)/(1) (3)
A. *Labour productivity*			
Steel (ton/person)	600–900	30	0.03–0.05
Electricity (kW/person)	2132[b]	244	0.114
Synthetic rubber (ton/person)	200–300	20–50	0.067–0.25
Ethylene (ton/person)	150	30	0.2
B. *Energy consumption*[a]			
Steel (kg/ton)	629	1034	1.64
Oil refinery (kg/ton)	19	22	1.16
Ethylene (1000 kal)	420–550	840	1.53–2.0
Electricity (g/kWh)	325	417	1.28

[a] standard coal equivalent;
[b] USA.
Source: IIE (1996, p. 40, and tables A and B).

In fact, Chinese policy-makers has clearly realized the increasing role of technology in the Chinese economy and paid much attention to the acceleration of technological progress. Since the mid-1980s, China has implemented a package of plans for the development of new technology, high-technology and traditional technology.[27] However, many problems still exist in the science and technology Chinese sector. The expenditure on research and development (R&D) refers to all actual expenditure made for R&D (fundamental research, applied research, and experimental development). In 1995, China spent 28.6 billion yuan on R&D activities, which was only 0.50 per cent of GNP, compared with the R&D/GNP ratios of 0.93 per cent in 1979 and 1.12 per cent in 1986.[28] Obviously, China's proportion of R&D expenses to GNP has been reduced substantially since the mid-1980s. According to UNESCO (1995, table 5), the R&D/GNP ratio of China was much lower than that of many advanced countries, such as USA (2.9 per cent, 1988), Japan (3.0 per cent, 1991), France (2.4 per cent, 1991), UK (2.1 per cent, 1991), and so on. Even though Minami (1994, p. 116) finds that the R&D/GNP ratio rises sharply with respect to per capita GNP in developing countries when the per capita GNP is less than US$11,000 and in the NIEs, it is impossible for us to estimate any significant correlation between the R&D/GNP ratio and the per capita GNP for China. The main causes may derive from two aspects:

(1) from the late 1970s to the mid-1980s, China spent large sums of money on R&D activities; (2) China's R&D/GNP ratio has declined rapidly since the mid-1980s alongside its GNP growth.[29]

BOX 5

Green Economics

Environmental concerns stem from two kinds of human activities: resource depletion which covers the activities of the losses reflecting the deterioration of land and depleting reserves of coal, petroleum, timber, underground water, and so on; resource degradation which covers the activities associated with air and water pollution, land erosion, solid wastes, and the rest. Resource depletion is a concern because it would mean the quantitative exhaustion of natural resources that are an important source of revenues, obtained through exploitation and the discovery of new reserves. In the case of resource degradation, the issue is not the quantitative exhaustion of natural resources, but rather the qualitative degradation of the ecosystem, for example, through the contamination of air and water as a result of the generation and deposit of residuals, and as a result of the environmental impact of producing rubbish and solid wastes.

Three elements are affecting sustainable development in China: population growth, self-sufficiency of the national economy and the coal-dominated energy structure. In 1949, the new government adopted the Soviet-type development model in which heavy industry was given priority while seeking maximum self-sufficiency in the national economy. The Chinese leadership believed that economic independence and national defence could only be guaranteed through heavy industry. But heavy industry is also the main pollution-making source. On the other hand, the quickly expanded population, followed by the increasing demand for energy and food, accelerated the deforestation and change of forestland and wetland into cropland. But the fragile ecosystem can only accelerate the vicious circle of poverty. In addition, the low and state-controlled prices also led to overexploitation and inefficient use of coal and other resources.

6 Can the Chinese Economy Be Spatially Optimized?

By the authority of our Lord Jesus Christ I appeal to all of you, my brothers, to agree in what you say, so that there will be no divisions among you. Be completely united, with only one thought and one purpose.

I Corinthians: 1: 10

6.1 SPATIAL SEPARATION IN CHINA

There have been two potentially contradictory metaphors pervading contemporary commentary on the nature and trajectory of the Chinese political economy. First of all, there is the more benign metaphor of the 'nationalization' of economic activities, which presents a picture of an environment in which economic agents, especially multiregional firms, are increasingly indifferent to political boundaries, competing in the 'national market' and satisfying the demands of consumers whose tastes are increasingly homogeneous across borders. Second, there is the view of the national economy as increasingly defined by different 'regional blocs' which are marked by high levels of intra-regional interdependence but which compete nationally. In principle, spatial economic separation may effectively be reduced to a minimum level within a sovereign country by the central government. Due to the diversified natural, geographical environments and the heterogeneous social and cultural conditions in China, however, the Chinese economy has been spatially separated by a series of natural and artificial barriers. This kind of spatial separation became particularly serious during the period when the centrally planned system was transformed into a decentralized administrative system. Let us look briefly at this spatial separation and its negative effects on the Chinese economy through three aspects – geography, institution and culture.

112

6.1.1 Geographical Barriers

China is one of the countries with the most complicated topography and diversified physical environment in the world. Glancing at the map of China, one may find that many administrative regions, especially FCADs, have been naturally bordered by geographical barriers such as mountains, rivers, lakes, and so on. This kind of geographical separation between adjacent FCADs could seriously affect the regional economic developments if the inter-FCAD transport and communication linkages are established inefficiently. After checking the highway networks of ten FCADs (Beijing, Shanghai, Tianjin, Hebei, Shanxi, Liaoning, Gansu, Qinghai, Inner Mongolia and Ningxia) in *China Atlas* published in 1983, for example, R. Guo (1993, p. 119) estimates that, of the 453 highways in the peripheral areas, about 60 per cent were transprovincially connected, whereas about 40 per cent terminated near the FCAD's border. Obviously, fragmentary communication networks have exacerbated the inconveniences for every sphere of the local inhabitant's lives and adversely affected the Chinese economy in particular.[1]

Another geographical barrier stems from the fact that many administrative borders were only informally demarcated by the political rulers in the long history of China. After 1986, the Ministry of Civil Affairs (MCA) conducted a series of field surveys on the FCADs of Xinjiang, Inner Mongolia, Ningxia, Gansu, Shaanxi, Qinghai, Jilin, Hebei and Shandong in order to provide legal, formal, geographical boundaries for those FCADs. Many problems, however, still remained unsolved. For example, after having compared the locally mapped borders, W. Zhang (1990, p. 8) points out that among China's 66 cross-FCAD border lines (about 52,000 km), 59 cross-FCAD borders have been discordantly portrayed and 54 cross-FCAD borders have been disputed by the relevant local governments along a section of about 9,500 km long borders. Non-cooperative cross-border relations between FCADs eventually could become a source of disturbance to economic development. Even worse, some inter-FCAD disputes led to armed conflicts and seriously affect the social security and economic sustainability in border regions regardless of the regulations concerning the resolution of border disputes between administrative regions issued by the State Council (1981 and 1988b). For example, there have been over 800 cross-FCAD border disputes in 333 counties (or about 39 per cent of the total border counties in all FCADs except for Hainan province) in mainland China. The total disputed areas (about 140,000 km^2) include grassland (about 96,000 km^2), mining areas (about 5,000 km^2), water (about 1000 km^2), and mixed grass-mining-forestland (about 30,000 km^2) and are distributed unevenly in the Western belt (about 130,000 km^2), the Central belt (about 17,000 km^2), and the Eastern belt (about 700 km^2).[2] Given the cross-border *imbroglios* between the FCADs, the multiregional cooperation in the exploitation and utilization of natural resources (such as energy, metals, forests, fishery, and so on) as well as the protection of environmental resources in the border regions will undoubtedly pose challenges to both central and local governments in China.

6.1.2 Institutional Barriers

There exist many multiregional differences in terms of natural and social resources, industrial structure, and economic development in China. For example, Shanxi (west Mt. Taihang) province has abundant coal resources but poor mineral, petroleum, and agricultural resources; except for petroleum, non-metals and agricultural resources, metals and coal resources are relatively not rich in the province of Shandong (east Mt. Taihang); Hebei (north R. Yellow) province has a surplus supply of metals and coal resources but lacks petroleum and non-metals; Henan (south R. Yellow) province has rich coal, metal and agricultural resources but low non-metals. To facilitate understanding of the multiregionally complementary conditions in China, let us introduce a quantitative index (Q_{ij}) as formulated in Table 6.1. Specifically, Q_{ij} has three circumstances: (1) when $Q_{ij} > 1$, it means that supply exceeds demand in the *j*th sector of the *i*th FCAD; (2) when $Q_{ij} < 1$, it means that supply is less than demand in the *j*th sector of the *i*th FCAD; and (3) when $Q_{ij} = 1$, it means that supply and demand are in equilibrium in the *j*th sector of the *i*th FCAD.

According to the principle of comparative advantage, the uneven distribution of natural resources and industrial structure among different FCADs enhances the mutual complementarities for the Chinese economy. However, administrative separation had formed, to some extent, a rigid self-reliant agricultural and industrial system for each FCAD and seriously affected cross-border economic relations, particularly during the high tide of administrative decentralization stemming from economic reform. In order to protect local market and revenue sources, it became very common in China

Table 6.1 $Q_{ij} = (x_{ij}/\Sigma_{j=1}^{6}x_{ij})/(\Sigma_{i=1}^{30}x_{ij}/\Sigma_{i=1}^{6}x_{ij})$

FCAD	Coal	Petroleum	Metal	Non-metal	Timber	Food
Anhui	1.42	0.00	0.93	1.61	0.18	1.34
Beijing	0.63	0.00	0.44	0.62	0.00	1.90
Fujian	0.43	0.00	0.33	1.55	6.23	1.45
Gansu	0.75	2.22	1.01	0.92	0.83	0.46
Guangdong	0.21	0.16	0.82	1.58	0.14	1.78
Guangxi	0.32	0.00	2.58	1.16	0.34	1.59
Guizhou	2.63	0.00	1.30	0.97	1.94	0.76
Hainan	0.04	0.00	3.58	0.83	0.54	1.59
Hebei	1.51	1.30	2.05	0.75	0.00	0.57
Heilongjiang	0.58	2.79	0.12	0.16	3.12	0.32
Henan	1.57	0.94	1.24	0.37	0.00	0.91
Hubei	0.23	0.71	0.66	2.45	0.17	1.37
Hunan	1.21	0.00	2.53	1.44	0.43	1.19
Inner Mongolia	1.48	0.38	1.33	0.95	5.60	0.78
Jiangsu	0.79	0.14	0.16	1.62	0.00	1.66
Jiangxi	1.08	0.00	3.43	1.36	1.38	1.05
Jilin	0.79	0.95	0.56	0.54	6.50	0.88
Liaoning	1.03	1.51	1.18	0.99	0.00	0.75
Ningxia	3.70	0.42	0.05	0.25	0.00	0.52
Qinghai	0.26	2.70	1.13	1.37	0.09	0.37
Shaanxi	1.22	0.58	3.47	0.64	0.67	0.82
Shandong	0.90	1.13	0.97	1.22	0.00	1.01
Shanghai	0.00	0.00	0.01	0.07	0.04	2.31
Shanxi	4.70	0.00	0.89	0.25	0.03	0.20
Sichuan	1.10	0.61	0.43	1.35	1.74	1.16
Tianjin	0.01	2.05	0.02	0.56	0.00	1.12
Tibet	0.03	0.00	5.05	1.88	10.7	0.53
Xinjiang	0.35	3.11	0.44	0.26	0.21	0.37
Yunnan	0.71	0.40	3.24	0.66	1.83	1.09
Zhejiang	0.21	0.00	0.62	2.21	0.01	1.82

Note: x_{ij} is the output value of the *j*th sector in the *i*th FCAD, as shown in SSB (1995b, pp. 118–36).

for some FCADs to restrict import (export) from (to) other FCADs by levying high, if informal, taxes and by creating non-tariff barriers on commodities ranging from tobacco to clothing, alcohol, washing machines, TV sets, refrigerators, and even automobiles whose production is seen as important to their provincially 'domestic' economies. Xinjiang autonomous region, for example, effectively banned the import of 48 commodities on the grounds that they would harm its local economy. Jilin refused to market beer produced in the neighbouring provinces of Heilongjiang and Liaoning. Hunan province prohibited the export of grain to its neighbour, Guangdong province ... In some FCADs, local authorities established, and provided finance for, a variety of schemes that promoted the sale of local products. Enterprises from other FCADs, however, often have difficulties in finding office spaces, accommodation or land for their business activities. These protectionist measures, which were often in violation of central directives, were enforced through a patchwork system of roadblocks, cargo seizures, *ad hoc* taxes, commercial surcharges, and licensing fees, and in a number of well-publicized cases, highway robbery across the inter-FCAD borders.[3] Moreover, this unfair competition between FCADs could be fierce in the 'battlegrounds' of their border regions and there were numerous tales of 'trade embargoes' or 'commodity wars' between FCADs over, among other items, rice, wool, tobacco, soy beans, and mineral products.[4]

Experience and lessons from advanced countries have shown that the success of a nation in promoting its economic development depends to a large extent on a complete legislative structure and effective instrumental incentives of its own. China's efforts to this end have achieved much progress, but some still remain to be done in depth. In fact, China's 'commodity wars' between FCADs stemmed from the fact that China does not have any constitutional clauses to specifically prohibit barriers against inter-FCAD commerce, even though the relevant regulations and laws have been issued time and again by the State Council (1980a, 1982, 1986 and 1990) and NPC (1993). More often than not, the state's orders were not accorded the priority status of a self-contained law, but took the form of less formal circulars, or were included as minor elements of larger pieces of portmanteau legislation.[5]

6.1.3 Cultural Barriers

Many sociologists and historians believe that the Chinese culture has not been homogeneous from its beginning. Besides the Han-Chinese who account for more than 90 per cent of the nation's total population, 55 minority groups which include Zhuang (15.6 million persons), Manchu (9.8 million persons), Hui (8.6 million persons), Miao (7.4 million persons), Uygur (7.2 million persons), Yi (6.6 million persons), and so on also exist in mainland China.[6] From a geographical perspective, the Han majority are dominant in the Eastern and Central belts with the only exception of Guangxi which is a Zhuang autonomous region. The other minority-dominated autonomous regions include Ningxia (Hui minority-based) and Xinjiang (Ugyur minority-based) in Northwest region, Inner Mongolia (Mongolian minority-based) in North region, Tibet (Tibetan minority-based) in Southwest region, and so on. In addition, China also has 78 minority-based autonomous prefectures and prefecture-level municipalities and further 641 minority-based autonomous counties and county-level municipalities under the administrations of the above autonomous regions and other FCADs.[7]

As a result, China's customs and culture vary from region to region. As shown in Table 1.1, some FCADs also have their own languages. What is more important, there are heterogeneous religious beliefs in China. For example, people in Tibet and its adjacent autonomous areas in Southwest China usually believe in Tibetan Buddhism, while most minorities in Northwest China are closely related to Islam. Nevertheless, the Han-Chinese representing the majority of the Chinese population in the Central and Eastern belts are traditionally in favour of Confucianism. Naturally, the chances of the adoption of a common standard and socioeconomic coordination between different groups of people are not likely to be enhanced if they have markedly differing attitudes as well as different cultural values. Apart from abstract questions of justice, this circumstance would not lead itself to an agreement between the cultural regimes concerned.

In addition, there have been many other factors spatially separating the Chinese economy. In order to have an in-depth understanding and present a quantitative and applicable approach to estimate the negative effects of spatial separation on the Chinese economy, we will introduce an *N*-dimensional spatial model in the next section.

6.2   A MATHEMATICAL DESCRIPTION

What are the functional differences between a region which is administered by a single political authority and one which is under the jurisdiction of two or more political authorities? How can regions differing in their number of political authorities be economically differentiated?[8] Theoretically, regions with different numbers of political authorities will yield different spatial mechanisms and, therefore, different economic performances. In order to explore these spatial economic problems, we will introduce an *N*-dimensional static model of spatial economies in this section and apply it to compare economically the spatial structures in China. Frankly, it is really not an easy task to construct such a complex model, to involve all FCADs differing in natural, geographic, social and political conditions. The only feasible way forward is to make some simplifications. To this end, we stipulate that the Chinese economy is composed of N sub-regions ($N = 1, 2, 3, \ldots 30$) and can be effectively administered by N independent policy-makers respectively. In order to build an N-dimensional spatial model ($N = 1, 2, 3, \ldots 30$) from which the optimal solutions of N sub-economies can be quantitatively derived, five necessary assumptions should be organized as below:

1. All necessary production factors (such as labour force, capital, technology, natural resource, information, and so on) are both scarcely and unevenly distributed within China.
2. Production factors cannot freely flow between the N sub-regions across the border(s) when $N \geq 2$.
3. Each of the N sub-regions has at least one comparatively advantageous (or disadvantageous) sector over other(s) when $N \geq 2$.
4. The transport and communication cost in the ith sub-region ($i = 1, 2, 3 \ldots N$) is too little to influence the ith policy-maker's locational preference within the ith sub-region.
5. The objective(s) of the policy-maker(s) is (are) to purely maximize its (their) profit(s) within its (their) own administrative division(s).

In fact, the first two assumptions are not *ad hoc* in China. Basically, they have characterized all FCADs in which border-related barriers exist. Assumption (3) is the *sine qua non* for the sub-regions to develop cross-border cooperation after the border-related barriers are removed. Assumption (4) allows the internal economic cooperation to become profitable within each of the N sub-regions when N decreases from 30 to 1. Finally, Assumption (5) serves as an indispensable condition under which the optimal solutions of the N sub-regions can be derived. Based on the above assumptions, we may build a generalized static model of N-dimensional spatial economies under $1, 2, \ldots,$ and N independent policy-makers respectively, from which the economic performances of China by different political authorities can be unambiguously differentiated.

6.2.1 The One-Dimensional Regional System

Consider a regional system (S) which is administered by a single policy-maker. For the sake of expositional ease, m policy variables are used here to denote the production factors like labour force, capital, technology, natural resource, information, and so on in the regional system, that is, $X^1 = (X_{111}, X_{112}, \ldots, X_{11m})$. In addition, the technical constraints for the m policy variables are noted as $g_1(X^1) \in g_1$ and the objective of the regional system is defined as a function of the policy variable set (X^1), that is, $f_1(X^1)$. According to Assumption (5), $\{f_1(X^1)\}$ should be maximized. Until now, we can organize a goal programming model for the one-dimensional regional economy:

$$\min d_1 \qquad\qquad (6.1)$$
subject to

$$\begin{cases} f_1(X^1) + d_1 = M_1 \\ g_1(X^1) \in g_1 \\ X^1 \in (0, \infty) \\ d_1 \in (0, \infty) \\ M_1 \to \infty \end{cases}$$

According to Assumptions 1 to 5 stated earlier in this section, there exists an optimal solution for the one dimensional regional system expressed by Model 6.1, that is $F_1^* = f_1(X^{1*})$, where $X^{1*} = (X_{111}^*, X_{112}^*, \ldots, X_{11m}^*)$.

6.2.2 The Two-Dimensional Regional System

Assume that the regional system (S) defined in Section 6.11 is now divided into two sub-regions ($S = S_1 + S_2$), the policy variables of which are defined as $S_1: X^{21} = (X_{211}, X_{212}, \ldots, X_{21m})$ and $S_2: X^{22} = (X_{221}, X_{222}, \ldots, X_{22m})$ respectively. The economic implications of X^{21} and X^{22} follow that of X^1. The technical constraints for the two sub-regional systems are noted as $g_{21}(X^{21})$ and $g_{22}(X^{22})$ respectively. As the two sub-regions are now economically separated each other, the technical constraints for each sub-region become more tightened than that for the one-dimensional regional system, that is, $g_{21}(X^{21}) \subset g_1$, $g_{22}(X^{22}) \subset g_1$ and $g_{21}(X^{21}) \cup g_{22}(X^{22}) = g_1$. $f_{21}(X^{21})$ and $f_{22}(X^{22})$ are defined as two independent objective functions for the sub-regions S_1 and S_2 respectively. According to Assumption 5, $f_{21}(X^{21})$

and $f_{22}(X^{22})$ should be maximized respectively. Finally, we obtain a goal programming model for the two-dimensional regional system

$$\min \ P^{21}d_{21} + P^{22}d_{22} \tag{6.2}$$

subject to

$$\begin{cases} f_{21}(X^{21}) + d_{21} = M_{21} \\ f_{22}(X^{22}) + d_{22} = M_{22} \\ g_{21}(X^{21}) \in g_{21}, \ g_{22}(X^{22}) \in g_{22} \\ X^{21} \in (0, \infty), \ X^{22} \in (0, \infty) \\ d_{21} \in (0, \infty), \ d_{22} \in (0, \infty) \\ M_{21} \to \infty, \ M_{22} \to \infty \\ P^{21} \in (0, \infty), \ P^{22} \in (0, \infty) \end{cases}$$

In model 6.2, P^{21} and P^{22} are set to identify the priorities under which the first and second sub-regional systems (S_1 and S_2) respectively are economically maximized. Obviously, when $P^{21} > P^{22}$, the economic maximization of S_1 is given a higher priority than that of S_2; when $P^{21} = P^{22}$, S_1 and S_2 are equally treated. According to Assumptions 1 to 5, the optimal solutions for S_1 and S_2 can be obtained from model 6.2: $F_{21}^* = f_{21}(X^{21*})$, where $X^{21*} = (X_{211}^*, X_{212}^*, \ldots, X_{21m}^*)$; $F_{22}^* = f_{22}(X^{22*})$, where $X^{22*} = (X_{221}^*, X_{222}^*, \ldots, X_{22m}^*)$. The total output value of the two dimensional regional system is $F_2^* = F_{21}^* + F_{22}^* = f_{21}(X^{21*}) + f_{22}(X^{22*})$. Based on Assumptions 1 to 5, we may prove that the maximized output of the two-dimensional regional system expressed by model 6.2 will not in any case exceed that of the one-dimensional regional system expressed by model 6.1, in other words $F_2^* \leq F_1^*$.[9]

6.2.3 The *N*-dimensional Regional System

Assume that the regional system (S) is now composed of N sub-regions ($S = S_1 + S_2 + \ldots + S_N$). The policy variable set of the ith sub-region (S_i) is defined as $X^{ni} = (X_{ni1}, X_{ni2}, \ldots, X_{nim})$ ($i = 1, 2, \ldots, N$). The economic implications of X^{ni} follow that of X^1. The technical constraints for the ith sub-regional systems are noted as $g_{ni}(X^{ni})$ ($i = 1, 2, \ldots, N$). In addition, as all sub-regions are now economically separated each other, the technical constraints for all sub-regions may be expressed as $g_{ni}(X^{ni}) \subset g_1$ and $g_{n1}(X^{n1}) \cup g_{n2}(X^{n2}) \cup \ldots \cup g_{nN}(X^{nN}) = g_1 . f_{ni}(X^{ni})$ ($i = 1, 2, \ldots, N$) stands for the objective function of the ith sub-region. As defined in

Assumption 5, $f_{n1}(X^{n1})$, $f_{n2}(X^{n2})$, ..., $f_{nN}(X^{nN})$ should be maximized respectively. Finally, a goal programming model for the N-dimensional regional system may be written as:

$$\min \sum_{i=1}^{N} P^{ni} d_{ni} \qquad (6.3)$$

subject to

$$\begin{cases} f_{ni}(X^{ni}) + d_{ni} = M_{ni} \\ g_{ni}(X^{ni}) \in g_{ni} \\ X^{ni} \in (0, \infty) \\ d_{ni} \in (0, \infty) \\ M_{ni} \to \infty \\ P^{ni} \in (0, \infty) \\ (i = 1, 2, \ldots, N) \end{cases}$$

In Model 6.3, P^{ni} is set to identify the priority under which the ith sub-regional system $(i = 1, 2, \ldots, N)$ is economically maximized. Obviously, when $P^{ni} \neq P^{nj}$ $(i = 1, 2, \ldots, N; j = 1, 2, \ldots, N;$ and $i \neq j)$ it implies that the ith and jth sub-regions (S_i and S_j) are unequally treated and that the larger the parameter of P^{ni} $(i = 1, 2, \ldots, N)$, the higher priority is given for the economic maximization of S_i, $(i = 1, 2, \ldots, N)$; when $P^{ni} = P^{nj}$ S_i and S_j are equally treated. Similarly, Model 6.3 yields an optimal solution for S_i, that is, $F^*_{ni} = f_{ni}(X^{ni*})$, where $X^{ni*} = (X^*_{ni1}, X^*_{ni2}, \ldots, X^*_{nim})$. The total output value of the N-dimensional regional systems is $F^*_N = F^*_{n1} + F^*_{n2} + \ldots + F^*_{nN}$. Applying the approach used by R. Guo (1995, pp. 38–43), we may prove that, under Assumptions 1 to 5, the largest output of an i-dimensional regional system (F_i) decreases with respect to i, that is:

$$F^*_N \leq F^*_{N-1} \leq \ldots \leq F^*_i \leq \ldots \leq F^*_2 \leq F^*_1, \text{ with}$$
$$F^*_i \geq 0 \text{ and } i = 1, 2, \ldots, N. \qquad (6.4)$$

6.2.4 Case Study[10]

Stemming from the heterogeneity of the physical environment, land productivity differs greatly from region to region in China.[11] For the sake of data availability and computational ease, we consider only five crops (cereal, oil bearing crops, cotton, tobacco and fruit) and one technical constraint, cultivable land.[12] Applying model 6.3, we may easily maximize China's agricultural output under

30-dimensional border and 1-dimensional border (or borderless) conditions.

(1) Under 30-d Border Condition

Let policy variable X_{ij} stand for the cultivable land input of the jth crop in the ith FCAD. The 30-d goal programming model is built as below.

(a) The cultivable land use for the five crops of the ith FCAD should not in any case exceed the total cultivable land area, that is:

$$\sum_{j=1}^{5} X_{ij} \leq CLA_i \tag{6.5}$$

where CLA_i is the total cultivable land area of the ith FCAD ($i = 1$, $2, \ldots 30$) for the five crops. Formula 6.5 generates 30 cultivable land constraints.

(b) In the 30-d spatial system, we suppose that each FCAD's output is no less than its previous year's one:

$$C_{ij}X_{ij} \geq PYO_{ij} \tag{6.6}$$

where C_{ij} (for the computational ease, let's fix it as a constant) is the annual output per ha of the jth crop ($j = 1, 2, \ldots, 5$) in the ith FCAD ($i = 1, 2, \ldots, 30$) in 1995; PYO_i is the previous year's output of the jth crop ($j = 1, 2, \ldots, 5$) in the ith FCAD ($i = 1, 2, \ldots, 30$). Based on the above definitions, we may derive 150 linear constraints for the 30 FCADs from Formula 6.6.

(c) The production function of each FCAD is to maximize its output in monetary value, that is:

$$\max F_{30i} = f_{30i}(X^{5i}) = \sum_{j=1}^{5} p_j C_{ij} X_{ij} \tag{6.7}$$

where C_{ij} is defined in Formula 6.6. p_j is the price of the jth product ($j = 1, 2, \ldots, 5$). For simplicity of computation, the price of the jth product is supposed to be a constant for all FCADs at all circumstances in the case study:[13] $p_1 = 1.16$ yuan/kg (cereal), $p_2 = 2.74$ yuan/kg (oil bearing crops), $p_3 = 11.73$ yuan/kg (cotton), $p_4 = 4.22$ yuan/kg (tobacco), and $p_5 = 1.58$ yuan/kg (fruit).[14] In addition, we assume that all FCADs are equally treated in the case study, that is, $P^{301} = P^{302} = \ldots = P^{3030} = 1$. Accordingly, we obtain min $Z_{30} = d_1 + d_2 + d_3 + \ldots + d_{30}$, where $d_1 = M_{301} - F_{301}$, $d_2 = M_{302} - F_{302}, \ldots, d_{30} = M_{3030} - F_{3030}$ (M_{30i} represents a figure that is larger than F_{30i}, $i = 1, 2, 3, \ldots, 30$). Finally, the goal programming model includes 150 policy variables and 180 production constraints. The optimal solution is listed in the 30-d column of Table 6.3.

(2) Under 1-d (borderless) Condition

Let us analyse the optimal solution for China's crop production under the borderless condition (that is, assume that the 30 FCADs are merged as a new economic community). In actual practice, the elimination of the 30-d economic border implies inter-FCAD economic cooperation and that trade can be freely conducted according to the principle of comparative advantages in China. Therefore, under this condition, Formula 6.6 becomes

$$\sum_{i=1}^{30} C_{ij} X_{ij} \geq PYO_j \qquad (6.8)$$

where PYO_j is the previous year's total output of the jth crop ($j = 1, 2, \ldots, 5$), that is, $PYO_j = \sum_{i=1}^{30} PYO_{ij}$. Formula 6.8 generates five linear constraints. Other production constraints are the same as that under the 30-d border condition.

The production function of each FCAD is to maximize its output in monetary value,

$$\max F_1 = f_1(X^5) = \sum_{i=1}^{30} \sum_{j=1}^{5} p_j C_{ij} X_{ij} \qquad (6.9)$$

where C_{ij} and p_j are defined in Formulas 6.6 and 6.7. Formula 6.7 may be transformed into a goal function, that is, min $Z_1 = d_1$, where $d_1 = M_1 - F_1$, (M_1 represents a figure that is larger than F_1). Finally, the new goal programming model includes 150 policy variables and 35 production constraints, which results in an optimal solution for each FCAD as shown in the 1-d column of Table 6.2. We are now able to compare the two spatial systems using their

Table 6.2 Maximized outputs under two different spatial systems (unit: billion yuan)

No	FCAD	(1) 30-d	(2) 1-d	(3) = (1)–(2)
1	Anhui	36.26	38.07	1.81
2	Beijing	3.78	4.24	0.46
3	Fujian	13.51	15.94	2.43
4	Gansu	9.02	9.74	0.72
5	Guangdong	26.27	30.22	3.95
6	Guangxi	22.13	21.91	−0.22
7	Guizhou	12.59	14.85	2.26
8	Hainan	2.71	3.06	0.35
9	Hebei	43.38	46.85	3.47
10	Heilongjiang	24.89	28.63	3.74
11	Henan	57.09	65.95	8.86
12	Hubei	40.69	41.10	0.41
13	Hunan	37.23	40.96	3.73
14	Inner Mongolia	12.87	14.28	1.41
15	Jiangsu	48.75	57.52	8.77
16	Jiangxi	22.53	24.56	2.03
17	Jilin	23.01	27.62	4.61
18	Liaoning	20.07	23.69	3.62
19	Ningxia	2.54	2.87	0.33
20	Qinghai	1.49	1.71	0.22
21	Shaanxi	15.77	15.77	0.00
22	Shandong	69.66	77.07	7.41
23	Shanghai	3.22	3.87	0.65
24	Shanxi	12.84	15.16	2.32
25	Sichuan	51.68	63.06	11.38
26	Tianjin	2.83	3.11	0.28
27	Tibet	0.86	0.84	−0.02
28	Xinjiang	22.99	27.13	4.14
29	Yunnan	16.69	20.20	3.51
30	Zhejiang	20.98	24.55	3.57
China		678.36	764.52	86.16

Notes: 30-d = the solution under the current administrative system; 1-d = the solution under a common market.

optimal solutions. The difference between the two systems' total output values is $F_1 - F_{30} = 86.16$ billion yuan, which means that, after the 30-d economic border were removed, China could have increased its production by about 12.70 per cent. Arguably this means that the production has been decreased by the same amount per year due to the existing border-related barriers. In Table 6.2, each FCAD obtains a different return when the 30-d condition is transformed to the 1-d condition. For example, Sichuan's production will increase by 11.38 billion yuan. In Guangxi, however, there will be a loss of 0.22 billion yuan. The net benefit from the enlarged and freely regulated national market is also different between other FCADs.

6.2.5 Conclusion

In theory, multiregional economic cooperation and trade must be mutually beneficial to all FCADs concerned, given the complementarity in natural resource endowments as well as other economic attributes. However, in China the costs arising from trans-FCAD transactions cannot be underestimated. Discoordinating factors are the differing sub-administrative systems of the FCADs and their specific internal social and cultural conditions. Thus, the extent of progress in economic cooperation between the FCADs must depend upon the extent to which the related sides pragmatically reorganize and respond to the economic and non-economic benefits and costs involved. In this section, we have estimated the economic impact of China's sub-political borders. The result shows that the multiregional complementarities have not been fully utilized and that the Chinese economy cannot be spatially optimized due to the existing cross-border separation. If the Chinese economy falls under the jurisdiction of a single political authority, the economic relationship between its internal locations and sectors may be easily regulated by means of unified economic policies, and the inefficiencies of allocation of production factors can, therefore, be eliminated. But as the Chinese economy is administered by different regional authorities, the problem cannot easily be solved.

6.3 CHINA's SEARCH FOR ECONOMIC INTEGRATION

Along with the increasing global participation of economic activity, the concept 'economic integration' has become a hot point in the political agenda of both developed and developing nations since the end of World War II, particularly in the late 1980s when the Cold War came to an end. During the last decades, international economic integration has achieved substantial progress, including the establishment of European Community (EC) and its transformation into the European Union (EU), the North America Free

Trade Agreement (NAFTA), Asia-Pacific Economic Cooperation (APEC), Association of Southeast Asian Nations (ASEAN), and so on.

Beside its active participation in APEC and other international economic organizations, the Chinese government has also recognized the importance of tearing down the internal barriers disrupting transprovincial trade and economic cooperation. In 1979 the CCPCC and State Council implemented a new spatial development strategy entitled 'evading weakness, exerting advantages, protecting competitiveness, and promoting unification'. This strategy first attempted to replace the traditional economic method by which the Chinese economy was constructed into several self-supported regional systems. On 20 October 1984, the Third Plenum of the twelfth CCPCC claimed that 'All administrative divisions should open up to each other, the barriers between economically developed and lagging regions, between coastal, inland and frontier regions, between urban and rural areas, and between different sectors and enterprises should be removed for economic unification according to the principle of evading weakness, mutual complementarity and joint development'.[15] Generally, it has been believed that multiregional economic cooperation was greatly promoted during the above period. From 1981 to 1985, more than 30 regional economic and technological cooperative organizations were established in China.

China's spatial economic integration drive was further promoted by the 'Regulations on Some Issues Concerning the Further Promotion of Horizontal Economic Unification' promulgated by the State Council in 1986. According to CASS (1992, pp. 561–7), more than 100 multiregional economic cooperative zones have been established by central and local government. Generally, China's multiregional economic cooperative zones are usually voluntarily established and jointly administered by adjacent local governments. Many of them also have liaison officers and convene regular (annual) meetings co-chaired by the participating sides. The main tasks of the meetings are to, *inter alia*, (1) discuss the key issues related to all sides concerned, such as the regional economic development strategy, regional economic structure, and so on; (2) coordinate the policies and measures concerning the promotion of regional economic development; (3) develop bilateral and multilateral economic cooperation; (4) study reconstruction and unification in the fields of production, circulation, science and technology, and (5) implement the specific coordination between all sides concerned.

According to their objectives and functions, the multiregional economic cooperative zones can be classified into seven categories: (1) synthesized economic cooperative zones, (2) resource-exploiting cooperative zones, (3) open economic zones, (4) municipal economic cooperative zones, (5) municipal economic cooperative networks, (6) cooperative zones for economically lagging areas, and (7) sectoral economic cooperative zones. In addition, these economic cooperative zones can generally be classified into three categories in terms of administrative level: first-class economic cooperative zones, each of which is usually composed of two or more adjacent FCADs; second-class economic cooperative zones (trans-FCAD border economic cooperative zones, or BECZs), each of which is composed of two or more adjacent prefectures, municipalities, or counties under different FCADs; and third-class economic cooperative zones, each of which is composed of two or more adjacent prefectures, municipalities, or counties within a single FCAD.

Among the above economic cooperative zones, the BECZs are worthy of further note, due to their special geographical locations and multidimensional administrative structures. The BECZs were a new entries to the regional economic sphere when the first BECZ in China was established in 1983. By the end of 1989, the total number of the BECZs had increased dramatically to 41.[16] The proliferation of BECZs has provided an efficient channel for provincially peripheral areas to develop cross-border economic ties and cooperation. From Table 6.3, we see that the average per capita NI is always higher in BECZs than in other border areas. Specifically, the per capita NI was only 473.79 yuan and 391.61 yuan in 2- and 3-FCAD border counties (an *i*-FCAD border county is one which is bordered by *i* FCADs) respectively, given the unavailability of trans-FCAD border economic cooperation; after trans-FCAD border economic cooperation, however, the per capita NI in the 2- and 3-FCAD border counties increased by 44.88 per cent and 49.17 per cent, to 686.42 yuan and 584.18 yuan respectively.[17]

Table 6.3 Average per capita NI by type of border-region, 42 counties

Type	2-FCAD border county		3-FCAD border county	
	non-BECZ	*BECZ*	*non-BECZ*	*BECZ*
Plain	489.79	942.40	391.61	467.69
Mountain	460.07	566.96	NA	623.01
All	473.79	686.42	391.61	584.18

Notes: (1) 'non-BECZ' denotes that trans-FCAD border economic cooperation is not available; (2) 'BECZ' denotes that the trans-FCAD border economic cooperation is available;
Source: calculated by the author based on R. Guo (1991, table 15).

BOX 6

Border-Regional Economics

Border-regional economics has broader content in both theoretical and practical perspectives. As a first step to investigate systematically this new subject, we should clarify the research objectives for the various economic aspects of the border-regions differing in natural, geographic, cultural and political dimensions. Generally, the tasks of border-regional economists are:[18]

1. To explore the spatial economic distributions in border-regions under the condition that production factors (such as capital, labour force, natural resource, technology, information, and the rest) are heterogeneously distributed and cannot freely flow across borders.
2. To reconstruct the spatial inter-relationship and regulate policy instruments for border-regions in an attempt to promote the socioeconomic development by appropriate approaches of rational coordination and management of border regions while not necessarily changing the political structure and social composition.
3. To propose strategies and policies for border-regional developments from both overall and local perspectives. Without the overall point of view, border-regional economics would not be a science. But if border-regional economists do not care about the interest of each independent sub-region, this kind of border-regional economics would lose its source of existence and become merely borderless economics.

7 China's Economic Internationalization

Have you not heard of the frog that lived in a shallow well? It said to a turtle coming from the East Sea: 'I am so happy! When I go out, I jump about on the railing beside the mouth of the well, and I rest in the holes on the broken wall of the well when I come home. If I jump into the water, it comes up to my armpits and holds up my cheeks. If I walk in the mud, it covers up my feet. I look around at the wriggly worms, crabs and tadpoles and non of them can compare with me. Moreover, I am lord of this trough of water and I stand up tall in this shallow well. My happiness is full. Why wouldn't you come here often and look around my place?'

Zhuangzi (369–286 BC)[1]

7.1 HISTORICAL REVIEW

China had been a typical autarkic society for a long time before it was forced to open up to the outside world at the end of the First Opium War (1840–42).[2] Since then, the Chinese economy has been transformed as a result of the destruction of feudalism. Foreign capital inflowed gradually into the mainland, followed by the penetration of Western culture, representing the first signal for Chinese industrialization. Unfortunately, because of the long civil wars as well as the Japanese invasion, Chinese economic construction had not been given priority in the first half of the twentieth century. During the First FYP period (1953–57), some economic progress was achieved. Thereafter, however, difficulties took place due to China's frequent domestic political struggles and fluctuating diplomatic relations with the capitalist bloc and then the socialist bloc.

As soon as the PRC was found on 1 October 1949, the Chinese government severed almost all economic ties with the capitalist world. Affected by the Korean War (1950–53) and the Taiwan strait crisis, the Eastern belt stagnated, compared with most parts of the Western belt which benefited geographically to a large extent from China's close relations with the former USSR. However, it should be noted that China's foreign trade with the CPEs usually remained at a minimum level, aiming at just supplementing any gap between domestic supply and demand. Such trade reflected natural resource endowments more than anything else. Therefore, China's close ties with the socialist economies did not result in significant economic effects on the Western belt. During the period from the early 1960s to the late 1970s, China practised autarkic socialism as a result of the Sino–USSR dispute as well as the 'self-reliance and independence' strategy.

China's economic internationalization strategy began to experience drastic changes in the late 1970s when the top Chinese policymakers suddenly found that the Chinese economy, after having been socialistically constructed for almost 30 years, had lagged far behind not only the Western but also those once-ever backward economies along the western coast of the Pacific ocean. It is now generally believed that the Chinese outward-oriented development policy has been borrowed, in part, from the NIEs. In order to attract foreign investment, China enacted the 'Law of the People's Republic of China Concerning the Joint Ventures with Chinese and Foreign Investment' in 1979. Also in this year, the CCPCC and State Council decided to grant Guangdong and Fujian provinces 'special policies and flexible measures' in foreign economic affairs. On 26 December 1979, the People's Congress of Guangdong province approved the Guangdong provincial government's proposal that a part of Shenzhen next to Hong Kong, Zhuhai next to Macau, and Santou be designed to experiment with a market-oriented economy with Chinese characteristics, namely, SEZ. This proposal was finally accepted by the NPC on 26 August 1980. At the same time, Xiamen in Southeast Fujian province *vis-à-vis* Taiwan also became a SEZ with the approval of NPC.[3]

Besides a 14,500 km coastline, China has over 22,000 km of international land boundaries through which nine frontier FCADs are directly exposed to the outside world (see Table 7.1). Generally, cross-border economic cooperation and trade are naturally facilitated by the geographical factor as well as that people on both sides of the border often belong to the same minority group and share the same language and customs across the border. China's rapid border development has mainly benefited from its open-door policy and *râpprochement* with the neighbouring countries since the mid-1980s. In 1984 the Chinese government promulgated the

Table 7.1   The boundary conditions for the Chinese economy

Frontier FCAD	Neighbouring countries (km of borderline)	Open towns
Heilongjiang	Russia (3045)	8
Inner Mongolia	Mongolia (3640), Russia (560)	10
Xinjiang	Russia (40), Mongolia (968), Pakistan (523), Kazakhstan (1533), Kyrgyzstan (858), Tajikistan (540), Afghanistan (76), India (1474)	10
Tibet	India (1906), Nepal (1236), Bhutan (470), Myanmer (188)	4
Yunnan	Myanmer (1997), Laos (710), Vietnam (1353)	4
Guangxi	Vietnam (1020)	4
Liaoning	North Korea (546)	1
Jilin	North Korea (870), Russia (560)	1
Gansu	Mongolia (65)	none

Sources: (1) Liu and Liao 1993, pp. 3–152; (2) *China Atlas*.

'Provisional Regulations for the Management of "Small-volume" Border Trade' and opened hundreds of frontier cities and towns. In contrast to the eastern coastal development which was mainly fueled by FDI, China's inland frontier development has been characterized by border trade with foreign neighbours. Inspired by Deng Xiaoping's Southern Speech in early 1992, China has embarked on a deeper outward-looking policy in an attempt to promote the development in the frontier regions of the four provinces of Heilongjiang, Yunnan, Jilin and Liaoning and the four autonomous regions of Inner Mongolia, Xinjiang, Tibet and Guangxi. Since the early 1990s, a series of favourable and flexible measures to manage cross-border trade and economic cooperation have been granted to those frontier FCADs.[4]

Since the reform and open-door policies were introduced in 1978, China has basically formed a pattern featuring gradual advance from east to west, from SEZs, then to other coastal areas, and finally to the inland area. Further progress has been made in opening border, riparian and inland areas to the outside world since 1992. This has also spread from processing industries to basic industries, infrastructure facilities and service trades, and is intended to develop toward a multilevel and all directional opening pattern. A glance at the PRC's history reveals that China's economic stagnation and prosperity have been closely related to its policy of economic internationalization.

More specifically, when the autarkic policy was implemented, economic stagnation occurred; when the outward-looking policy was introduced, economic prosperity would be achieved accordingly. China's regional economic performances have also been decided in this way.

7.2 FOREIGN TRADE

> Under a system of perfectly free commerce, each country naturally devotes its capital and labour to such employments as are most beneficial to each. This pursuit of individual advantage is admirably connected with the universal good of the whole... It is this principle which determines that wine shall be made in France and Portugal, that corn shall be grown in America and Poland, and that hardware and other goods shall be manufactured in England.
>
> David Ricardo (1817, ch. vii)

7.2.1 General Review

A country may benefit from exporting those commodities it can produce more cheaply and importing those which can be produced more efficiently abroad. This is particularly useful for China – a country with abundant natural and agricultural resources but lack of capital, technology – to import advanced scientific innovations, production techniques and management experience from advanced nations. To bring about socialist modernization in its own way, China did not adopt the strategy of 'founding a nation on trade' used by many industrially developed nations, rather, it was based on the principle of 'independence and self-reliance' during the first decades of the PRC. As a result, China lagged far behind the advanced nations. In order to achieve quickly the economic modernization, China must actively seek new technologies through foreign trade and cooperation.

China's foreign trade and economic relations during the early stage of the PRC reflected, to a large extent, the basic characteristics of a socialist economy. In the 1950s, because of a trade embargo imposed by the USA and other Western nations, most foreign trade was restricted to the Soviet bloc countries. Following the Sino–Soviet split in the early 1960s, foreign trade decreased dramatically. Guided by the principle of 'self-reliance and independence',

Figure 7.1 Foreign trade, 1952–95

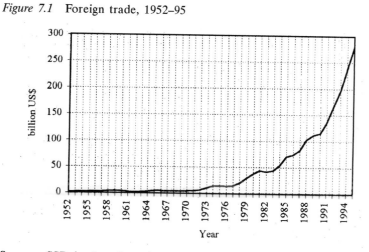

Sources: SSB (various issues)

Figure 7.2 Foreign trade as percentage of GNP, 1952–95

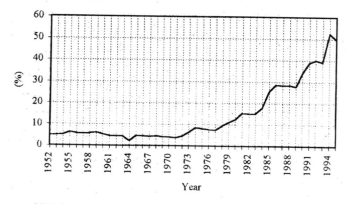

Sources: SSB (various issues) and Table 4.3

China's foreign trade and economic relations had not been improved significantly before the early 1970s. Since then, its trade with the capitalist market increased gradually, as a result of the *rāpprochement* with Japan, the USA, and some EC nations. However, because the autarkic economic policy had still been in operation before the late 1970s, both the volume of foreign trade and the ratio of it to GNP were still very small at that time in China, as demonstrated in Figures 7.1 and 7.2.

Table 7.2   China's foreign trade with major countries (regions), 1995

Country or region	*Billion US$*						
	iMport		*eXport*		*X + M*		*X − M*
Hong Kong and Macau	8.72	(6.60)	36.78	(24.72)	45.50	(16.20)	28.06
Japan	29.01	(21.96)	28.46	(19.13)	57.47	(20.46)	−0.55
USA	16.12	(12.20)	24.71	(16.61)	40.83	(14.54)	8.59
Taiwan	14.78	(11.19)	3.10	(2.08)	17.88	(6.37)	−11.68
South Korea	10.29	(7.79)	6.69	(4.50)	16.98	(6.05)	−3.6
Germany	8.04	(6.09)	5.67	(3.81)	13.71	(4.88)	−2.37
Others	45.12	(34.16)	43.36	(29.15)	88.48	(31.50)	−1.76
Total	132.08	(100.00)	148.77	(100.00)	280.85	(100.00)	16.69

Note: Figures in parentheses are percentages.
Source: SSB (1996, pp. 586–8).

Since the late 1970s, China has made many efforts to import advanced production equipment from abroad and use it to kick-start its economic take-off. Except for a few years such as 1982–83 and 1989–90, China's foreign trade during the reform period has grown with exceptional rapidity: the values of commodity imports (CIF) and exports (FOB) increased from US$10.9 billion and US$9.8 billion in 1978 to US$132.1 billion and US$148.8 billion respectively in 1995. In 1979, China's major export partners were Hong Kong and Macau (28%), Japan (20.2%), EC (12.6%), and the USA (4.4%), while the major sources of imports were Japan (25.2%), EC (21.3%), and the USA (11.9%).[5] In 1995, China's major six trading partners (measured by total commodity imports and exports) were Japan (20.46%), Hong Kong and Macau (16.20%), the USA (14.54%), Taiwan (6.37%), South Korea (6.05%), and Germany (4.88%) which accounted for more than two-thirds of China's total foreign trade (see Table 7.2).

7.2.2   Structural Analysis

When exports exceeds imports, a trade surplus occurs. During the early period of the PRC, the Chinese economy sustained a large trade deficit. This seems to be reasonable because China, after many years of wars, needed more consumer goods as well as production materials than it could supply. From 1955 to 1977, China obtained a high level of trade surplus, with the exceptions of 1960, 1970, and 1974–75. Obviously, this beneficial foreign trade pattern had

Figure 7.3 Foreign trade surplus (deficit) as percentage of total trade, 1952–95

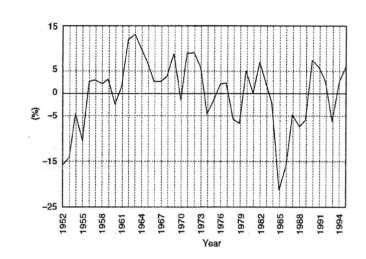

Sources: SSB (1989, pp. 29, 633; 1994, pp. 33, 506; 1996, pp. 42, 580).

to large extent been shaped by China's 'self-reliance' policy for much of that period. China's attempt at speeding up economic development based on the 'imported' method was mainly responsible to the trade deficit in the late 1970s. A long-lasting trade deficit occurred between 1984–89. Trade surplus has accompanied the strong and growing exports since 1990, with the exception of 1993 (see Figure 7.3). This has also increased China's foreign deposits. However, this trade surplus has also led to large trade deficits for its trade partners, sometimes resulting in retaliations.[6]

Generally, foreign trade can be classified into four types according to the composition of imported and exported commodities in kind: (1) both imports and exports are dominated by primary goods; (2) imports are dominated by primary goods while exports by manufactured goods; (3) exports are dominated by primary goods while imports by manufactured goods; and (4) both imports and exports are dominated by manufactured goods. China's foreign trade has effectively transformed from pattern (1) to pattern (4) over the past decades. In the early 1950s, the shares of primary and manufactured goods were about 80 per cent and 20 per cent of the total exports respectively. Since then, the share of manufactured products to total exports has grown steadily and it eventually overtook

Figure 7.4 Shares of manufactured commodity imports (exports) to total imports (exports), 1980–95

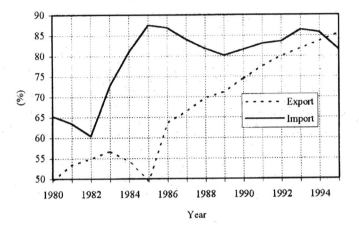

Sources: SSB (1996, pp. 581–2).

that of primary products in the early 1980s. In 1995, the share of manufactured goods to the total exports increased to more than 80 per cent (see Figure 7.4). This structural change of exports has been largely ascribed to China's strong push towards industrialization since 1949 (as discussed in Chapter 5). The composition of imported commodities, includes a very small share of primary products compared with that of manufactured products, due to China's abundance in natural resources as well as its large agricultural sector.

7.2.3 Regional Analyses

It is very obvious from international evidence that (1) countries with high per capita GNP usually have a high ratio of foreign trade to GDP, as high per capita GNP may lead to increased international competitiveness and a high volume of exports resulting in the increased importation of raw materials and fuel; (2) the larger the economy, the smaller the ratio of foreign trade to GDP in a nation, as smaller countries must depend on foreign trade for economic development but larger ones can develop their economic activities from within. Using this hypothesis that the ratio of foreign trade to GDP (δ) is determined by per capita GNP (y) and population

(*P*), R. Minami (1994, p. 129) obtains a log-form regression equation as below:

$$\ln\delta = 3.977 + 0.0695\ln y - 0.217\ln P \quad (R^2 = 0.598) \qquad (7.1)$$
$$\quad\quad (2.40) \quad\quad (-6.86)$$

where, ln represents a natural logarithm, R^2 is a multiple correlation coefficient and the figures in the parentheses under the parameters are the *t* statistics. Obviously, empirical estimates are consistent with the hypothesis. What do these estimates reveal about the ratio of China's foreign trade to GDP? If we substitute *y* (US$573) and *P* (1211.2 million) into Equation 7.1, a value of 17.78 per cent is obtained for δ. This is smaller than the actual value of δ (40.48 per cent), indicating that China has a strong tendency to import or/and export despite its low level of per capita GNP.

Foreign trade has been found to be very important to the Chinese economy. In different regions of China, however, the ratio of foreign trade (total imports and exports) to GDP varies greatly, from only 6.2 per cent in Henan to as high as 221.7 per cent in Beijing in 1995. Using the same specification as in Equation 7.1 and the data of China's 30 FCADs given in Table 7.3, we obtain the following log-form regression equation:

$$\ln\delta = -8.164 + 1.415\ln y - 0.234\ln P$$
$$\quad\quad (6.66) \quad\quad (-2.05)$$
$$(N = 30, \; R^2 = 0.65, \; F = 24.61) \qquad (7.2)$$

Although the empirical estimates in Equation 7.2 show a positive parameter for *y* and a negative parameter for *P*, which are similar to that in Equation 7.1, the elasticity of *y* on δ in China (1.415) is much larger than that in the world (0.0695). This arguably indicates that China's regional import and export performances have been more heavily decided by the per capita GDP than the rest of the world. Substituting the values of *y* and *P* into Equation 7.2, we obtain two groups of the values of δ for the 30 FCADs: (1) the estimated values of δ are smaller than the actual values, including Beijing (84.1% *v.* 221.7%), Liaoning (31.5% *v.* 39.4%), Jilin (18.7% *v.* 19.3%), Fujian (32.6% *v.* 55.8%), Shandong (20.9% *v.* 23.3%), Guangdong (34.3% *v.* 161.3%), Guangxi (12.2% *v.* 16.1%), Hainan (31.0% *v.* 54.0%), Guizhou (5.0% *v.* 8.8%), Yunnan (10.1% *v.* 14.9%), Tibet (13.5% *v.* 32.4%), Shaanxi (10.1% *v.* 14.1%), and Gansu (7.6%

v. 9.0%); (2) the estimated values of δ are larger than the actual values, including Tianjin (74.5% *v.* 73.0%), Hebei (15.5% *v.* 11.5%), Shanxi (13.5% *v.* 10.7%), Inner Mongolia (15.0% *v.* 10.0%), Heilongjiang (23.6% *v.* 9.9%), Shanghai (153.3% *v.* 82.6%), Jiangsu (30.8% *v.* 26.4%), Zhejiang (40.4% *v.* 27.3%), Anhui (10.5% *v.* 8.4%), Jiangxi (9.7% *v.* 9.2%), Henan (9.4% *v.* 6.2%), Hubei (14.5% *v.* 11.9%), Hunan (10.8% *v.* 7.8%), Sichuan (8.3% *v.* 8.2%), Qinghai (19.9% *v.* 7.8%), Ningxia (18.6% *v.* 10.8%) and Xinjiang (25.5% *v.* 11.7%).

Until now, we have been able to conclude that China's foreign trade has been developed unevenly from region to region during the past decades and that the FCADs in the first group have a stronger tendency to import and export than the FCADs in the second group. In order to quantitatively examine the causes of China's differing regional foreign trade patterns, we build a spatial model involving more variables. Assume that L denotes the distance of a FCAD's capital city to the nearest coastal port (in kilometre) and D (a dummy variable) denotes whether or not a FCAD shares a common border with the foreign economy(ies). Using the data shown in Table 7.3, we obtain a non-linear regression equation:

$$\ln\delta = -8.24 + 10.12D + (14.78 + 17.31D)/L + (1.30 - 1.20D)\ln y$$
$$(2.33) \quad (2.25) \quad (1.58) \qquad (5.68)(-2.29)$$
$$(N = 30, \ R^2 = 0.78, \ F = 17.43) \tag{7.3}$$

It is evident from Equation 7.3 that, beside the per capita GDP (y), the variable L also plays a role in the trade dependence, that is, the larger L, the smaller the ratio of foreign trade to GDP (δ), indicating that China's regional foreign trade follows a decreasing pattern with respect to the distance of a FCAD's capital city to the nearest coastal port (L). Moreover, the dummy variable (D) plays two different roles in China's regional foreign trade performances: (1) from the geographical dimension, when $D = 1$, the FCAD has a stronger growth tendency of foreign trade with respect to L (that is, $14.78 + 17.31D$) than that when $D = 0$; (2) from the economic dimension, the elasticity of per capita GDP (y) on δ ($1.30 - 1.20D$) is largely reduced when $D = 1$, which intuitively illustrates that regional foreign trade performance is less connected to per capita GDP for most of the frontier FCADs in China.

Table 7.3 An interregional comparison of foreign trade, 1995

FCAD	y	D	δ	L	P
Shanghai	17403	0	82.6	27	14.15
Beijing	11150	0	221.7	108	12.51
Tianjin	9768	0	73.0	27	9.42
Zhejiang	8161	0	27.3	162	43.19
Guangdong	7836	0	161.3	13.5	68.68
Jiangsu	7296	0	26.4	270	70.66
Liaoning	6826	1	39.4	135	40.92
Fujian	6674	0	55.8	27	32.37
Shandong	5747	0	23.3	297	87.05
Heilongjiang	5443	1	9.9	648	37.01
Hainan	5030	0	54.0	13.5	7.24
Xinjiang	5025	1	11.7	2430	16.61
Hebei	4427	0	11.5	270	64.37
Jilin	4356	1	19.3	432	25.92
Hubei	4143	0	11.9	675	57.72
Inner Mongolia	3647	1	10.0	513	22.84
Shanxi	3550	0	10.7	405	30.77
Guangxi	3535	1	16.1	405	45.43
Qinghai	3437	0	7.8	1350	4.81
Hunan	3435	0	7.8	540	63.92
Anhui	3332	0	8.4	378	60.13
Ningxia	3309	0	10.8	945	5.13
Henan	3300	0	6.2	513	91
Sichuan	3121	0	8.2	1188	113.25
Yunnan	3024	1	14.9	810	39.9
Jiangxi	2966	0	9.2	432	40.63
Shaanxi	2846	0	14.1	1053	35.14
Tibet	2333	1	32.4	1998	2.4
Gansu	2270	1	9.0	1188	24.38
Guizhou	1796	0	8.8	621	35.08

Notes: y = per capita GDP (yuan); P = population (million); δ = the ratio of foreign trade to GDP (%); L = the distance of a FCAD's capital city to the nearest coastal port (kilometre); D = 1 (denotes that a FCAD shares a common border with foreign country(ies)) or 0 (denotes that a FCAD does not share a common border with foreign country(ies)).
Sources: SSB (1996, pp. 43, 580, 594 for ∂; pp. 43, 70 for y; p. 70 for P) and *China Atlas* for the calculations of D and L.

7.3 FOREIGN INVESTMENT

China has made continuous efforts to attract foreign capital in the forms of both foreign loans and FDI. Foreign loans include foreign government loans, loans from international financial institutions, buyers' credits and other private loans. In order to attract foreign investment, the NPC enacted the 'Law of the People's Republic of China Concerning the Joint Ventures with Chinese and Foreign Investment' in 1979. In the SEZs and other economic and technological development zones, foreign investors were afforded preferential treatment. Moreover, the government assumes responsibility for improving the landscape and constructing infrastructure such as water-supply and drainage systems, electricity, roads, post and telecommunications, warehouses, and so on.

Joint venture, cooperative and foreign enterprises are three major forms of foreign investment. Since 1979, FDI in China has expanded dramatically, from a total amount of US$1,120 million in 1979–81 to US$37,521 million in 1995 (see Table 7.4). The scope of foreign investment has now been extended from investments in tourism, textile and building industries to cooperative ventures in oil exploration, transportation, telecommunications, machine building, electronics and other industries.[7] Regarding the origins of FDI, Hong Kong and Macau were the largest investors and contributed 43.30 per cent of the total foreign investment, followed by Japan (10.62%), Taiwan (6.58%), USA (6.51%), Singapore (3.87%), South Korea (2.47%), and UK (2.10%) in 1995.[8]

Foreign investment has played an increasing role in the Chinese economy. The shares of foreign trade, GVIO, and employees of the foreign-funded enterprises to China were only 17.4 per cent, 2.1 per cent and 1.4 per cent in 1990. In 1995, they increased drastically to 39.1 per cent, 16.6 per cent and 10.8 per cent, up by 1.25, 6.67, and 6.71 times that in 1990 respectively.[9] What is more, foreign enterprises have promoted the importation of advanced technology, equipment and management and, above all, competition mechanisms from the advanced economies. It is worth noting that there have also existed some problems in relation to foreign investment in China. First foreign-funded enterprises have focused on the non-productive sectors (such as hotels and public housing) rather than the productive (especially high-tech) sectors.[10] Second, the incomplete economic systems (such as taxation, auditing, customs, and so on) existing in China's transition from traditional socialism

Table 7.4 Utilization of foreign capital in China, 1979–95, US$ million

Year	Total	Foreign loans[a]	FDI[b]	Others[c]
1979–82	12,457	10,690	1,166	601
1983	1,981	1,065	636	280
1984	2,705	1,286	1,258	161
1985	4,647	2,688	1,661	298
1986	7,258	5,014	1,874	370
1987	8,452	5,805	2,314	333
1988	10,226	6,487	3,194	545
1989	10,059	6,286	3,392	381
1990	10,289	6,534	3,487	268
1991	11,554	6,888	4,366	300
1992	19,202	7,911	11,007	284
1993	38,960	11,189	27,515	256
1994	43,213	9,267	33,767	179
1995	48,133	10,327	37,521	285

[a] includes government loans and loans from international organizations;
[b] includes joint ventures, cooperative and foreign enterprises;
[c] includes financial leasing, compensation trade, and processing and assembly.
Sources: Ma and Fang (1993, p. 1004) and SSB (1996, p. 597).

to the socialist market mechanism have on one hand disturbed regular businesses and made it possible on the other hand for foreign businessmen to transfer profits illegally from China to other countries.[11] Last but not the least, the fragmentary legal structure and the ineffectiveness of law enforcement and supervision have always been the major obstacle in the absorption of foreign capital.

It should be noted that foreign investment has been unevenly distributed in China. In 1995, Guangdong province received the largest share (26.86%) of the total foreign capital, followed by Jiangsu (13.41%), Fujian (10.45%), Shanghai (7.57%), and Shandong (6.96%). The five FCADs receiving the least foreign capital were Qinghai (0.045%), Ningxia (0.16%), Gansu (2.08%), Inner Mongolia (2.23%), and Guizhou (2.27%).[12] Not surprisingly, the most important determinant for the irregular absorption of foreign capital is geographical location. For example, the Eastern belt received most of the foreign capital, while less than 10 per cent of the total foreign capital flowed into the Central and Western belts which cover more than 85 per cent of China's territory. Nevertheless, this uneven pattern has gradually improved as a result of government efforts to internationalize the inland economy. From 1990 to 1995, the foreign capital which was actually used by the Eastern belt decreased from 93.2 to 86.1 per cent of that by China as a whole, while the shares of foreign capital which was actually used by the Central and Western belts to China jumped from 4.0 and 2.8 per cent to 9.2 and 4.7 per cent respectively during the same period.[13]

7.4 CHINESE ECONOMIC LIBERALIZATION

Prior to the early 1980s, the management of foreign economic affairs rested in the hand of one government ministry that controlled things too finely and rigidly. In the first years when China implemented the outward-oriented development strategy, reform of the foreign economic system was conducted via three aspects. First, under the unified control of the state, a closer relationship between production and marketing and between industry and trade were arranged, which enabled production units to participate directly in foreign trade. Second, the special policies and measures relating to foreign trade were handed to the local governments. A third type of reform was to expand the autonomy of the SOEs to act on their own initiatives and have direct links with foreign traders at meetings arranged by specialized export SOEs. In 1982, the Ministry of Foreign Trade (MFT) was renamed the Ministry of Foreign Economic Relations and Trade (MFERT). At the same time, trade bureaux at provincial and local levels were established to manage both foreign trade and FDI.

In 1984, the trade management system was further reformed. Foreign trade enterprises were given autonomy to deal with international trade. The MFERT and local trade bureaux were, in principle, not allowed to interfere in the management of foreign trade enterprises. Many large SOEs received permission to engage in foreign trade. Local enterprises were also able to establish their own foreign trade companies. In 1988, foreign trade was reformed by a system of contracts under which the separation between ownership (state) and management (enterprise) was maintained and thus the foreign trade enterprises were able to operate independently. Despite these reforms, the fundamental structure of central planning and state ownership has not been changed fundamentally, particularly in large- and medium-sized SOEs.

In parallel with the gradual intensification of its economic reforms, China has increasingly amplified its foreign-related legal system, steadily improved its trade and investment environment and enforced the intellectual property rights protection system. On the issue of trade system transparency, China has sorted out and publicized all management documents that used to be deemed confidential. In 1993, the Ministry of Foreign Trade and Economic Cooperation (MFTEC) was established to reform laws and regulations on the management of foreign trade and economic cooperation. Import restrictions were further eased. By the end of 1995, China had rescinded import licensing and quota control on 826 tariff lines.

It must be pointed out that, however, China's foreign economic affairs have not been guided by a *laissez-faire* approach even since the outward-oriented development strategy was implemented in the 1980s. Intervention in the form of trade restrictions such as tariffs and licensing, subsidies, tax incentives and active contact with the world economy exists in both import and export sides. China used to manage its foreign trade through high tariff rates. This policy effectively promoted the development of its domestic industries which were still in the initial stage. However, it also negatively affected the Chinese economy. For example, under the high tariff rates, the products made in abroad have not an equal opportunity to enter the Chinese market as that made in China, which will inevitably prevent the importation of high-quality and cheap commodities from the advanced nations, harm the Chinese consumers, and finally provide less incentives for the Chinese producers to improve their competitiveness. China's import-regulating tax system was finally abolished in 1992. Since then, the Chinese government has reduced the tariffs three times. However, the average tariff rate had been still higher than that of other developing countries before April 1996 when China began to reduce the tariff rates on more than 4000 items of imported commodities with an average reduction of over 30 per cent. Meanwhile, the preferentialities of tax exemption and reduction for the foreign-funded enterprises have been also abolished. After the reduction, China's average tariff rate was cut to 23 per cent from the previous level.

China's foreign exchange system used to be controlled severely by the government. Since China started its economic reform in the late 1970s, the foreign exchange system has been liberalized gradually. In the early 1980s, Chinese currency renminbi (RMB) was non-convertible and foreign exchanges were strictly supervised by the state. There existed two exchange rates at that period: an official rate published by the government and another special one for foreign trade. Such a system was aimed at enhancing the country's exports and restrict its imports, for then China suffered from a serious lack of foreign exchange. In 1984, a new exchange retaining policy was adopted by the government as a result of the improvement in China's foreign trade and economy. It allowed domestic enterprises and institutions to retain a part of their foreign currency earnings, compared with the previous one in which these units turned in all their foreign currency earning to the state. Although a larger part of foreign exchanges was still in the control of the government, the new retaining policy stimulated domestic enterprises to increase their exports, and hence the foreign trade performance of China improved significantly. On 1 January 1994, China established a new unitary and floating exchange-rate system. Although it is based on market supply and demand, this system is still to a large extent determined by the government, as the People's Bank of China (PBC), China's central bank, takes the position of the largest demander of foreign exchange and the Bank of China (BOC) which is also owned by the state is the largest supplier of foreign exchange. What is more, the newly established foreign exchange rate system is still officially controlled and the central bank is one of the biggest participants in the market so as to keep RMB rate at a reasonable level.[14]

Last but not least, China's economic liberalization has been hindered by both 'super-national remuneration' and 'sub-national remuneration' since the early 1980s. On one hand, the foreign-funded enterprises have been greeted by a series of favourable policies such as tax exemption and low tax rates; on the other hand, they also have faced some unequal treatments and economic discriminations in such fields as communication, transportation, housing, advertising, and so on. Obviously, the Chinese government should solve these problems before or shortly after it joins the World Trade Organization (WTO).

BOX 7

How to Apply for Going Abroad.

Since the late 1970s when the open-door policy was introduced, Chinese citizens have been freeer to go abroad. However, problems still remain due to both the border control policy of China and the unavailability of visa-free access to most foreign nations. At present, Chinese citizens going abroad for public affairs are able to apply for special passports which may, with the help of the government, be easily visad by the foreign embassies and consulates in China. Unfortunately, those who intend to go abroad for private affairs have to apply for passports and visas through a complicated procedure shown in the diagram as below:

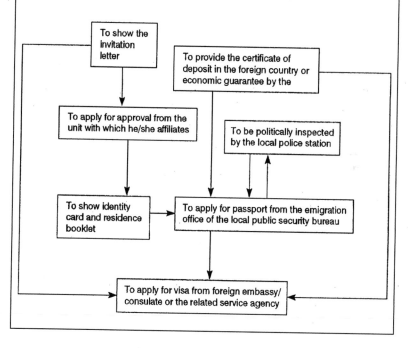

8 An Economic Analysis of the Greater China Area

Just as a clam came out to bask in the sun a snipe pecked at its flesh. The clam closed its shell and gripped the snipe's beak. The snipe said: 'If it does not rain today and tomorrow, you will become a dead clam'. 'If you cannot free yourself today and tomorrow, you will become a dead snipe,' replied the clam. Neither one would give way and eventually a fisherman caught both the clam and the snipe.

Zhanguoce (475–221 BC)

8.1 HISTORICAL EVOLUTION

The greater China area is defined in this chapter as one which includes Taiwan, Hong Kong, Macau and mainland China.[1] Against their common history, cultural and linguistic homogeneity, during the past decades the four Chinese areas have followed divergent political systems, from which different social and economic performances have resulted. As soon as the PRC was founded in 1949, mainland China had effectively adopted and practised a Marxist–Leninist command economy as imposed by the Soviet Union, before it decided to introduce structural reform in the late 1970s. As two colonial economies under British and Portuguese administrations respectively, Hong Kong and Macau have been fundamentally westernized, whereas the Chinese culture and language are still accepted by most of the citizens living there. Taiwan had been colonially ruled by the Japanese for 50 years before it was liberated and returned to China in 1945. With the Civil War (1946–49) coming to an end, however, the newly reunified nation was separated by two ideologically rival regimes – the Nationalists (KMT) in Taiwan and the Communists (CCP) in the mainland. Backed by the United States, Taiwan followed the capitalist road of economic development. While both sides of Taiwan strait have declared that there is only one *China* in the world and that their motherland

146

should be reunified sooner or later, many political issues arising from the bloody war which was eventually detrimental to national cooperation remain unresolved.

In order to have an in-depth understanding of the economic mechanisms of the greater China area, let us briefly review the historical evolution of Hong Kong, Macau and Taiwan.

8.1.1 Hong Kong

Hong Kong was initially included in Bao'an county, while the latter also included nowadays Dongguan county and the Shenzhen municipality of Guangdong province. In 1573, Xin'an county was established and had administered Hong Kong before Hong Kong island and Kowloon peninsula were ceded to Great Britain in 1842 and 1860 respectively. In 1898, the British government rented an area of the southern part of Bao'an county for 99 years as its New Territories from Qing dynasty (1644–1910). Including Hong Kong island, Kowloon peninsula, and the New Territories, Hong Kong had a 1,068 square kilometres land area and 6.06 million population in 1995.

During the past decades, there existed a special geopolitical scenario for the two sides of Shenzhen river. Even though the Chinese character, Shenzhen, means a deep gutter, no one would have expected that the 'gutter' had served as a forbidden frontier between the socialist China and the capitalist Hong Kong in the middle of the twentieth century, and also has been still fuelling up the industrialization of the South China area. On 19 December 1984, the Chinese and British governments jointly declared the transference of the sovereignty of Hong Kong from UK to PRC on 1 July 1997.[2] Upholding national unity and territorial integrity, maintaining the prosperity and stability of Hong Kong, and taking account of its history and realities, China has decided that upon its resumption of the exercise of sovereignty over Hong Kong, a special administrative region (SAR) will be established in Hong Kong in accordance with the provisions of Article 31 of the Constitution of the PRC. Under the principle of 'one country, two systems', 'the socialist system and policies shall not be practised in the Hong Kong special administrative region, and the previous capitalist system and way of life shall remain unchanged for 50 years'.[3]

8.1.2 Macau

Located in the western side of Zhujiang (Pearl river) mouth, Macau
was included in Xiangshan county, Guangdong province before it
was occupied by the Portuguese in 1533 and formally became a
Portuguese colony in 1887. With a 16.92 square kilometres land
area including Macau peninsula and Taipa and Toloane islands, Macau
had a 411,000 population in 1995. According to the Sino–Portugal
Joint Declaration signed on 15 January 1988, Macau will be handed
over from the Portuguese administration to China on 20 December 1999. After then, Macau will become the second SAR of the
PRC to exercise 'one country, two systems'.

8.1.3 Taiwan

With 36,000 square kilometres of land and more than 20 million
population, Taiwan is composed of Taiwan, Penghu, Quemoy, Mazu
and other small islands adjacent to mainland China. The Sino–
Japanese War was ended with the signing of the Shimonoseki Treaty
on 17 April 1895. Under the Treaty, Japan seized Taiwan and the
Penghu islands from China, subjecting Taiwan to colonial rule for
half a century. At the end of the World War II, together with the
Allied forces, China defeated Japan. On 25 October 1945, Taiwan
and Penghu islands returned unconditionally to the Chinese government, marking the end of Japan's colonization. However, with
the civil war coming to an end, Taiwan and mainland China were
again politically separated in 1949 when the Nationalist-led government fled to Taiwan and, consequently, the Communists took
power in the mainland.

Since the late 1940s, China has been in practice ruled by two
ideologically antagonistic regimes, each of which has laid claim to
the sole sovereignty of the whole nation and treated the other side
as its 'local' government.[4] The division of the Chinese nation ex-
tends through many phases of Chinese life – political, economic
and social. The 50 year-long cross-strait separation destroyed national unity, led to tragic conflicts and produced mutual distrust
and many other human and national agonies. Since the 1980s, it
has become the inviolable mission and long-term goal for the two
regimes to achieve peaceful the reunification and promote the all-
around revitalization of the nation.

In short, the greater China area is undergoing a major transformation.

Sino–Hong Kong and Sino–Macau relations will be no longer treated internationally after 1997 and 1999 respectively. Regardless of the political separation, non-governmental relations between the two sides of the Taiwan strait have developed gradually since 1979 when the Standing Committee of the NPC publicized 'Message to the Taiwan Compatriots', especially since 1988 when private visits from Taiwan to the mainland were permitted by the Taiwanese government. Indirect links (mainly via Hong Kong and Macau) will be automatically transformed into, if they still exist, direct links after the sovereignties of Hong Kong and Macau return to mainland China.[5] In the remainder of this chapter, we will examine economic relations between Hong Kong, Macau, Taiwan and mainland China.

8.2 AN ECONOMIC COMPARISON OF TAIWAN, HONG KONG, MACAU AND MAINLAND CHINA

Against the common historical, cultural, and linguistic homogeneity, the greater China area has followed different routes of economic development. Hong Kong and Macau have been under the colonial administrations of the UK and Portugal respectively. Taiwan served as the Japanese colony during 1895 and 1945 and, after a short reunification with mainland China, has been an independent entity. As a result, economic differences and mutually complementary conditions have existed significantly between the four parts of the area.

8.2.1 Macroeconomic Indicators

In 1994, the greater China area comprised US$1,014,083 million GNP and 1226.15 million population. The per capita GNP of this area was thus averaged at US$822, which is only between that of the Solomon Islands (US$800) and Indonesia (US$880) in the *World Bank Atlas*. Geographically, economic wealth has been unevenly distributed in this area. For instance, Hong Kong, Macau and Taiwan, as a result of the earlier introductions of the *laissez-faire* approach, shared 38 per cent of the GNP with only about 2 per cent of the population and less than 0.04 per cent land area of the greater China area in 1994. Naturally, their levels of per capita GNP were much higher than mainland China's, as demonstrated in Tables 8.1 and 8.2.

Table 8.1 Major economic indicators of Taiwan, Hong Kong, Macau and mainland China, 1994

Item	Taiwan	Hong Kong	Macau	Mainland China	Greater China[a]
GNP (million US$)[b]	251080	126290	6513[d]	630200	1014083
(Annual growth rate, %)[c]	(6.1)	(5.4)	(5.72)[d]	(12.6)	(10.11)
Per capita GNP (US$)[b]	11930	21650	15864[d]	530	822
Trade (million US$)[c]	178398	312835	3992	236620	731845
where, Import[c]	85349	161632	2126	115610	364717
Export[c]	93049	151203	1866	121010	367128
Trade/GNP (%)[a]	71.05	247.71	6141.54	37.55	72.63
Per capita electricity generation (kWh)[b]	5080	6233		711	817.43[e]
Energy intensity in GDP (toe/'000 93 US$)[b]	0.26	0.11		204.70	128.10[e]

[a] calculated by the author based on ([b]), ([c]), and ([d]);
[b] ADB (1996, pp. 17, 28) except for Macau;
[c] SSB (1996, pp. 42, 580, 776);
[d] SSB (1996, pp. 803, 808) for GDP;
[e] excluding Macau.

From the dynamic view, all parts of the greater China area have enjoyed higher annual GNP growth rates than most of the remaining economies in the world. Particularly praiseworthy is the fact that mainland China's GNP growth rate was among the highest. Moreover, if all goes according to plan, mainland China will continue to increase its GNP at a higher rate than the other parts.

Hong Kong's economy was seriously affected by the Japanese occupation during the World War II. The population decreased sharply from 1.6 millions in 1940 to 0.60 million in August 1945 and 60 per cent of the buildings were destroyed.[6] Restricted by the shortage of land and other natural resources of its own and the closed-door policy in mainland China, Hong Kong's economy grew very slowly before the 1970s. Since then, however, it has grown rapidly, as a result of its favourable geographical location and free market system. Hong Kong's per capita GNP has now been amongst the highest of the Asian economies.

For the past 400 years, the mixture of Western and Chinese societies has resulted in a unique cultural landscape for Macau. However, Macau's industrialization only began at the 1960s and had been restricted by the trade protectionism imposed on Hong Kong by the United States and the European Community before the early

Table 8.2 Major social indicators of Taiwan, Hong Kong, Macau and mainland China, 1994

Item	Taiwan	Hong Kong	Macau	Mainland China	Greater China[h]
Land area (1000 km²)[a]	36	1.068	0.017	9564	9601.1
Population (million persons)[a]	21.18	6.06	0.41	1198.50	1226.15
Population density (persons/km²)[a]	605.56	5674.16	24231.68	124.84	127.24
Life expectancy, female/male (years)	77/71.8[a]	81.2/75.8[a]		71/68[b]	71.2/68.1[i]
Adult literacy rate, female/male (%)[c]	86/96	88/96	95.7[g]	73/90	73.2/90.1[i]
Unemployment rate (%)[a]	1.6	1.9		2.9	2.8[i]
Per capita energy consumption (kgoe)[c]	2730	2184		676	719[i]
Population with access to electricity (%)[c]	100	100	100.00[e]	80	80.45
Doctors per 1000 persons[a]	539.3	126.6	56.8	158.0[a]	164.4
Durables per 100 households[d]					
Colour TV sets	99.36	100.00[e]	100.00[e]	94.14[f]	94.26
Refrigerators	99.14	100.00[e]	100.00[e]	27.26	28.88
Washing machines	92.31	100.00[e]	100.00[e]	43.00	44.11

[a] SSB (1996, pp. 69, 114, 769, 785, 803);
[b] 1990 data from SSB (1996, p. 812);
[c] ADB (1996, pp. 11, 28), SSB (1996, pp. 769, 781, 803);
[d] as for Table 5.7, SSB (1996, p. 782);
[e] based on various news from CCTV;
[f] black/white and colour TV sets;
[g] H. Xie (1992, p. 115) for the labour population;
[h] calculated by the author based on [a]–[g];
[i] excluding Macau.

1980s.[7] Since then, Macau's economy has grown steadily. In sum, the economic development of Macau has benefited from its proximity to both Hong Kong (one of the freest markets) and mainland China (one of the cheapest sources of labour and raw materials). Today, trade, tourism and casino, and estate and construction had been Macau's three major industries and accounted for 36.9 per cent, 25.0 per cent, and 8.8 per cent of the GDP respectively.[8]

During the past decades, economic development in Taiwan faced many obstacles such as lack of energy and industrial resources, high population density, large amount of defence expenditure to sustain a balance with mainland China (as shown in Table 8.4), a series of failures in foreign affairs, increasing political pressure from the mainland, affects of regional protectionism, and so on. Guided by the capitalist mechanism as well as an outward-oriented policy, Taiwan has been successfully transformed from an agriculturally based economy to a newly industrialized economy and been known as one of the 'Asian dragons'. In 1953, its per capita GNP was only US$167, but this figure grew dramatically to US$12,439 in 1995.

8.2.2 Real Living Standards

With the heterogeneous natural and social conditions, there exist great differences of real living standards in the greater China area. However, due to the differing regional personal consumption structures and purchasing powers, we can only conduct a rough comparison of the four parts. In brief, Hong Kong and Macau, as two municipal economies, have the highest, while mainland China has the lowest level of living standards in the greater China area. Regarding the socioeconomic gap between Taiwan and mainland China, one may roughly compare according to Tables 8.1 and 8.2. In 1994, the per capita GNP of Taiwan was 22.51 times that of mainland China. However, this economic gap would be narrowed substantially if purchasing power differences are considered. We will discuss this in detail below.

Mainland China's per capita energy consumption (one of the most comprehensive indicators representing the level of living standards) was about one-quarter Taiwan's. If taking the number of consumer durables per 100 households into account, the gaps between the sides would be further narrowed. For instance, the number of refrigerators per 100 households in Taiwan was about 3.64 times and that of washing machines in Taiwan is about 2.15 times that in mainland China. Moreover, the difference of the number of TV sets per 100 households between mainland China and Taiwan would be significantly reduced if mainland China's black and white TV sets are included. Other indicators, such as life expectancy, literacy, and other physical quality-of-life indexes, not to mention political freedom of the individual (which is the most valuable criterion in many nations), however, seem to indicate that there are still significant differences within the greater China area.

8.2.3 Mutually Complementary Conditions

Mutually complementary conditions obviously exist in the greater China area in terms of natural resources, labour force, technology, and industrial structure, as demonstrated in Table 8.3. For example, mainland China has adequate and various agricultural products and oil, coal, building materials, some high-tech products, excess and cheap labour, and a huge domestic market; while it lacks capital, advanced equipment, technology, and management experience. Taiwan, with high capital saving, advanced equipment ready to move out, and vanguard agricultural and industrial products and management experience, is scarce in energy and industrial resources, and facing increasing insufficiency and high costs of labour supply. Furthermore, its economic development seems to have been restricted by the limited domestic market. As one of the freest economies in the world, Hong Kong has capital surplus, favourable conditions for international trade, and advanced management experience in commercial and financial markets; while it is severely lacking agricultural and industrial resources, especially fresh water, foodstuff, energy and land. In addition, like Taiwan, Hong Kong and Macau are also facing a serious deficiency and high cost of labour.[9] Under the mutually complementary conditions, the positive effects on the economic development of the greater China area can be achieved through trade and spatial relocation of production factors such as labour, raw materials, technology, capital, and so on within the area.

Table 8.3 Mutually complementary conditions in the greater China area

Part	Advantages	Disadvantages
Mainland China	Adequate and various agricultural products, energy, industrial materials, excess labour, some high-tech products, and huge domestic market.	Shortage of capital, equipment, technology, management experience, and less developed economic infrastructures.
Taiwan	High capital saving, advanced equipment ready to move out, vanguard agricultural and industrial products, and management experience.	Shortage of energy and industrial resources, limited domestic market, and insufficiency and high costs of labour supply.
Hong Kong and Macau	Capital surplus, favourable convenient conditions for international trade, the freest economic environment, and management experience in commercial and financial markets.	Severe shortage of agricultural and industrial resources, especially fresh water, foodstuff, energy, and land and shortage of labour.

8.3   CROSS-TAIWAN STRAIT ECONOMIC RELATIONS

8.3.1   Historical Evolution

The Taiwan strait became a forbidden boundary in 1949 when the Nationalist-led government fled to Taiwan and, at the same time, the Communist-led government was founded on the mainland. Since then, Taiwan and mainland China have been under two divergent regimes. Against the common cultural and linguistic homogeneity, mainland China chose essentially socialism, while Taiwan followed the route of market-oriented capitalism. Furthermore, the sides have antagonistically treated each other, particularly during the high tide of military confrontation, when the mainland claimed to liberate the Taiwan compatriots from the *black* society sooner or latter, while Taiwan maintained that it would use the 'three democratisms' to re-occupy the mainland eventually.[10]

Table 8.4 A comparison of military expenses between Taiwan and mainland China, 1993[a]

Item	Taiwan	Mainland China
Defence expense (US$ 100 million)	104	562 (74)[b]
Forces (1000 persons)	442	3,031
Defence expense as % of GNP	4.7	2.7 (1.2)[b]
Defence expense as % of budget	20.0	16.2 (9.2)[b]
Per capita defence (US$)	494	48 (6)[b]
Forces per 1,000 population	21.0	2.6

[a] the US Arm Control and Disarmament Agency (1993);
[b] SSB (1996, pp. 230, 580).

The Taiwan-based Nationalists had been the internationally recognized government representing China as a whole before 15 October 1971 when the UN seat was changed from Taiwan to mainland China according to UNs Resolution No. 2758. Since then, the international positions of Taiwan and mainland China have been reversed. Following the United States' transference of its diplomatic relations with China from the KMT-led Taiwan to the CCP-led mainland in December 1978, almost all Western nations began to establish their formal ties with the mainland. As a result, Taiwan lost most of its friends.

Even though '[the cross-Taiwan strait] reunification does not mean that [the] mainland will swallow up Taiwan, nor does it mean that Taiwan will swallow up the mainland',[11] many critical issues relating to the cross-strait relations still remain unresolved. For instance, even though both mainland China and Taiwan have declared to the outside world that they are pursuing the 'one China' policy, the contents of which are absolutely different from each other. Mainland China proudly stresses that the 'People's Republic of China' (PRC) has been one of the five permanent members of the UN's Security Council and of course should be and has already been the only legal government representing China of which, to be sure, Taiwan is only a province;[12] Taiwan, however, strongly argues that the 'Republic of China' (ROC) founded by Dr. Sun Yatsen has existed since 1911 and is still in *râpport* with a certain number of independent nations. What is more important, along with Taiwan's remarkable economic growth and social progress, the Taiwanese government, after a long silence, has increasingly realized that it is time to expand internationally its political space and to let the outside world know the fact that there exists the 'Republic of China on Taiwan' in the international community.

Nevertheless, progress towards the peaceful reunification has been registered in negotiations on specific issues. Since the 1980s, the 'Wang Daohan–Koo Chenfu talks'[13] have represented forward steps in the relations between the two sides of the Taiwan strait. The major obstacles are that Taiwan has resisted the 'One country, two systems' and that the PRC has opposed Taiwan's activities to 'internationally expand living space' which is aimed, as claimed by mainland China, at creating 'two Chinas' or 'one China, one Taiwan' and states that 'only after peaceful reunification is accomplished can Taiwan compatriots and other Chinese truly and fully share the international dignity and honour attained by our great motherland.'[14] Moreover, Beijing has strongly resisted any effort to multilateralize the cross-strait relations, even at informal levels, insisting that this is a purely domestic matter.[15] However, where there is patience and willingness to compromise, there is still hope. The hope emerges when the two sides find that they are not fundamentally so different after all. Both sides will come to understand this 'sameness' and their basic heterogeneity if they can make further progress in the cross-strait cooperation by establishing exchanges of, *inter alia*, sport, culture, education, science and technology, and high-level political groups.

8.3.2   Bilateral Trade and Economic Exchanges

Bilateral trade and economic exchanges between Taiwan and mainland China had been frozen before 1979, except for small amounts of indirect trade of, among others, Chinese medicine and other native products from mainland China to Taiwan (mainly conducted via Hong Kong). In 1979, mainland China's 'Taiwan policy' was transformed from 'liberating Taiwan' to 'peaceful reunification'. Since then, indirect trade between the two sides and the Taiwanese investment in mainland China via Hong Kong and other regions have grown rapidly as a result of the cross-strait *détente*. In addition, tourism, technological and labour cooperation between the sides have also developed rapidly.

Indirect trade

Table 8.5 demonstrates that the total amount of cross-strait trade increased by 125 times, from US$77.8 million in 1979 to

Table 8.5   Re-exports between Taiwan and mainland China via Hong
Kong, 1979–94, million US$

Year	Total volume		To the mainland		To Taiwan		Surplus
		AGR		*AGR*		*AGR*	*(2)–(3)*
	(1)	*(%)*	*(2)*	*(%)*	*(3)*	*(%)*	*(4)*
1979	77.8	66.36	21.5	992840	56.3	20.54	−34.8
1980	311.2	300.2	235.0	994.4	76.2	35.4	158.8
1981	459.3	47.6	384.2	63.5	75.2	−1.4	309.0
1982	278.5	39.4	194.5	−49.4	84.0	11.8	110.4
1983	247.7	−11.1	157.9	−18.8	89.9	6.9	68.0
1984	553.2	123.3	425.5	169.6	127.8	42.2	297.7
1985	1102.7	99.3	986.9	132.0	115.9	−9.3	870.9
1986	955.6	−13.4	811.3	−17.8	144.2	24.4	667.1
1987	1515.5	58.6	1226.5	51.2	288.9	100.4	937.6
1988	2720.9	79.5	2242.2	82.9	478.7	65.7	1763.5
1989	3483.4	28.0	2896.5	29.9	586.9	22.6	2309.6
1990	4043.6	16.1	3278.3	13.2	765.4	30.4	2512.9
1991	5793.1	43.3	4667.2	42.4	1126.0	47.1	3541.2
1992	7406.9	27.9	6287.9	34.7	1119.0	−0.6	5169.0
1993	8689.0	17.3	7585.4	20.6	1103.6	−1.4	6481.8
1994	9809.5	12.9	8517.2	12.3	1292.3	17.1	7224.9

Note: AGR = annual growth rate
Source: Statistical Division of Hong Kong Government (various years).

US$9809.5 million in 1994. As a result, the trade dependency ratio
of Taiwan on mainland China rose by more than five times between 1981 and 1994, jumping to 5.50 per cent from only 1.05 per
cent, as shown by the official statistics in Table 8.6. It should be
noted that, if the 'small-size direct trade' (that is, 'illegally' conducted by the fishermen from the two sides) is taken into account,
the actual trade volume would be much larger.[16] According to an
estimation by the Mainland Commission (1995, July), the cross-
strait trade accounted for 10.02 per cent of Taiwan's total foreign
trade and 7.5 per cent of mainland China's total foreign trade in
1994. Taiwan and mainland China have been each other's fourth
largest trade partner, and mainland China has been the major source
for Taiwan's trade surplus. In 1994, 93.9 per cent of Taiwan's trade
surplus (US$7697 million) came from the indirect cross-strait trade.

Since 1985 when the Taiwanese government carried out the 'non-
interference' policy to Taiwan's exportation to mainland China, the
restrictions of the cross-strait trade have been gradually torn down

Table 8.6   Trade dependency ratios of Taiwan to mainland China[a],
1981–94, %

Year	Official statistics			Estimated by MC (1995)		
	Export	*Import*	*Total*	*Export*	*Import*	*Total*
1981	1.70	0.35	1.05	1.70	0.35	1.05
1982	0.88	0.44	0.68	0.88	0.44	0.68
1983	0.63	0.44	0.55	0.80	0.44	0.64
1984	1.40	0.58	1.06	1.40	0.58	1.06
1985	3.21	0.58	2.17	3.21	0.58	2.17
1986	2.04	0.60	1.49	2.04	0.60	1.49
1987	2.28	0.83	1.71	2.28	0.83	1.71
1988	3.70	0.96	2.47	3.70	0.96	1.47
1989	4.38	1.12	2.94	5.03	1.12	3.31
1990	4.88	1.40	3.32	6.54	1.40	4.23
1991	6.10	1.79	4.16	9.84	1.79	6.20
1992	7.72	1.55	4.83	12.95	1.55	7.60
1993	8.93	1.43	5.36	16.47	1.43	9.32
1994	9.15	1.51	5.50	17.22	2.18	10.02

[a] expressed by the shares of the export, import, and export plus import to
the mainland in Taiwan's total export, import, and export plus import
respectively.
Source: Z. Yan (1995, p. 57).

under the principle of 'indirect trading', that is, the direct trade
partners should be located outside mainland China and trade movements should be via third countries (regions). On the mainland,
foreign trade companies are not allowed to deal directly with Taiwanese companies outside Hong Kong and Macau. This policy,
nevertheless, has promoted the two sides' foreign trade companies
to open up either sub-companies or branches in Hong Kong and
Macau.

Indirect Taiwanese investment on the mainland

During the early period, Taiwanese investment in mainland China
was usually conducted under the names of investors from Hong
Kong, Macau, overseas Chinese and others who would nominally
be accepted by the two sides.[17] In order to absorb the Taiwanese
capital, mainland China promulgated the 'Regulations Concerning
the Promotion of the Taiwanese Compatriots' Investment' in July
1988 and the 'Law of Protecting the Taiwanese compatriots investment' in March 1994 respectively. In October 1990 the Taiwanese

government formally allowed businessmen to invest in mainland China under the names of their sub-companies housed in the third areas. According to Table 7.4, Taiwanese investment in the mainland increased from US$471.89 million in 1991 to US$3165.16 million in 1995, which has already made Taiwan the third largest investor (behind Hong Kong and Macau as a whole and Japan) in the mainland. As Taiwanese businessmen were only allowed to invest indirectly (that is, via third regions or countries) in mainland China, this kind of investment is in theory one between the third region (country) and mainland China, which might result in many unsolved issues. We will discuss them in Section 8.3.3.

Financial movement between Taiwan and mainland China had been strictly prohibited by the Taiwanese government before May 1990 when South China Bank (in Taiwan) was allowed to indirectly (via a British bank in Hong Kong) offer individual remittance from Taiwan to mainland China. In July 1993, financial movements were able to extend from individual to business activities and in addition banks in the Taiwan area were able to receive funds coming indirectly from mainland China. Table 8.7 shows an increasing tendency of financial movements between Taiwan and mainland China. From 1990 to 1994, individual funds sent indirectly from Taiwan to mainland China increased at an average rate of 79.28 per cent annually from US$18,903,697 to US$350,107,310. However, the amount of business funds sent indirectly to the mainland (US$100,396,939) shown in Table 8.7 was much smaller than the actually received amount (US$3,391,340,000)[18] in 1994, which implies that many Taiwanese businessmen must have used other channels to invest on the mainland.[19]

Other economic exchanges

In Taiwan, the population is mainly identified by two groups – native Taiwanese and Han- and other ethnic Chinese who fled to Taiwan when the Nationalists (KMT) lost the mainland in 1949. Most of the latter have relatives in mainland China. Besides the cross-strait trade and Taiwanese investment in the mainland, other economic exchanges between the two sides have also grown rapidly during the past years. Since November 1987 when Taiwanese citizens were allowed to pay private visits to mainland China, visitors from Taiwan to the mainland have increased year by year. In addition, exchanges in labour, science and technology between the sides have also developed rapidly.

Table 8.7 Indirect financial movements between Taiwan and mainland China, US$

| | From Taiwan to the mainland | | | | From the mainland to Taiwan[c] | |
| | Individual[a] | | Business[b] | | | |
Year	Piece	Total amount	Piece	Total amount	Piece	Total amount
1990	15,815	18,903,697				
1991	57,706	82,018,131				
1992	90,290	204,473,361				
1993	73,665	238,343,222	505	15,898,145	809	26,132,382
1994	99,665	350,107,310	2,521	100,396,939	2,342	88,626,917
1995[d]	53,689	203,779,380	1,790	59,620,721	500	17,408,236

[a] since 21 May 1990, including funds sent to family members and relatives, donations and other transferable payments, excluding traveling expenses.
[b] since 29 July 1993;
[c] since July 1993;
[d] January–June.
Source: Mainland Commission (1995, August).

8.3.3 Unresolved Issues

Dividing the Chinese nation into two economically complementary but politically antagonistic counterparts, the Taiwan strait may have been perhaps one of the special political borders in the world. The nearest distance between Taiwan and mainland China is within 1800 metres. However, due to the unavailability of direct links, cross-strait trade and economic relations have to be indirectly conducted via third countries (regions). As a result, transaction costs have increased accordingly, not to mention the extra expenses resulting from the increased distance of transportation.[20]

Direct links for postal, air and shipping services and trade between the sides are the objective requirements for their economic development and contact in various fields, and since they are in the interests of the people on both sides, it is absolutely necessary to adopt practical measures to speed up the establishment of such direct links. Since the 1980s, efforts have been made to promote negotiations on the basis of reciprocity and mutual benefit and signing non-governmental agreements on the protection of industrialists and businessmen. However, substantial progress has not been achieved. According to research conducted by CEC (1996), the indirect cross-strait links have sustained a net loss of US$731.5 million per annum for postal, remittance, air and shipping services between the sides.[21]

It should be noted that both cross-strait trade and Taiwanese investment in mainland China have still been to a large extent affected by the political uncertainties across the strait. In order to avoid 'putting all their eggs into one basket', the Taiwanese government carried out a 'South-oriented' policy in 1993, encouraging Taiwanese businessmen to invest in ASEAN and other Southeast Asian nations.[22] This situation will be further accelerated by Taiwanese independency on one hand and political pressure from the mainland on the other hand.[23]

8.3.4 Concluding Remarks

In view of the development of the world economy in the twenty-first century, cross-strait economic exchanges and cooperation should be further accelerated. Only this can achieve prosperity for both sides and benefit the entire nation. The two sides have promised that political differences should not affect or interfere with economic cooperation between the sides. Under the principles of peace, equality and bilateralism, the Taiwanese government is willing to promote cross-strait economic exchanges and treat the mainland as its hinterland. In order to seek the most efficient way of raising the level of the national economy, the PRC government seems intent to continue to implement, over a long period of time, the policy of encouraging industrialists and businessmen from Taiwan to invest in the mainland. Along with the enforcement of the 'Law of the People's Republic of China for Protecting the Investment of the Compatriots of Taiwan' and safeguarding the legitimate rights and interests of industrialists and businessmen from Taiwan, the contacts and exchanges between the sides will definitely increase and, surely, so too will mutual understanding and trust.

In concluding this section, two remarks concerning cross-strait reunification by Mr. Jiang Zemin and Mr. Lee Tenghwei are worth quoting to highlight future milestones on cross-strait relations:

It has been our consistent stand to hold negotiations with the Taiwan authorities on the peaceful reunification of the motherland. Representatives from the various political parties and mass organizations on both sides of the Taiwan Strait can be invited to participate in such talks. I said in my report at the fourteenth

National Congress of the Communist Party of China held in October 1992, 'On the premise that there is only one China, we are prepared to talk with the Taiwan authorities about any matter, including the form that official negotiations should take, a form that would be acceptable to both sides.' ... We have promised time and again that negotiations should be held on officially ending the state of hostility between the sides and accomplishing peaceful reunification step by step. Here again I solemnly propose that such negotiations be held. I suggest that, as the first step, negotiations should be held and an agreement reached on officially ending the state of hostility between the two sides in accordance with the principle that there is only one China. On this basis, the two sides should undertake jointly to safeguard China's sovereignty and territorial integrity and map out plans for the future development of their relations. As regards the name, place and form of these political talks, a solution acceptable to both sides can certainly be found so long as consultations on an equal footing can be held at an early date. (Jiang Zemin, Beijing, 31 January 1995.)

Since the thirty-eighth year of the Republic of China, Taiwan and the mainland have been governed by two non-interrelated political entities, which has resulted in the separation and divisive governance of the two sides of Taiwan strait and then raised the national reunification issue accordingly. Therefore, regarding the resolution of the reunification issue, we should seek the truth from facts and respect history so as to find a feasible form of national reunification under the situation of the divided governance of the two sides. If this reality is treated properly, a more unanimous point of view on the 'one China' could be reached by the two sides as soon as possible ...

Facing the tide of global participation in economic development, all Chinese should mutually complement, and benefit from, each other's experience. The economic development of Taiwan should treat the mainland as its hinterland; while the economic development of the mainland may take that of Taiwan as reference. We are willing to provide technologies and experience and help the mainland to improve agriculture for the benefit of the farmers; at the same time, we should also take the ongoing investment and trade as the basis and continue to help the mainland economy to prosper and raise the level of the living standards. ... (Lee Tengwei, Taipei, 8 April 1995.)

8.4 FUTURE PERSPECTIVE

When viewed with a belief that things are bound to change, there is not even a single element in the heaven and earth that does not change, while all materials in this world and the existence of myself who lives and dies are eternal when viewed from the standpoint that things do not change.

Su Dongpo (1037–1101 AD)

It is close to a rule among practitioners and theorists that multilateral conflicts frequently arise from narrow individual interests and expectations of different communities on one hand, and a chaotic interdependent system on the other hand. Notwithstanding the political, economic and social differences within the greater China area, it looks more and more possible for all Chinese, under growing comparative advantages, mutually complementary conditions as well as the tendency towards the unanimity of political, social, especially economic points of view among different parts of the area, to find an appropriate approach that can maximize the benefits for all the parties concerned, while also taking into account their respective articulated objectives.

After the return of Hong Kong and Macau from the British and Portuguese governments to mainland China in 1997 and 1999 respectively, the economic development of the PRC will have gone ahead by 2 to 3 years, given an average per capita GNP growth rate of 6 to 9 per cent for the mainland.[24] Accordingly, the existing indirect cross-strait links (that is, via Hong Kong and Macau) will, if they still exist, be transformed automatically into 'direct links'. However, nobody can predict when the cross-strait reunification will become a possibility. But the successful transition of Hong Kong is believed to be the critical factor on which the future reunification of the greater China area will depend.[25] With the Cold War coming to an end and private and semi-official cross-strait contacts being guaranteed by the both sides, all Chinese see no reason why their country should be left out of the surging tide of *détente* and further divided by the man-made barriers. Regarding the possible direct links between the sides, mainland China has intended to open as the first step six coastal ports (Qingdao, Dalian, Tianjin, Shanghai, Xiamen and Guangzhou) for cross-strait shipping businesses; while Taiwan had also a plan in which a foreign shipping centre is established in Kaohsiung. Both sides also tried to reduce the political sensitiveness to the minimum level by, among other actions, not hanging up the national flags.

While the Chinese economic areas are developing at an exceptional rate, all Chinese people have never forgotten that their motherland is still being artificially divided. Nevertheless, the creation of political harmony and reunification between Taiwan and mainland China may still require time and patience from both parties. It is a hopeful sign that the two political leaders (Mr. Jiang Zemin and Mr. Lee Tenghwei) have promised to reunify the two sides of Taiwan strait peacefully. Chinese people on both sides of the strait and the outside world as well will watch carefully to see how sincerely the two political leaders make the attempt. Of course, both sides know quite well about the clam-snipe story, an ancient Chinese fable stated at the beginning of the chapter, and don't want themselves to be caught by the 'fisherman' eventually.

Surely, the 'sleeping giant' is awake!

BOX 8

Overseas Chinese Economics

There have been more than 50 million overseas Chinese living in over one hundred countries (regions). Since World War II, especially the 1970s, the overseas Chinese wealth has been growing rapidly and played an increasing role in the world economy. An incomplete estimate shows that the overseas Chinese already had US$223.1 billion of foreign currency deposits by the end of 1993, which is mainly distributed in Taiwan (US$90.6 billion), Hong Kong (US$32.7 billion), Singapore (US$43.7 billion), Thailand (US$23.4 billion), Malaysia (US$15.4 billion), Indonesia (US$11.0 billion), the Philippines (US$4.3 billion), and other nations (US$2.0 billion).[26] An even more optimistic estimation reveals that, excluding Taiwan and Hong Kong, the total capital owned by overseas Chinese could exceed US$150 to 200 billion.[27] Since the early 1980s, the overseas Chinese have contributed greatly to the economic development of mainland China, especially the coastal area with which they have close ties. Studies show that overseas

Chinese investment has provided more than two-thirds of the total direct foreign investment (DFI) in mainland China during the past years. China's growing exports have also been greatly promoted by the overseas Chinese.

Briefly, several factors can explain this remarkable growth of the overseas Chinese economy: (1) thriftiness and hard working of the overseas Chinese, (2) an élite group of intellectuals, (3) the positive role of overseas Chinese organizations, and (4) the closer socioeconomic ties with mainland China.

Notes

Notes to Introduction

1. The major events that occurred in the Chinese society during the twentieth century are listed below in a chronological order: 1912, China's last dynasty, Qing, was replaced by the Republic of China (ROC); 1937, Japan invaded China and the War of Resistance Against Japan (WRAJ) began; 1945, Japan surrendered unconditionally and, thereafter, the Civil War between the Nationalists and the Communists broke out; 1949, the People's Republic of China (PRC) was founded, followed by the large-scale land reform and socialist transformation of capitalist industry and commerce in mainland China; 1958, the Great Leap Forward (GLF) movement was started, followed by a three year famine (1959–61); 1966, the Great Cultural Revolution (GCR) was launched by Mao Zedong; 1978, China began to gradually reform its centrally planned economy (CPE); 1992, stimulated by Deng Xiaoping's Southern Speech in February, China decided to build up a socialist market economy (SME) with the Chinese characteristics.
2. All data are measured at current prices based on SSB (1987, p. 670; 1996, p. 280).
3. This first of the World Bank reports was given prominence in *The Economist* (28 November 1992). Subsequent reports appeared in *Financial Times* (26 April 1993) and *The Economist* (15 May 1993).
4. Under the best guess projection, the US share of the world output falls down to 19.2 per cent in 2003, Japan experiences a declining share to something on the range of 7.6 to 8.1 per cent. In contrast, China's share jumps unambiguously up to 13.0 per cent in the best guess scenario and 15.5 per cent in the high-growth scenario (Noland, 1995, p. 95, tab. 1).
5. Definitely, given China's relatively low prices for most of the commodities and services, the PPP-based economic gaps between China and those countries will be narrowed considerably.
6. See, for example, Tang (1982, p. 8) for a detailed explanation of this cycle.
7. There have been slightly different explanations on China's *fang–shou* cycle. For example, Shirk (1990, p. 26), Dittmer and Wu (1993, pp. 10–12) reached a similar conclusion, sketching out four relatively complete, synchronous cycles of *fang* and *shou* during 1980 to 1987: *fang* predominated in 1979–80, 1984, and 1988, while *shou* predominated in 1981, 1985–86, 1987, and 1988–89.
8. More evidences may be found in Z. Sun (1993, pp. 95–104), L. Feng (1993, pp. 87–94) and R. Guo (1993, pp. 201–5).
9. Data source: SSB (1993, p. 72, tab. T3.9).
10. It is interesting to note that the number of the peasants' uprisings is

closely related to governmental corruption during 1796 to 1911 in the late Qing dynasty (see Z. Liang (1978, ch. 1) and Jin and Liu (1984, pp. 119–23)).

11. In what follows, unless stated otherwise, the term 'first-class administrative division' (FCAD) will be used to denote 'province', 'autonomous region' or 'municipality directly under the central government'.

12. The discussion of the Chinese environmental situation and policies has appeared in another draft entitled 'Chinese Economic Sustainability' (*Occasional Papers* No. 10, University of Trier, Germany) and, therefore, will not be included in this book.

13. *Lunyu–weizheng*

Notes to Chapter 1

1. *Cihai* (1988, p. 94). More often than not, the Chinese nation, as it is now called *zhongguo* (central state) in pinyin form, had another name, *jiuzhou* (nine states). The reason for the latter may be plausibly explained by the fact that the remaining three states (Binzhou, Youzhou and Yingzhou) had been independent from China before the central and peripheral states were unified as a single nation.

2. *Zhongshu-xingsheng* and *xingsheng* (the latter evolved to *sheng*) referred to the central government ministerial representative agencies to the FCADs.

3. Notice that the Chinese character *dao* is being used as 'province' in Korea and that *sheng* is used as 'ministry' in Japan.

4. It has been virtually the most important power body in making decisions on Chinese state affairs.

5. See K. Yang (1993, p. 248).

6. See *People's Daily* (1992, p. 1).

7. Examples of literature on the application of the six great regions would include Hu, Shao and Li (1988, pp. 171–381), K. Yang (1989, p. 92), and H. Wei (1992, pp. 62–3).

8. NPC is the highest legislature in China. It includes a Standing Committee housed in Beijing and more than two thousand formal members representing all regions and sectors of China. The latter meet regularly in the Great Hall of the People in Beijing to discuss state affairs, issue laws and key regulations and appoint central government officials.

9. See *Guangming Daily*, 6 April 1986, p. 1.

10. For example, Wu and Hou (1990, p. 116), Hu, Shao, and Li (1988, pp. 182–4), S. Yang (1990, pp. 38–43), G. Liu (1994, pp. 1–13), and T. Hsueh (1994, pp. 22–56) give the same definition.

11. The first major Han-Chinese migration from the northern to the southern part of Yangtze river took place during Wei, Jin, and South and North dynasties (220–589), and was accelerated during Five Dynasties and Ten States period (907–960) when China's northern part became the field of battle. Since then, large-scale Han-Chinese migration was promoted by the frequent wars between the Chinese and Liao, Jin, Mongol and other minorities in North Song (960–1126) and South

Song (1127–1279) dynasties. In the wars with their far northern en-
emies, the Han-Chinese first lost their northern part after the late
North Song dynasty.
12. More details and comments on these suggestions may be found in
J. Liu (1996, pp. 153–6).

Notes to Chapter 2

1. China's cultivated land could have been under-estimated due to incomplete statistics and insufficient exploration efforts. For instance,
after summing up the official data from the provincial statistics, the
total cultivated land area is no more than 100,000,000 ha, while other
estimates (such as 120,000,000 ha, 133,333,000 ha, and 146,667,000
ha) have been also conducted by different institutions based on satellite photographs and sample surveys respectively (H. Cheng, 1990, pp.
1–18).
2. There has been different estimates on the forestland area. In 1979,
the Chinese official statistics defined the forestland area at 1,220,000
km^2, while the World Bank (1992) puts the figure at 1,150,000 km^2 for
the year 1980. According to S. Vaclav (1992, p. 434), China's forestland area was estimated as 124,650,000 km^2 ha in the third national
survey (1984–88) and were reported by SSB and Ministry of Forestry
of China as 1,246,000 km^2 and 1,092,000 km^2 respectively for the year
1989. NEPA (1993, p. 4; 1994, p. 5) evaluates it at 1,309,000 km^2 in
1992 and 1,337,000 km^2 in 1993 respectively.
3. The 15 metals include copper, lead, tin, zinc, iron ore, manganese,
nickel, chromium, cobalt, molybdenum, tungsten, vanadium, bauxite,
titanium, and lithium.
4. Data source: W. Zhu (1990a, pp. 727–36).
5. Notice that the monetary values of the mineral resources might have
been under-estimated due to the use of low and officially fixed prices
for mineral products before the 1990s. But it does not matter here.
Our aim is only to multiregionally estimate the relative shares, nothing more.
6. Data source: SSB (1996, p. 4).
7. For more discussions about the interregional separation and its affects on the Chinese economy, see Chapter 6.
8. K. Wakabayashi (1989, p. 14) estimates that 14 million people died
from starvation between 1959 and 1961. In addition, R. Minami (1994,
p. 197, fn. 8) puts the number of deaths higher.
9. The literature of this arguments would include Wang and Dai (1958,
pp. 10–4), He, Zhu and Liao (1960, pp. 20–5), and L. Zhang (1982,
pp. 12–14).
10. Cited from Z. Mao (1949, pp. 453–4).
11. Cited from R. Minami (1994, p. 197).
12. If considering the contribution of capital saved as a result of the reduced birth rate, this figure would be higher.
13. According to a sampling survey conducted on 1 October 1995, the
birth gender proportions for population at the ages of 0, 1, 2, 3, 4

years were 116.57:100, 121.08:100, 121.26:100, 119.17:100, and 115.01:100 respectively (SSB, 1996, p. 72).

14. According to the PRC's Constitution, women and men shall have the same right to be employed and paid the same wage if they do the same job. However, this does not always apply in rural areas where labour productivity is to a large extent physically determined.

15. Data source: SSB (1993, p. 153). The population age composition also differs among regions. In 1982, Shanghai became the first FCAD whose population aged 65 years or over exceeded 7 per cent of the total population (which is generally known to be an aged society) (Lin and Liu, 1996, p. 12). In 1995, the old-aged FCADs further covered Beijing, Tianjin, Jiangsu, Zhejiang, Shandong, Guangdong, Liaoning and Sichuan. Examples of FCADs with low ratios of the aged population to the total population were Qinghai (3.58%), Ningxia (3.78%), Gansu (4.34%), Xinjiang (4.42%), Heilongjiang (4.58%), and Inner Mongolia (4.70%) (SSB, 1996, p. 73).

16. To illustrate the long-term effect of rural-urban imbalance of population growth, let's assume that r_A (P_A) and r_B (P_B) are the population growth rates (number of population) of urban (A) and rural (B) areas respectively ($r_A < r_B$). Let $r_A = 1\%$ and $r_B = 2\%$. Assume $P_A = P_B = 1$ when t = 0; then when t = 1, $P_A:P_B$ = 1:1.01; t = 10, $P_A: P_B$ = 1:1.10; t = 20, $P_A: P_B$ = 1:1.22; t = 30, $P_A: P_B$ = 1:1.34; t = 40, $P_A: P_B$ = 1:1.48; t = 50, $P_A: P_B$ = 1:1.63. The above figures simply suggest that, given population growth rates in urban and rural areas of 1 per cent and 2 per cent respectively, the number of population of the rural area which is equal to that of the urban area at the year zero will be 1%, 10%, 22%, 34%, 48%, and 63% larger than that of the urban area after 1, 10, 20, 30, 40, and 50 years respectively.

17. Data source: SSB (1996, p. 114). According to the Chinese definition, registered unemployment rate in urban areas refers to the ratio of the number of the registered unemployed persons to the sum of the number of employed persons and the registered unemployed persons. The registered unemployed persons in urban areas refer to persons who are registered as permanent residents in the urban area engaged in non-agricultural activities, aged within the range of labouring age (for male, 16 years or older but younger than 50 years; for female, 16 years or older but younger than 45 years), capable of work, unemployed but desirous to be employed and have been registered at the local employment service agencies to apply for a job.

18. The unemployment rates for some countries were 6.6% (USA), 9.4% (France), 10.9% (Italy), 15.2% (Spain), and 8.1% (UK) (ILO, 1993). However, the definition of 'unemployment' differs from country to country, so it is difficult to conduct meaningful international comparisons.

19. Data source: SSB (1996, p. 69).

20. Calculated by the author based on SSB (1996, p. 70).

21. Data source: SSB (1996, p. 71).

22. Data source: SSB (1996, p. 336).

23. Notice that only in 1995 did the Chinese government decide to implement a nine-year compulsory education system (six years of primary

school and three years of junior middle school), aiming at universal access to junior middle school within six years in urban and coastal areas and within ten years in the remaining areas.

24. In the years when class struggle was taken as the key line, the Chinese workers, poor and low-middle peasants, and other revolutionary groups were classified by order of importance into nine groups of which the intellectuals were treated as the 'notorious number nine' (*chou laojiu*).

25. According to R. Guo (1986, p. 234), the 'break-point' for China's university teachers will occur at the beginning of the twenty-first century.

26. According to the PRC's Constitution, workers are the leading class in China.

27. According to Chenery and Syrquin (1975, p. 20), when the per capita GNP grows from US$100 to US$400 in developing countries, the ratio of educational expenditure to GNP increases from 3.3% to 3.5% accordingly.

28. Data source: SSB (1996, pp. 42, 232).

29. Data source: UNESCO (1995, table 4.1).

30. Calculated by the author based on SSB (1996, pp. 120–1). Ironically, this fact has not been able to satisfy the basic requirements of the newly promulgated Law of the PRC on Teachers in which 'the average wage of teachers should be higher or no lower than that of the government functionaries'.

31. See Li, Zhang and Zhong (1989, p. 37).

32. Cited from Knight and Li (1993, p. 300).

33. For a deeper discussion see Chapter 6.

34. Data source: SSB (1993, p. 72, table. T3.9).

35. Data source: UN (1994). The HDI is calculated in terms of mean value of education, ratio of adult literacy, life expectancy of population and PPP-adjusted per capita GNP.

Notes to Chapter 3

1. 'Qinceer'. Based on K. Liu (1991, p. 155).

2. The centralized planning model is based upon the supposition that 'society' (in practice the planning agencies, under the authority of the political leadership) knows or can discover what is needed, and can issue orders incorporating these needs, while allocating the required means of production so that the needs are economically met – cited from A. Nove (1987, p. 881).

3. Even though the term 'commodity' in the Chinese understanding is closely related to the concept of market economy, we may assume that it was used here to literally distinguish the Chinese economy from the Western style market system.

4. The term was firstly publicized in bold headlines in the CCP's official newspapers, such as *People's Daily, Workers' Daily*, in early 1988.

5. For details of the Speech, see X. Deng (1992, pp. 370–83).

6. See *China Daily*, 17 November 1993, Art. 16.

7. Ibid., Art. 17.

8. See H. Gu (1997, pp. 52–5). Notice that it is difficult for reasons of

statistical coverage, ambiguous ownership categories and price distortions to determine with any high degree of precision the shares of planning and market activities.

9. Data source: SSB (1990). The concepts GVIO, GVAO, and NI are based on the MPS used during the pre-reform period. For more details about the MPS, see Chapter 4.
10. Data source: S. Liu (1982, p. 31).
11. For more detailed analysis of the GLF and its impacts on the Chinese economy, see Chapter 5.
12. See, for example, S. Liu (1982, p. 28–51) for more details.
13. This boring bargaining between state planners and the managers usually reached a high tide during the national planning meetings arranged by the SPC annually.
14. On the dual pricing system, see Box 3.
15. Data source: State Council (1988a, p. 198).
16. Data source: T. Liu (1995, p. 53).
17. As a result of the complementarities of the state and non-state sectors, more and more people are keenly considering 'one household, two systems' (*yijia liangzhi*) as their optimal pattern of employment, that is, in a household, some member(s) is (are) engaged by the non-state sector, while the other(s) is (are) working in the state sector.
18. Data source: R. Minami (1994, p. 77).
19. As noted by C. Lin (1995), China s SOEs enjoyed far less autonomy than their Soviet antecedents, as the Soviet enterprises operated under the Economic Accounting System (*khozraschet*) which endowed state enterprises with a limited degree of financial autonomy with them being allowed to retain a proportion of profits, depreciation reserves, and major repairs funds. But national shortages of productive resources and severe weakness in enterprise management in China during the 1950s compelled a much more centralized system which left SOEs without any substantive decision-making or financial autonomy.
20. According to SICA (1995), the number of *getihu* grew by over 11 times, from 1,828 thousand in 1981 to 22,390 thousand in 1995, while that of *shiyingqiye* grew by over five times, from 91 thousand in 1989 to 563 thousand in 1995. Notice that the actual number could be larger as some IOEs could have reported under the name of 'COEs' in order to evade the 'individual income' tax.
21. Notice that as soon as the Tian'anmen Square incident (May–June 1989) was calmed down, the Chinese leadership began to re-emphasize the role of the working class in the Chinese economy.
22. The literature of the evolution in central–local fiscal arrangement over the pre-reform era would include N. Lardy (1975, pp. 25–60), A. Donnithorne (1976, pp. 328–54) and Oksenberg and Tong (1991, pp. 1–32).
23. That is, the marginal and average propensity to tax each FCAD from its collected revenue ranged between 12 per cent and 90 per cent (Oksenberg and Tong, 1991, p. 24).
24. In what follows in this paragraph, the fiscal parameters in parentheses are defined in Table 3.4.

25. Data source: W. Wei (1994, pp. 297–9).
26. Knight and Li (1995, p. 16) explain three main reasons for why the FCADs have retained an increasing proportion of the revenue they collect: (1) the growing importance of extra-budgetary revenue in total revenue; (2) under the lump-sum contract system the marginal rate of tax was unity if the target was not achieved and zero for revenue in excess of the target; and (3) the increasing cross-section responsiveness of budgetary expenditure to budgetary revenue.
27. Cited from G. Liu (1994, p. 3). More detailed analysis will be given in Chapter 5.
28. Data source: K. Yang (1993, p. 179).
29. Cited from Knight and Li (1995, p. 5).

Notes to Chapter 4

1. It is worth noting that the SNA has some shortcomings and is not a complete measure of economic welfare from which humankind may benefit. In fact, as illustrated in UN (1990a and b), the SNA-based GNP (or GDP) indicator ignores the costs of both the depletion and degradation of natural and environmental resources.
2. More evidences may be found in K. Tsui (1993, pp. 30–1).
3. See, for example, Guo and Han (1991, pp. 10–21) for a more detailed explanation and the critical evaluation on the quality of Chinese GDP data.
4. Therefore, NI equals GVSP minus all material costs including depreciation of capital.
5. According to a survey conducted by Jilin Provincial Statistical Bureau (1990, pp. 27–8), the rural GVIO data reported to the SSB might have been 21.8 per cent higher than the real data in Jilin province in 1989.
6. See, for example, Guo and Wang (1988), D. Yang (1990, 230–57), Denny (1991, pp. 186–208), F. Dong (1992, pp. 63–4), Lyons (1992, pp. 471–506), Tsui (1991, pp. 1–21), H. Wei (1992, pp. 61–5), W. Yang (1992a, pp. 70–4; 1992b, pp. 65–6), P. Zhang (1994, pp. 296–312), Wei and Liu (1994, pp. 28–36), and X. Song (1996, pp. 38–44).
7. See, for example, K. Yang (1991, pp. 504–9; 1993, pp. 129–45), Liu, Gong, Li and Wu (1994, pp. 141–66), and Tsui (1993).
8. Data source: ADB (1996, p. 17). All data are estimated according to the *World Bank Atlas* method of converting national currency to current US dollars.
9. As a matter of fact, the reason why the Chinese government has rejected the PPP-enlarged GDP may arise from, among others, the fears that it could affect China as a less-developed country obtaining the favourable loans and economic assistance from the international organizations – J. Zheng (1996, p. 1).
10. Data sources: SSB (1989, p. 29; 1994, p. 33; 1996, p. 42; and 1996b, pp. 13 and 15). As the SNA-based data for the period from 1978 to 1984 had been only crudely estimated by the SSB, we exclude them from estimation.

11. For more evidences of the overstatement on China's GNP for the post-1992 period, one may also refer to Ling *et al.* (1995, pp. 18–19), *China Youths* (1995, p. 2), *The Economist* (1995, p. 19), *People's Daily* (1995, p. 2), W. Huang (1996, pp. 157–62), and so on.

12. The size of underground economic activities varies enormously from country to country. Obviously, it is impossible to get precise estimates because, by their very nature, the details have been largely hidden from the authorities. Nevertheless, the following factors determine the size of the underground economy: (1) The level of taxes and regulations. The greater their level, the greater the incentive for people to evade the system and 'go underground'. (2) The determination of the authorities to catch up with evaders, and the severity of the punishments for those found out. (3) The size of the service sector relative to the manufacturing sector. It is harder for the authorities to detect the illicit activities of motor mechanics, gardeners and window cleaners than the output of cars, bricks and soap. (4) The proportion of the population that is self-employed. It is much easier for the self-employed to evade taxes than it is for people receiving a wage where taxes are deducted at source. Cited from J. Sloman (1991, p. 574).

13. Cited from *Asia-Pacific Economic Times*, 22 October 1996.

14. Of course, this approximation is only a crude one, but it would be at least better than taking no action at all, when one tries to measure the economic inequalities for the FCADs in China (see Section 4.4).

15. For more details on this research project, see Griffin and Zhao (eds., 1993) and Zhao and Griffin (eds., 1994).

16. Data source: SSB (1986, p. 563 and 1996, p. 282).

17. According to World Bank (1981, p. 49), the income differentials between rural and urban areas were much larger in China than in many other low income Asian countries and Latin American countries.

18. Notice that according to Khan *et al.* (1993, p. 34), the difference between the incomes of an average urban household and an average rural household is much higher than the officially estimate. The true ratio of urban to rural incomes, for instance, would be 2.42 in 1988 as compared to a ratio of 2.05 estimated by the SSB (1989, p. 719).

19. Obviously, after black and white TV sets are excluded, the urban–rural gap is still very large.

20. Data source: SPC (1996, pp. 37–40).

21. See, for example, K. Yang (1989, pp. 95–6) and Liu, Gong, Li and Wu (1994, pp. 142–3) for the application in the Chinese economic analyses.

22. Examples of literature for the application in the Chinese economic analyses would include N. Lardy (1980, pp. 153–90), Lyons (1992, pp. 471–506), Denny (1991, pp. 186–208), K. Tsui (1991, pp. 1–21), and W. Yang (1992, pp. 70–4).

23. For instance, after having mathematically illustrated the Gini and CV indices with Lorenz curve, F. Zhou (1994, pp. 193–200) concludes that when the Gini coefficient slightly changes, it may not be consistent with CV, whereas when Gini coefficient changes at a relatively large rate, it may be consistent with CV.

24. In the extreme case when $c \to \infty$, the ranking of the corresponding

GE is same as that of Rawls' maximum criterion, that is, to focus exclusively on the well-being of the worst-off province (Shorrocks, 1980, pp. 613–25).

25. Literature of the multidimensional measurement of regional inequalities would include Atkinson (1970, pp. 244–63), Atkinson and Bourguigon (1992, pp. 140–53), Maasourmi (1986, pp. 771–9), and Kolm (1976a, pp. 416–42; 1976b, pp. 82–111; and 1977, pp. 1–13). In addition, as a demonstration in which two indices (per capita GDP and per capita hospital beds) are considered, K. Tsui (1994, pp. 181–92) applies the multidimensional GE method to calculate China's regional disparities between 1978 and 1989. Due to the complexity of the multidimensional measurement, we will not conduct it here.

26. Data source: SSB (1990b). All data are based on comparable prices.

27. The per capita GDPs are estimated according to the method in Section 4.2.2 for the FCADs whose GDP data are not officially reported.

28. See Khan *et al.* (1993, p. 69).

29. An economic comparison of Taiwan, Hong Kong, Macau and mainland China will be conducted in Chapter 8.2.

30. Data sources: Ottolenghi and Steinherr (1993, p. 29), Savice (1992, p. 191), Smith (1987, p. 41), B. Higgins (1981, pp. 69–70), Nair (1985, p. 9), Hill and Weidemann (1989, pp. 6–7), Kim and Mills (1990, p. 415), and Hu, Wang, and Kang (1995, p. 92).

31. Data source: N. Li (1997, p. 12).

Notes to Chapter 5

1. Data source: J. Liao (1982, p. 130).

2. Among the pre-reform FYPs, the First FYP (1953–57) has been generally known to be most successful, because many key macroeconomic issues, such as the relationship between industry and agriculture and the setting of an appropriate rate of accumulation, were properly handled in this FYP. However, some economic problems in relation to over-centralized administration and non-economic methods of management that have been reformed since the late 1970s had their origins in that period.

3. Cited from Mao (1956, p. 285).

4. See Mao (1957, p. 491).

5. Data source: S. Liu (1982, p. 32).

6. Data source: SSB (1990b).

7. During the GLF period, large amounts of material and labour were invested in heavy industry at the expense of agriculture and light industry. Millions of peasants abandoned farming to dig for ore and fell trees in order to make steel using indigenous methods. The harvest was poor despite the high yields, which eventually resulted in a three-year famine.

8. Data source: W. Liang (1982, p. 60).

9. Data source: Jao and Leung (1986, pp. 3, 6).

10. Examples of literature on the third-front area would include Lardy (1978), Leung (1980), Maruyama (1982, pp. 437–71), Z. Liu (1983),

Riskin (1987), Naughton (1988, pp. 227–304), Bo (1991, pp. 1202–3, 1209), and Z. Chen (1994, pp. 329–42).
11. Data source: Hu, Wang and Kang (1995, p. 5).
12. Data source: G. Liu (1984, p. 270).
13. Data source: W. Liang (1982, pp. 61–2). This clearly went too far beyond the real capacities of this country. For example, the proposed targets for grain, steel and oil production were far higher than the 1985 actual outputs as listed in Table I.1.
14. Data source: W. Liang (1982, p. 56, table 3).
15. More detailed information is given in SSB (1996, p. 89).
16. See SSB (1996, pp. 405–1).
17. The units used are yuan for Y and K and person for L.
18. Data source: UNFAO (1992).
19. Data source: SSB (1996, p. 354). Rural labourers are classified by main activity: for example, those engaged primarily in agriculture and secondly in commerce are classified under agriculture.
20. Data source: SSB (1996, pp. 387–90).
21. World Bank (1996, p. 51) lists five factors contributing to the remarkable growth and superior record of efficiency of the TVEs:

    (a) *Kinship and implicit property rights.* Strong kinship links among rural Chinese villagers encourage responsibility in entrepreneurs. The sharing of implicit, if fuzzy, property rights leads to a productive combination of risk and reward sharing between entrepreneurs and local government. None the less, incentives facing TVEs are more like those of private firms in that the residual profits accrue to a limited group: a traditionally stable local community and, in particular, its government and TVE managers.

    (b) *Decentralization plus financial discipline.* The 1984 decentralization of fiscal power in China allowed sub-national governments to retain locally generated revenues, creating powerful incentives for the development of local industry. Under this system a non-performing TVE becomes an unaffordable drain on a limited local budget. In the end persistent money-losers are closed and the work force is shifted to more profitable lines.

    (c) *Competition.* Studies also show intense competition for investment (including foreign investment) among communities with TVEs. Success in attracting investment is affected by reputation and local economic performance.

    (d) *Market opportunities and rural saving.* A past bias against light industry and services has created vast market opportunities, buttressed by high rural saving and demand following the agricultural reforms of 1978 and by the limited scoop for emigration from rural areas.

    (e) *Links with the state enterprise sector.* The large state-owned industrial sector provides a natural source of demand, technology and raw materials for many TVEs. Foreign investment from Hong Kong and Taiwan (China) plays the same role for many others.

22. More details may be found in He, Gu, Yan and Bao (1991, pp. 124–41).
23. Lu Xun, a well-known writer, ironically noted that while the Western nations used gunpowder to make firearms and the compass for navigation, China used gunpowder to make firecrackers and compass to align the spiritual location within the landscape (*fengshui*).
24. Data source: J. Liao (1982, p. 138).
25. Data source: SSB (1987, p. 100).
26. Data source: W. Huang (1996, p. 11).
27. These plans include, *inter alia*, (1) '*863' Plan*, which aims to track the frontiers of high-tech, research and development; (2) *Torchlight Plan*, which aims to promote the commercialization, industrialization and internationalization of high-tech products; (3) *The Climbing Plan*, which aims to organize the research and application of new and high technologies; (4) *Spark Plan*, which aims to spread applicable technologies to small- and medium-sized enterprises, TVEs, and other rural areas, and (5) *Harvest Plan*, which aims to popularize various kinds of technology contributing to agriculture, herd and fishery.
28. Data sources: (1) SSB (1996, p. 661) for the data of 1995; (2) SSTC (1988, p. 267) for the data of 1986; (3) As Ma and Sun (1981, p. 614) estimate that China's R&D expenses were 0.54 per cent of GVIAO in 1979, using the estimated GVIAO/GNP ratio in Equation 4.3, we can obtain an approximation of R&D/GNP ratio ($0.54/0.58 \approx 0.93$).
29. According to UNESCO (1986), the R&D/GNP ratio of China was, although lower than that of USA, Japan, West Germany, UK and Switzerland whose R&D/GNP ratios exceeded 2.0, higher than that of Pakistan, Indonesia, Thailand and the Philippines whose R&D/GNP ratios ranged from 1.0 to 0.4, and much similar to that of Austria, Australia, Denmark, Italy and South Korea whose R&D ratios ranged from 1.0 to 1.2 during 1980–85.

Notes to Chapter 6

1. Examples of literature on the cross-border communications in China would include *Economic News* (1987, p. 1; 1988, p. 1), W. Zhu (1990b, pp. 20–4), Y. Hu (1992, p. 1), and R. Guo (1993, pp. 118–23; 1996, pp. 70–1).
2. See *Baokan Wenzhai* (1989, p. 4).
3. This phenomenon has been described as *Zhuhou Jingji* (feudal prince economy) or *Duli Wangguo* (independent kingdom). See, for example, Shen and Dai (1990, p. 12), Z. Li (1993, pp. 23–36) and Wedeman (1993, pp. 1–2) for more detailed analyses.
4. More detailed evidences may be found in Z. Sun (1993, pp. 95–104), L. Feng (1993, pp. 87–94), R. Guo (1993, pp. 201–5), and D. Goodman (1994, pp. 1–20).
5. See Young and Ho (1993, pp. 9–13).
6. Data source: SSB (1996, p. 56).
7. Data source: SSB (1996, p. 54).
8. In what follows in this section, we will use the number of political authorities, spatial structure, or border dimension involved in a region interchangeably.

9. More details on the mathematical proof may be found in R. Guo (1995, pp. 38–43).
10. The aim of the case study is to demonstrate the application of the model built in Section 6.2. Given the availability of all necessary data, one can also quantitatively calculate the impact of spatial separation on the Chinese economy as a whole.
11. Unless stated otherwise, all data used in this Section are Based on SSB (1995, pp. 347–9; 1996, pp. 368–70 and 374).
12. Other factors, such as labour force, fertilizer, conditions of irrigation and cultivation, and so on, are also very important in agricultural production. But their influences on the optimal solutions will be insignificant if they are not the critical constraints
13. In market economies, the price of a product is never a constant but a function of both supply and demand, while the latter are also determined by spatial locations.
14. Data source: PYC (1995, pp. 246–54). The price of cereal is a weighted mean of the prices of rice, wheat and corn, the price of oil bearing crops is a weighted mean of the prices of peanuts, rapeseed and sesame), and that of fruit is a weighted mean of apples and oranges.
15. See CCPCC (1984).
16. Examples of the literature would include CASS (1992) and R. Guo (1993, pp. 189–95; 1996, pp. 146–50).
17. The per capita NI differences between the BECZs and the non-BECZs can, *ceteris paribus*, approximately reflect the economic effects of cross-border cooperation.
18. Cited from R. Guo (1996, pp. 38–9, 41, 44).

Notes to Chapter 7

1. 'Qiushui'. Cited from K. Liu (1991, p. 13).
2. According to *Guangxu Da Qing Huidian Shili* (vol. 775, p. 4 and vol. 776, p. 13), *haijin* (close-door) policy includes: (1) the export of cereals and five metals (gold, silver, copper, iron and tin) were strictly prohibited; (2) private trade and contacts between Chinese and foreign businessmen were illegal; (3) foreigners' activities in China were only allowed on the conditions that 'At most ten foreigners may take a walk together near their hotel three days a month on the 8th, 18th and 28th', 'Overseas businessmen should not stay in Guangdong in winter', and 'Women from foreign countries are prohibited to enter this country', and so on; (4) Chinese businessmen going abroad were subject to the conditions that 'At most one litre of rice may be carried by a seaman a day' and 'At most two guns may be installed in a ship'; and (5) manufacture of seagoing vessels of more than 500 *dans* in weight and 8 metres in height was prohibited. (Translated from P. Zheng (1992, pp. 30–1).)
3. Thereafter, a series of open-door measures were implemented in the coastal area: in October 1983, Hainan island, Guangdong province, was allowed to conduct some of the special foreign economic policies granted to the SEZs; in April 1984, 14 coastal cities (including Tianjin, Shanghai, Dalian, Qinhuangdao, Yantai, Qingdao, Lianyungang,

Nantong, Ningbo, Wenzhou, Fuzhou, Guangzhou, Ganjiang and Beihai) were designated by the CCPCC and the State Council as 'open cities'; in February 1985, three deltas of Yangtze River, Pearl River and South Fujian were approved as coastal economic development zones (EDZs); in March 1988, the EDZs of the three deltas were again approved to extensively cover larger areas while at the same time some cities and counties in Liaodong and Shandong peninsulas and Bohai Basin area were allowed to open up economically to the outside world; in April 1988, the NPC approved the establishment of Hainan province which was organized as an SEZ with even more flexible policies than other SEZs; in April 1990, Shanghai's suggestion of speeding up the development of Pudong area using some of the SEZ's mechanisms was approved by the CCPCC and the State Council.

4. These measures include, *inter alia*, (1) 'Measures Concerning the Supervision and Favourable Taxation for the People-to-People Trade in Sino-Myanmer Border' (25 Jan. 1992, Office of Custom, PRC); (2) 'Notification Concerning the Further Opening up of the Four Frontier Cities of Heihe, Shuifenhe, Hunchun and Manzhouli' (1992, State Council); (3) 'Notification Concerning the Further Opening up of the Five Frontier Cities and Towns of Nanning, Kunming, Pingxiang, Ruili and Hekou' (June 1992, State Council); (4) 'Some Favourable Policies and Economic Autonomy Authorized to the Frontier Cities of Heihe and Shuifenhe' (June 1992, Heilongjiang); (5) 'Resolution of Some Issues Concerning the Extension of Open-door and Promotion of Economic Development' (20 Apr. 1991, Inner Mongolia); (6) 'Notification of Promoting Trade and Economic Cooperation with Neighbouring and Eastern European Countries' (9 Feb. 1992, Xinjiang); (7) 'Resolutions Concerning the Further Reform and Opening up to the Outside World' (14 July 1992, Tibet); (8) 'Provisional Regulations Concerning the Border Trade' (1991, Yunnan province). (Based on *Bulletins of the State Council, People's Republic of China*, various issues).

5. Data source: W. Teng (1982, pp. 169–70).

6. There have been some remarkable differences in estimating China's imports and exports due to differing statistical systems. For instance, statistics from the US Department of Commerce indicated that Sino–US trade had been in favour of the US side during the 1979–82 period, but the US started registering deficit in 1983, and the figure amounted to US$39.5 billion in 1996. Chinese statistics from the Customs of the PRC, however, suggested that China had recorded deficit in the bilateral trade between 1979 and 1992. Surplus first appeared in 1993, and rose to US$10.5 billion in 1996 – Cited from SCIO (1997, p. 21).

7. See C. Chen (1992, p. 58).

8. Data source: SSB (1996, pp. 598–9).

9. See IIE (1996, pp. 274–5).

10. On 20 June 1995, the SPC, SETC and MFTEC jointly promulgated the Interim Provisions on Guidance for Foreign Investment and the Industrial Catalogue Guiding Foreign Investment'. According to these Interim Provisions, foreign investment policy is represented via four major categories (prohibiting, limiting, permitting and encouraging).

Foreign business people are encouraged to participate in key economic construction projects and technical transformation of existing enterprises. Key project construction should favour basic industries, agriculture and industries related to agriculture.

11. For example, some foreign-funded enterprises tended to overvalue the imported equipment and parts and/or reduced the prices of the exported products (L. Xiao, 1993).
12. Data source: SSB (1996, p. 600).
13. Calculated by the author based on SSB (1991–96). The foreign capital used by ministries are excluded from the analysis.
14. In 1978, one US dollar was equivalent to RMB¥1.6. Since then, the Chinese government has depreciated the RMB several times, attempting to promote exports. RMB was devalued by 118.75 per cent from 1978 to 1986, falling down to US$1 = RMB¥3.5 and was further devalued by 38.55 per cent from 1986 to 1990. In 1993, one US dollar was equivalent to RMB¥5.76. In 1994 when the unitary and floating rate system was established, RMB was devalued to the lowest level (US$1 = RMB¥8.62). Since then, RMB has appreciated slightly.

Notes to Chapter 8

1. There have been different names for the greater China area, such as 'the Chinese circle' (Y. Wen, 1987), 'the Chinese community' (B. Zhou, 1989; and Z. Hwang, 1988, p. 924), 'the greater China community (Z. Zheng, 1988), 'China economic circle' (Y. Feng, 1992, pp. 6–9; Fei, 1993, p. 54), 'Chinese economic area' (Segal, 1994, p. 44), 'China economic zone' (J. Zhou, 1992, pp. 18–21), In addition, Dong and Xu (1992, pp. 10–13) and Wei and Frankel (1994, pp. 179–90), while among others, add Singapore, Malaysia, Indonesia, Thailand and the Philippines to this area.
2. See 'Joint Declaration of the Government of the United Kingdom of Great Britain and Northern Ireland and the Government of the People's Republic of China on the Question of Hong Kong', Beijing, 19 December 1984.
3. See 'Basic Law of the Hong Kong Special Administrative Region of the People's Republic of China', Art. 5, the Third Session of the Seventh NPC, 4 April 1990.
4. For example, the Mainland Commission has still been established by the Taiwanese government so as to officially manage its 'mainland affairs', while in mainland China, the Office for Taiwan Affairs is also authorized by the State Council to deal with the 'Taiwan affairs'.
5. More details in this regard will be discussed in Section 8.3.
6. See Wu and Liang (1990, p. 235).
7. See R. Cremer (1989, p. 21).
8. Data source: Hwang and Cheng (1994, p. 179).
9. During the early 1990s, average labour cost in Hong Kong, Macau and Taiwan was 10–20 times that in mainland China (X. Yang, 1992, p. 3).
10. A comparison of military expenditures between Taiwan and mainland China is illustrated in Table 8.4.

11. See Jiang (1995, p. 2).
12. The PRC's attitude towards the Taiwan's position in the international community may be briefly summarized by Z. Jiang (1995, p. 2) as that 'Under the principle of one China and in accordance with the charters of the relevant international organizations, Taiwan has become a member of the Asian Development Bank, the Asian-Pacific Economic Cooperation Forum and other international economic organizations in the name of 'Chinese Taipei.'
13. Wang Daohan has been President of Association for Relations across the Taiwan Strait (ARATS) in the mainland and Koo Chenfu has been Chairman of Strait Exchange Foundation (SEF) in Taiwan.
14. Cited from Z. Jiang (1995, p. 2).
15. For an orthodox presentation of the PRC case, see S. Wei (1994, pp. 1–7).
16. For example, Kao and Shong (1994) estimate that re-exports via other regions (excluding Hong Kong) were approximately US$8200 million in 1994. F. Lee (1995) notes that the total trade between Taiwan and mainland China would reach US$14,400 million in 1994, of which re-exports via Hong Kong are US$8,700 million, rating about 60 per cent of the total amount, and the remainder is 'semi-directly' conducted by the two sides, rating about 40 per cent of the total amount.
17. In 1985, Chen Guoshun, a Taiwanese businessman was sentenced in Taipei to 12 years in prison for 'rebellious' activities. The prosecutor charged Chen with illegally entering mainland China in 1984, signing a contract, and engaging in direct investment in the mainland. Chen's sentence sent a shock wave to those who had engaged or intended to conduct direct business activities (*Pai Shing Semimonthly*, 1 March 1986, p. 52).
18. Data source: SSB (1996, p. 598).
19. According to Chen, Yee and Shu (1993), many Taiwanese businessmen prefer to use their Hong Kong-based sub-companies to 'directly' fund the business activities in the mainland.
20. For instance, the mainland's export of raw coal to Taiwan has been nominally 'organized' by Japanese and South Korean companies. According to China National Coal Industry Import and Export Corporation (CNCIE), US$0.5 has been charged by Japan and South Korea for each ton of coal re-exported to Taiwan.
21. Which includes US$248.0 million for shipping service, US$437.5 million (6.95 million hours) for air service, US$24.0 million for postal service, and US$22.0 million or more for remittance service (*Cankao Xiaoxi*, 1996, p. 8).
22. Until 1995, the number of the Taiwanese funded projects in the ASEANs was 4,249, the total investment of which reached US$28.02 billion, accounting for more than 11 per cent of Taiwan's total foreign investment (Y. Li, 1996, p. 2).
23. A sample survey conducted in Taiwan in July 1994 reveals that, when the responders were asked if they were Chinese or Taiwanese, 34 per cent replied 'Taiwanese', 20 per cent answered 'Taiwanese first and then Chinese', 16 per cent said 'Chinese first and then Taiwanese',

and only 27 per cent were willing to consider themselves as 'Chinese' (*Yuan Jian Monthly*, March, 1994, p. 12).

24. Let *GNP* = gross national product, *POP* = population, *mc* = mainland China, *x* = Hong Kong, Macau or Taiwan, r_{mc} = the average annual growth rate of per capita GNP for mainland China within a certain period in the future, and $T(x)$ = time period (in years) by which the per capita GNP of mainland China will reach that of mainland China and *x* as a whole, the average economic level for a territorially enlarged China is determined mathematically by an equation as

$$\frac{GNP_{mc} + GNP_x}{POP_{mc} + POP_x} = \frac{GNP_{mc}}{POP_{mc}} (1 + r_{mc})^{T(x)}, \text{ with } \frac{GNP_x}{POP_x} >> \frac{GNP_{mc}}{POP_{mc}} \text{ and } r_{mc} > 0.$$

Using the above equation and the data in Tables 8.1 and 8.2, we can calculate $T(x)$ for a constant rate $r_{mc} = 7$ per cent: T(Hong Kong) = 2.51 years, T(Macau) = 0.03 year and T(Taiwan) = 4.58 years.

25. See C. Kan (1994, p. 173).
26. See *The Economic Research Materials* (1996, p. 62).
27. See *The Economist* (1992, p. 17).

References

(*Note*: the titles of Chinese references are listed in English translations followed by *pinyin* forms in parentheses.)

Agarwala, Ramgopal (1992) 'China: Reforming Intergovernmental Fiscal Relations', *World Bank Discussion Papers*, no. 178, Washington DC: World Bank.

Asia-Pacific Economic Times, 22 October 1996.

Asian Development Bank (1996) *Key Indicators of Developing and Asian Countries 1996*, vol. XXVII, Economics and Development Resource Center, ADB, Manila, published for the ADB by Oxford University Press.

Atkinson, A.B. (1970) 'On the Measurement of Inequality', *Journal of Economic Theory*, 2, 244–63.

Atkinson, A.B. and Bourguigon, F. (1992) 'The Comparison of Multidimensional Distributions of Economic Status', *Review of Economic Studies*, 140–53.

Baokan Wenzhai (1989) 'The Armed Disputes in China's Internal Borders' (zhongguo bianjie da xiedou), *The Digest of Newspapers and Magazines*, 13 June, 4.

Baum, Richard (1994) *Burying Mao: Chinese Politics in the Age of Deng Xiaoping*, Princeton: Princeton University Press.

Bo Yibo (1991) *A Retrospect of Some Key Decisions and Incidents of China* (ruogan zongda juece yu shijian de huigu), vol. I, Beijing: The CCPCC Literature Press.

Brown, Lesely (1993) *The New Shorter Oxford English Dictionary*, Oxford: Clarendon Press.

Cankao Xiaoxi (1996) 'Reference News-Taiwan', 16 October p. 8.

CASS (1992) *China's Yearbook for Horizontal Economy* (zhongguo hengxiang jingji nianjian), Beijing: China Social Sciences Press.

CCPCC (1984) 'Decision of the CCPCC Concerning the Reform of Economic Structure', the third Plenum of the twelfth CCPCC, Beijing, 21 October.

CCPCC Party School (ed.) (1988) *The Basic Plans for China's Economic Reform, 1979–87* (zhongguo jingji tizhi gaige guihuaji, 1979–87), Beijing: CCPCC Party School Press.

Chen, C. (1992) 'Modernization in Mainland China', *American Journal of Economics and Sociology*, 51 (1), 57–68.

Chen Gongyan (1994) *China's Regional Economic Development: A Comparative Study of the East, Central, and West Belts* (zhongguo quyu jingji fazhan: dongbu zhongbu he xibu de bijiao yanjiu), Beijing: Beijing University of Technology Press.

Chen Zhenguang (1994) 'An Analysis of the Industrial Development in the Third-front Area', in Liu, Li and Hsueh (eds.), pp. 329–42.

Chen, Long-qi, Yee Yan-liang and Shu Ru-qin (1993) 'A Study of the

Feasibility of Opening the Indirect Commercial Funds Sent to the Mainland Area' (kaifang dui dalu diqu shangye xing jianjie huikuan kexing xing zhi yanjiu), Research Project prepared to the Mainland Commission, Taipei.

Chenery, Hollis and Moises Syrquin (1975) *Patterns of Development, 1950–1970*, published for the World Bank, New York: Oxford University Press.

Cheng Hong (1990) 'A Brief Introduction to China's Natural Resources' (zhongguo zhiran zhiyuan gaishu), in CISNR (ed.), pp. 1–20.

China Daily, 17 November 1993.

China Enterprise Evaluation Centre (1990) *China's Top 500 Enterprises*, published by *Management World* magazine for the Development Research Centre of the State Council, Beijing.

China Youths, 3 January 1995.

Chinese Society for Administrative Divisions (ed.) (1991) *Studies of China's Administrative Divisions* (zhonguo xingzheng quhua yanjiu), Beijing: China Social Press, 1991.

Cihai (1988) 'State' (*zhou*), *Cihai*, Shanghai: Shanghai Cishu Press.

Commission of Economic Construction (1996) 'The Opening of the Three Direct Links of the Special Economic and Trade Zones May Save US$700 million' (kaitong jingmao tequ santong, niansheng qiyi meiyuan), Taipei, cited in *Central Daily*, 14 October.

Commission of Integrated Survey on Natural Resources (ed.) (1990) *Handbook of Natural Resources in China* (zhongguo zhiran zhiyuan shouche), Chinese Academy of Sciences, Beijing: Science Press.

Cremer, Rolf D. (1989) 'The Industrialization of Macau', in Jao, Mok and Ho (eds.), pp. 18–32.

Denberger, R.F. (ed.) (1980) *China's Development Experience in Comparative Perspective*, Cambridge: Harvard University Press.

Deng Xiaoping (1992) 'The Key Points of the Speeches in Wuchang, Shenzhen, Zhuhai, Shanghai, etc.' (zai wuchang, shenzhen, zhuhai, shanghai deng di de jianghua yiaodian), in Literature Editing Committee of CCPCC (ed.), pp. 370–83.

Denny, David L. (1991) 'Provincial Economic Differences Diminished in the Decade of Reform', in U. S. Congress Joint Economic Committee (ed.), vol. 1, pp. 186–208.

Development Research Centre of the State Council (ed.) (1994) *The Regional Coordinate Development Strategy in China* (zhonguo quyu xietiao fazhan zhanlue), Beijing: China Economy Press.

Dittmer, Lowell and Yu-shan Wu (1993) 'The Political Economy of Reform Leadership in China-Macro and Micro Informal Politics Linkages', Paper presented to the Annual Meeting of the Association of Asian Studies, Los Angeles.

Dong Fan (1992) 'Some Comments on Analyses of Interregional Income Gaps' (guanyu diqu jian shouru chaju biandong fenxi de jidian shangque yijian', *The Economic Research* (jingji yanjiu), 7, 63–4.

Dong Fureng (1982) 'Relationship between Accumulation and Consumption', in Xu and others (eds.), pp. 79–101.

Dong Suosheng and Xu Cunmao (1992) 'Some Issues Relating to the Greater China Economic Cooperation' (da zhonguo jingji xiezuo de jige wenti), in Youths Committee of CSNR (ed.), pp. 10–3.

Donnithrone, A. (1976) 'Centralization and Decentralization in China's Fiscal Management', *China Quarterly*, 66, pp. 328–54.

Du Peng (1994) *A Study of the Process of Population Aging in China* (zhongguo renkou laohua yanjiu), Beijing: The People's University of China Press.

Eatwell, John, Murray Milgate and Peter Newman (eds) (1987) *The New Palgrave: A Dictionary of Economics*, London: Macmillan.

Economic News, 11 February 1987; 21 December 1988.

Fei Wumei (1993) 'Economic Analysis of China Economic Area' (dui zhongguo jingji quan de fenxi), *Asia-Pacific Economic Review*, 2, 54–9.

Feng Lianggang (1993) 'On the "Wars" over the Purchase of Farm and Subsidiary Products', *Chinese Economic Studies*, 26, (5), 87–94.

Feng Yiquan (1992) 'The Trends of Asian–Pacific Regional Cooperation and the Formation and Development of the Chinese Economic Circle', in Youths Committee of CSNR (ed.), pp. 6–9.

Financial Times, 26 April 1993

Goodman, David S.G. (1994) 'The Politics of Regionalism: Economic Development Conflicts and Negotiation', in Goodman and Segal (eds), pp. 1–20.

Goodman, David S.G. and Gerald Segal (eds) (1994) *China Deconstructs: Politics, Trade, and Regionalism*, London and New York: Routledge.

Griffin, Keith and Zhao Renwei (eds) (1993) *The Distribution of Income in China*, New York: St. Martin's Press.

Gu Haibing (1997) 'China's Economic Marketization: An Estimate and Forecast' (zhonguo jingji shichang hua chengdu de zuixin guji yu yuce), *Management World*, 2, 52–5.

Gu Jirui (1995) 'Analyses on the Causes of Variable Income among Regions in China', Proceedings of the Fifth Annual Meeting of the Congress of Political Economists (COPE), International, pp. 45–51, Seoul, South Korea, 5–10 January .

Guo Fansheng and Wang Wei (1988) *Poverty and Development* (pinkun yu fazhan), Hangzhou: Zhejiang People's Press.

Guo Rongxing (1986) 'A System Dynamics Analysis of China's University Teachers' (woguo gaoxiao shizhi duiwu de xitong dongtai fenxi), Proceedings of the First National Meeting of System Dynamics Society of China, Shanghai.

Guo Rongxing (1991) 'A Preliminary Study of Border-Regional Economics: Theory and Practice of China' (bianjie diqu jingji xue cutan: lilun yu zhongguo shijian), PhD thesis, CUMT.

Guo Rongxing (1993) *Economic Analysis of Border-Regions: Theory and Practice of China* (zhongguo shengji bianjie diqu jingji fazhan yanjiu), Beijing: China Ocean Press.

Guo Rongxing (1995) 'The Impacts of Provincial Borders on the Economic Development of China: The N-dimensional Model of Spatial Economies' (shengji bianjie dui zhongguo jingji de yingxiang), *Xitong Gongcheng Lilun Yu Shijian* (Journal of China System Engineering Society), 15, (4), 38–43.

Guo Rongxing (1996) *Border-Regional Economics*, Heidelberg: Physica-Verlag.

Guo Shuqing and Han Wenxiu (1991) *The Distribution and Utilization of China's GNP* (zhongguo GNP de fenpei he shiyong), Beijing: The People's University of China Press.

He Baoshan, Gu Jirui, Yan Yinglong and Bao Zongshun (1991) *Studies on the Non-agricultural Development in Jiangsu's Rural Area* (jiangsu nongcun feinonghua yanjiu), Shanghai: Shanghai People's Press.

He Jianzhang, Zhu Zhongyan and Liao Jiren (1960) 'Criticizing Ma Yinchu's Reactionary "New Population Theory"' (pipan Ma Yinchu fandong de 'xin renkou lun'), *The Economic Research* (jingji janjiu), 4, 20–5.

Higgins, Beijamin (1981) 'Economic Development and Regional Disparities: A Comparative Study of Four Federations', in R. Mathews (ed.), pp. 69–70.

Hill, Hall (ed.) (1989) *Unity and Diversity: Regional Economic Development in Indonesia Since 1970*, Singapore: Oxford University Press.

Hill, Hall and Anna Weidemann (1989) 'Regional Development in Indonesia: Patterns and Issues', in H. Hill (ed.), pp. 1–7.

Hong Fuyu (1945a) 'On the New Provincial Regions' (xin shengqu lun), *Dagong pao*, 2 October.

Hong Fuyu (1945b) 'Reconstruring Provincial Regions: A Preliminary Discussion' (chonghua shengqu fang'an chuyi), *Oriental Journal*, 43, (6).

Hsueh, Tien-tung (1994a) 'A Synthesized Development Index System for China's Regions' (zhongguo diqu zhonghe fazhai zhibiao tixi), in Liu, Li and Hsueh (eds), pp. 22–56.

Hsueh, Tien-tung (1994b) 'The Regional Economic Development Pattern in China and Its International Comparison' (zhongguo diqu jingji fazhan de xingtai, jianyu guoji jian de biaojiao), in Liu, Li and Hsueh (eds), pp. 74–99.

Hsueh, Tien-tung, Li Qiang and Liu Shucheng (1993) *China's Provincial Statistics*, Boulder: Westview Press.

Hu Angang, Wang Shaoguang and Kang Xiaoguang (1995) *Regional Disparities in China* (zhonguo diqu chayi baogao), Shenyang: Liaoning People's Press.

Hu Huanyong (1991) 'The Past, Present, and Future Administrative Divisions in China' (zhongguo xingzheng qu de guoqu, xianzai he weilai), in CSAD (ed.), pp. 144–67.

Hu Huanyong and Ding Jinhong (1990) 'The Past, Present, and Future of China's Administrative Divisions' (woguo xingzhengqu de guoqu, xianzai he jianglai), *Journal of East China Normal University*, 2, 10–17.

Hu Naiwu and Yang Ruilong (eds) (1994) *Studies of the Disequilibrated Development Issues in the Chinese Economy* (zhongguo jingji feijunheng fazhan wenti yanjiu), Taiyuan: The United Press of Shanxi Universities.

Hu Xin, Shao Xin and Li Fuzheng (1988) *Chinese Economic Geography* (zhonguo jingji dili), Lixin Financial Economics Series, Shanghai: Lixin Accounting Books Press.

Hu Xuwei (1993) 'On the Typology and Organization of Economic Regions in China' (lun zhonguo jingjiqu de leixing yu zhuzhi), *ACTA Geographica Sinica*, 48 (3), 193–202.

Hu Xuwei and Yang Guanxong (eds) (1990) *China's Coastal Port Cities* (zhongguo yanhai gangkou chengshi), Beijing: Science Press.

Hu Yueping (1992) 'Guizhou Recovers its Broken Roads with the Neighboring Provinces' (Guizhou yu linsheng xiutong duantou lu), *People's Daily*, 20 September, p. 1.

Huang Weiding (1996) *The Hidden Economy in China* (2nd edn) (zhongguo de yinxing jingji), Beijing: China Commercial Press.

Hwang Qichen and Cheng Weiming (1994) *The 400 years of Macau Economy* (aomen jingji sibai nian), Macau: The Macau Foundation.

Hwang, Eui-Gak (1993) *The Korean Economies: A Comparison of North and South*, Oxford: Clarendon Press.

Hwang, Zhi-lian (1988) *The United States' 203 years: An Analysis of the History and Future for the 'American System'* (meiguo 203 nian: dui 'meiguo tixi' de lishi yu weilai xue de fenxi), Hong Kong: Zhongliu Press.

Institute of Industrial Economics (1996) *China's Industrial Development Report* (zhongguo gongye fazhan baogao), Beijing: The Economics and Management Press.

International Labor Office (1993) *Statistical Yearbook*, Washington DC.

Jao, J.C. and C.K. Leung (eds) (1986) *China's Special Economic Zones: Policies, Problems and Prospects*, Oxford: Oxford University Press.

Jao, Y.C., V. Mok and L.S. Ho (eds) (1989) *Economic Development in Chinese Societies: Models and Experiences*, Hong Kong: Hong Kong University Press.

Jian Tianlun (1996) 'The Disequilibrated Regional Economic Development and the Reform of the Fiscal System in China' (zhongguo quyu jingji bu pingheng fazhan yu shuizhi gaige), *Economic Highlights* (jingjixue xiaoxi bao), 18 October 198, p. 2.

Jian, Tianlun, Jeffrey D. Sachs and Andrew M. Warner (1996) 'Trends in Regional Inequality in China', *China Economic Review*, 7, (1), 1–22.

Jiang Zemin (1995) 'Continue to Promote the Reunification of the Motherland', *China Daily*, 2 February, 1–2.

Jilin Provincial Statistical Bureau (1990) 'Please Read the Results of An Investigation to Evaluate the Quality of Data for the Three Indices' (sanxiang zhibiao shuju zhiliang ruhe, qingkan diaocha pinggu jieguo), *China Statistics* (zhongguo tongji), 2, 27–8.

Jin Guantao and Liu Qingfang (1984) *Prosperity and Crises – On the Ultrastable Structure of the Federal System in China* (xingsheng yu weijilun zhongguo fengjian shehui de chao wending jiegou), Changsha: Hunan People's Press.

Kan, Chak-Yuen (1994) *The Emergency of the Golden Economic Triangle – Mainland China, Hong Kong and Taiwan*, Taipei: Lifework Press.

Kao, Chang and Shong En-rong (1994) 'A Positive Analysis of the Indirect Trade between the Two Sides of the Taiwan Strait via the Third Areas', *Journal of the Chunghua Institution for Economic Research*, Taipei, September.

Kee, Woo Sik, In-Taek Hyun and Kisoo Kim (eds) (1995) *APEC and A New Pacific Community: Issues and Prospects*, Seoul: The Sejong Institute.

Keidel, Albert (1995) *China's Regional Disparities*, World Bank.

Khan, A. Rahman., Keith Griffin, Carl Riskin and Zhao Renwei (1993) 'Household Income and Its Distribution in China', in Griffin and Zhao (eds), pp. 25–73.

Kim, Kyung-Hwan and Edwin S. Mills (1990) 'Urbanization and Regional Development in Korea', in J. Kwon (ed.).

Knight, John and Li Shi (1993) 'The Determinants of Educational Attainment in China', in Griffin and Zhao (eds), 285–330.

Knight, John and Li Shi (1995) 'Fiscal Decentralization, Redistribution and Reform in China', *Working paper*, no. 168, Institute of Economics and Statistics, Oxford University.

Kolm, S-C. (1976a) 'Unequal Inequalities I', *Journal of Economic Theory*, 12, 416–42.

Kolm, S-C. (1976b) 'Unequal Inequalities II', *Journal of Economic Theory*, 13, 82–111.

Kolm, S-C. (1977) 'Multidimensional Equaliterianisms', *Quarterly Journal of Economics*, 91, 1–13.

Kwon, Jene K. (ed.) (1990) *Korean Development*, New York: Green Press.

Lardy, N.R. (1975) 'Centralization and Decentralization in China's Fiscal Management', *China Quarterly*, 61, 25–60.

Lardy, N.R. (1978) *Economic Growth and Income Distribution in the People's Republic of China*, New York: Cambridge University Press.

Lardy, N.R. (1980) 'Regional Growth and Income Distribution in China', in R. Denberger (ed.).

Lee, Fei (1995) 'The Development of the Cross-Taiwan Strait Trade Relations: Present Situation, Issues, and Measures', *Taiwan Studies*, 2.

Leung, C.K. (1980) *China: Railway Patterns and National Goals*, Department of Geography, The University of Chicago, Research Paper no. 195.

Li Ning (1997) 'Pearl River Delta Heading Towards Modernization', *Beijing Review*, 40 (4), 12–13.

Li Jingwen and Fan Mingtai (1994) 'A Comparison of the Regional Structures for the Economic Development in China During Pre- and Postreform Periods' (gaige kaifang qianhou zhongguo jingji fazhan quyu jiegou de bijiao), in Liu, Li, and Hsueh (eds), pp. 57–73.

Li Shantong, Wu Zhengzhang and Wu Chong (1994) 'A Quantitative Analysis of the Inter-Regional Linkages in China' (zhongguo quji lianxi de shuliang fenxi), in State Council's Development Research Centre (ed.), pp. 139–75.

Li Xuezheng, Zhang Wenmin and Zhong Jiyin (1989) 'Set-up the Wage System Oriented at Improving Efficiency' (jianli yi tigao xiaolu wei daoxiang de gongzhi zhidu), *The Economic Research*, 2, 34–40.

Li Yanjun (1996) 'Taiwan to Enhance the "South-Oriented Policy" and Enlarge the Investment Area' (Taiwan kuoda 'nanxia zhengce' touzhi fanwei), *International Trade News*, 16 May, p. 2.

Li Zhengyi (1993) 'In-Depth Exploration of the Question of Regional Blockades', *Chinese Economic Studies*, 26 (5), pp. 23–36.

Li Zhisheng (1988) 'Influences, Disadvantages and Suggestions' (yingxiang, lieshi he jianyi), in P. Zhang (ed.), pp. 338–9.

Liang Wensen (1982) 'Balanced Development of Industry and Agriculture', in Xu *et al.* (eds), pp. 152–78.

Liang Zuo-jing (1978) 'The Political Corruption and Social Uprisings in the Late Qing Dynasty: A Quantitative Analysis' (wanqing zhi zhengzhi yu shehui shaoluan), *Journal of the Research Institute for Chinese Culture*, 9, Chinese University of Hong Kong.

Liao Jianxiang (1982) 'Size of Industrial Enterprises Operation and Choice of Technology', in Xu *et al.* (eds), pp. 130–44.

Lin Fude and Liu Jintang (1996) 'Towards the 21st Century: the Regional Disparities of China's Population' (maixiang 21 shiji: zhongguo renkou de diqu chayi), *Population Studies* (renkou yanjiu), 2, 10–14.

Lin, Cyril (1995) 'The Reform of State-owned Enterprises in China', unpublished draft, University of Oxford, Oxford.

Ling Yunzhi, Xu Feng and Chen Jiaqing (1995) 'Be Attention to the Overstatement Wind!' (jingti! fukua feng), *Economic Tribune* (jingji luntan), 7, 18–19.

Literature Editing Committee of CCPCC (ed.) (1993) *Selected Works of Deng Xiaoping* (Deng Xiaoping wenxue), Beijing: The People's Press.

Liu Baorong and Liao Jiasheng (eds) (1993) *China's Frontier Opening and the Neighbouring Countries* (zhongguo yanian kaifang yu zhoubian guojia shichang), Beijing: The Legal Press.

Liu Guoguang (1984) *A Study of China's Economic Development Strategy Issues* (zhonguo jingji fazhan zhanlue wenti yanjiu), Shanghai: Shanghai People's Press.

Liu Guoguang (1994) 'China's Regional Economic Development Strategy – An Evaluation and Prospect' (zhongguo diqu jingji fazhan zhanlue de pinggu yu zhaiwang), in Liu, Li and Hsueh (eds), pp. 1–13.

Liu Junde (1996) *China's Administrative Divisions: Theory and Practice* (zhongguo xingzheng quhua de lilun yu shijian), Shanghai: East China Normal University Press.

Liu Shucheng, Gong Yi, Li Qiang and Wu You (1994) 'The Regional Income Disparity in China: Measurement, Analysis, and Policy Suggestions' (zhongguo ge diqu shouru chayi de jishuan, fenxi yu zhengze jianyi), in Liu, Li and Hsueh (eds), pp. 142–3.

Liu Shucheng, Li Qiang and Hsueh Tien-tung (eds) (1994) *Studies on China's Regional Economic Development* (zhongguo diqu jingji yanjiu), Beijing: China Statistical Publishing House.

Liu Suinian (1982) 'Economic Planning', in Xu *et al.* (eds), pp. 28–51.

Liu Tiemin (1995) 'Changes to China's Economic System Structure' (zhongguo jingji tizhi jiegou de yanbain), *Management World*, 3, 51–6.

Liu Zaixing (1983) 'On the Construction of the Third-front Area' (lun shanxian jianshe), Department of Planning and Statistics, The People's University of China, Beijing.

Liu Zaixing (1994) 'The Overall Production Allocation and the Regional Coordinate Development' (zhongti shengchanli peizhi he quyu xietiao fazhan), in Development Research Centre of the State Council (ed.), pp. 15–63.

Liu, K.L. (1991) *100 Ancient Chinese Fables*, Beijing: China Foreign Translations Publishing House and the Commercial Press (Hong Kong) Ltd.

Lyons, Thomas (1992) 'Interprovincial Disparities in China: Output and Consumption, 1952–1957', *Economic Development and Cultural Change*, 39, 471–506.

Ma Hong and Fang Weizhong (eds) (1993) *The Economic Development in China: Present and Future* (zhongguo jingji kaifa: xianzhai yu weilai), Beijing: The Economics and Management Press.

of China (zhonghua renmin gonghe guo 1985 nian gongye pucha zhiliao), Beijing: China Statistical Publishing House.

SSB (1988b) *China Population Statistical Yearbook* (zhongguo renkou nianjian), Beijing: China Statistical Publishing House.

SSB (1989b) *China Yearbook for Price Statistics* (zhongguo jiage tongji nianjian), Beijing: China Statistical Publishing House.

SSB (1990b) *A Compilation of Historical Statistical Materials of China's Provinces, Autonomous Regions and Municipalities (1949–89)* (quanguo ge sheng, zhiziqu, zhixiashi lishi tongji zhiliao huibian 1949–1989), Beijing: China Statistical Publishing House.

SSB (1991b) *China Energy Statistical Yearbook* (zhongguo nengyuan tongji nianjian), Beijing: China Statistical Publishing House.

SSB (1991c) *Some Statistical Materials of Social Development for the Major Countries and Regions 1990* (shijie zhuyao guojia he diqu shehui fazhan bijiao tongji zhiliao 1990), Beijing: China Statistical Publishing House.

SSB (1993) *China Population Yearbook* (zhongguo renkou nianjian), Beijing: China Statistical Publishing House.

SSB (1994b) *The 1993 Abstracts of International Economic and Social Statistics* (guoji jingji he shehui tongji tiyao 1993), Beijing: China Statistical Publishing House.

SSB (1996b) *China Industrial Economic Statistical Yearbook 1995*, Beijing: China Statistical Publishing House.

SSB (1981–96) *China Statistical Yearbook*, Beijing: China Statistical Publishing House.

Standing Committee of NPC (1979) 'Messages to the Taiwanese Compatriots' (gao Taiwan tongbao shu), Beijing: National People's Congress of PRC, January.

State Council (1980a) 'Provisional Regulations Relating to the Development and Protection of Socialist Competition' (guanyu fazhan yu baohu shehui zhuyi jingzheng de zhanxing tiaoli), Beijing.

State Council (1980b) 'Provisional Regulations Concerning the Promotion of Economic Unification', Beijing.

State Council (1981) 'Contemporary Regulations Concerning the Resolutions of the Border Disputes of the Administrative Divisions of the P. R. China' (zhonghua renmin gongheguo xingzhengqu bianjie zhengyi culi tiaoli), Beijing, China.

State Council (1982) 'Notice Relating to the Prohibition of Blockades in the Sale of Industrial Products' (guanyu jinzhi gongye chanpin xiaoshou bilei de tongzhi), Beijing.

State Council (1984) 'Provisional Regulations on the Enlargement of Autonomy of State Industrial Enterprises', 10 May, Beijing.

State Council (1986) 'Regulations on Some Issues Concerning the Further Promotion of Horizontal Economic Unification', 26 March.

State Council (1988a) 'Contemporary Regulations Concerning the Resolutions of the Border Disputes of the Administrative Divisions of the P. R. China', Beijing, China, revised version.

State Council (1988b) 'A Retrospect on the Reforms of the Economic System and the Prospects on the Basic Thought of the Future Reforms' (jingji tizhi gaige de huigu yu jinhou gaige de jiben shilu), in CCPCC Party School (ed.).

State Council (1990) 'An Administrative Order to Remove all Regional Blockades to Trade', Beijing.

State Council (1992) 'Regulations on the Transformation of the Operating Mechanisms of State-owned Industrial Enterprises', Beijing, 22 July.

State Council (1993) 'Resolution Concerning the Promotion of the Development of the TVEs in the Central and Western Area', Beijing, December.

State Council Information Office (1996) 'On Sino–US Trade Balance', *Beijing Review*, 40 (14), 20–7.

State Industrial and Commercial Administration (1995) *A Compilation of Industrial and Commercial Statistics* (gongshang xingzheng guanli tongji huibian), Beijing.

State Science and Technology Commission (1988) *Guide to China's Science and Technology Policy* (zhongguo kexue jishu zhengce zhinan), Beijing: Science and Technology Compilation Press.

Statistical Division of Hong Kong Government *Re-exports by All Countries of Origin by Importing Countries by Items*, various years.

Study Group of CASS (1994) 'Theoretical Thinking and Policy Choice on Chinese Economy Towards the 21st Century' (zhongguo jingji jinru 21 shiji de lilun shikao yu zhengce xuanzhe), *Economic Research Journal* (jingji yanjiu), 8, 1–14.

Summers, R. and A. Heston (1991) 'The Penn World Table (Mark 5): An Expended Set of International Comparisons, 1950–1988', *Quarterly Journal of Economics*, 327–68.

Sun Jin (1987) *Territory, Resources, and Regional Development* (guotu, zhiyuan kaifa he quyu fazhan), Beijing: People's Education Press.

Sun Shangqing (ed.) (1991) *The Economic Structure: Theory, Application and Policy* (jingji jiegou de lilun, xingyong yu zhengce), Beijing: China Social Science Press.

Sun Ziduo (1993) 'Causes of Trade Wars over Farm Products, Their Effects, and Suggested Solutions', *Chinese Economic Studies*, 26 (5), 95–104.

Taiwanese Economic Department (1994) 'The Regulations Concerning the Permission of the Trade with the Mainland Area', July, Taipei.

Tang, Tengxiang (1982) 'The Economic Responsibility System and Accounting in China's Enterprises', *Caiwu Yu Kuaiji* (Property and Accounting) 20 January 1982, pp. 7–11.

Teng Weizao (1982) 'Socialist Modernization and the Pattern of Foreign Trade', in Xu *et al.* (eds), pp. 167–92.

The Economic Research Materials (1996) 6, p. 62.

The Economist, various issues.

Topping, Audrey R. (1995) 'Ecological Roulette: Damming the Yangtze', *Foreign Affairs*, September/October, 132–46.

Tsui, Kai-yeun (1991) 'China's Regional Inequality, 1952–1985', *Journal of Comparative Economics*, 15, 1–21.

Tsui, Kai-yuen (1993) 'Economic Reform and Interprovincial Inequalities in China' *Working paper* no. 31, Economics Department, the Chinese University of Hong Kong, Hong Kong.

Tsui, Kai-yuen (1994) '*A Multiregional Measurement of China's Inequalities*', in Liu, Li, and Hsueh (eds), pp. 180–98.

U.S. Congress Joint Economic Committee (ed.) (1991) *China's Economic Dilemmas in the 1990s: the Problems of Reforms, Modernization, and Interdependence*, vol. 1, pp. 186–208, Washington DC: the U.S. Government Printing Office.

UNDP (1994) *China Environment and Sustainable Development Resources Book: A Compendium of Donor Activities*, Beijing, China, April.

UNESCO *Statistical Yearbook*, 1986, 1989, 1992, 1995.

UNFAO *Statistical Yearbook*, various issues.

United Nations (1988) *World Population Prospect*.

United Nations (1990a) *SNA Handbook on Integrated Environmental and Economic Accounting*, Preliminary draft of Part I: 'General Concept', New York.

United Nations (1990b) *Revised System of National Accounts*, Preliminary draft, New York.

United Nations (1994) *Human Development Report 1994*, New York: Oxford University Press.

Vaclav, Smil (1992) 'China's Environment in the 1980s: Some Critical Changes', *Ambio*, 21 (6), 431–6.

Wakabayashi, Keiko (1989) *China's Population Problem*, Tokyo: University of Tokyo Press (in Japanese).

Walker, T. (1995) 'Five Nations in Pact to Develop NE Asian Region', *Financial Times* (News: Asia–Pacific), 31 May.

Wang Wenxiang (ed.) (1986) *China's Special Economic Zones and 14 Coastal Cities*, Beijing: China Zhanwang Press.

Wang Zuo and Dai Yuanchen (1958) 'A Critique on the "New Population theory"' ('xin renkou lun' pipan), *The Economic Research* (jingji yanjiu) 2, 10–14.

Wedeman, A.H. (1993) 'Editor's Introduction to Chinese Economic Studies', *Chinese Economic Studies*, 26 (5) (special issue on regional protection), 1–2.

Wei Houkai (1992) 'On the Changing Pattern of Interregional Income Gaps in China' (lun woguo quji shouru chaju de biandong geju), *The Economic Research* (jingji yanjiu), 4, 61–5.

Wei Houkai and Liu Kai (1994) 'The Analysis of Regional Differences in China and the forecast of their changing trends' (woguo diqu chayi biandong qushi fenxi ji yuce), *China Industrial Economic Research*, 3, 29–36.

Wei Shiyan (1994) 'Comrade Deng Xiaoping's Concept of "One country, two systems" and Its Practice', *Foreign Affairs Journal*, 33, September, 1–7.

Wei Wei (1994) 'The Imbalance of Regional Economic Development and Disequilibrated Growth of China' (woguo diqu jingji fazhan shiheng yu feijunheng zhengzhang), in Hu and Yang (eds), pp. 279–309.

Wei, Shang-jin and Jeffrey Frankel (1994) 'A "Greater China" Trade Block?', *China Economic Review*, 5 (2), 179–90.

Wen, Yong (1987) 'The Prospects of the Asia–Pacific Area and the Chinese Circle: An Interview with Chen Kunyao, Director of Asian Studies

Center of Hong Kong University' (yatai diqu jingji qianjing he zhongguo: fang xianggang daxue yazhou yanjiu zhongxin zhuren Chen Kunyao), *Economic Review*, 30 November.

Williamson, Jeffrey G. (1965) 'Regional Inequality and the Process of National Development: A Description of the Patterns', *Economic Development and Cultural Change*, 13 (4), 165–204.

Wolf, Thomas (1985) 'Exchange Rates, Foreign Trade Accounting and Purchasing Power Parity for Centrally Planned Economies', *World Bank Staff Working Papers*, no. 779.

Work Bank (1991) 'Mexico in Transition: Towards a New Role for the Public Sector', Report 8770-ME, Washington DC.

World Bank (1981) *China: Development of a Socialist Economy* (zhonguo: shehui zhuyi jingji de fazhan). Beijing.

World Bank (1990) *China: Revenue Mobilization and Tax Policy*, Washington DC.

World Bank (1992) *STAR – World Development Indicators 1991, Socioeconomic Time-series Access and Retrieval System*, Version 2.5, April 1992

World Bank (1993) *World Development Report*, Washington DC.

World Bank (1996) *From Plan to Market: World Bank Development Report 1996*, New York: Oxford University Press.

World Bank Atlas 1996.

World Resources Institute (1992) *World Resources 1992–93*, Oxford: Oxford University Press.

Wright, Tim (1984) *Coal Mining in China's Economy and Society 1895–1937*, Cambridge: Cambridge University Press.

Wu Chuanjun and Hou Feng (1990) *Territorial Development and Planning* (guotu kaifa ahengzi yu guihua), Nanjing: Jiangsu Educational Press.

Wu Rende and Liang Yi (1990) 'Hong Kong – The First Financial and Trade Centre in the Far East' (yuandong diyi jinrong maoyi zhongxin-xianggang), in Hu and Yang (eds), 234–44.

Xiao Lian (1993) 'China's Economic Internationalization: A Prospect', unpublished draft, Institute of American Studies, Chinese Academy of Social Sciences.

Xie Hanguang (1992) 'Industrial Development in Macau', in Youths Committee of CSNR (ed.), pp. 110–16.

Xu Dixin *et al.* (eds) (1982) *China's Search for Economic Growth: The Chinese Economy Since 1949*, Beijing: New World Press.

Yan, Zong-da (1995) 'The Cross-Taiwan Strait Financial relations: Situation, Issues, and Prospect', *The Central Bank Quarterly*, 17 (4), 54–74.

Yang Kaizhong (1989) *A Study of Regional Development in China* (zhongguo quyu fazhan yanjiu), Beijing: China Ocean Press.

Yang Kaizhong (1991) 'The Theory and Application of Regional Structure – An Application of the Regional Structure in China' (quyu jiegou lilun yu yingyong-zhongguo quyu jiegou yanjiu), in S. Sun (ed.), pp. 504–9.

Yang Kaizhong (1993) *For A Spatial Integration: China's Market Economy and Regional Development Strategy* (maixiang kongjian yiti hua: zhongguo shichang jingji yu quyu fazhan zhanlue), 'Across the Century Series', Chengdu: Sichuan People's Press.

Yang Weimin (1992a) 'An Empirical Analysis of the Changes in Inter-regional Income Inequalities' (Diqu jian shouru chaju biandong de shizheng fenxi), *The Economic Research* (jingji yanjiu), 1, 70–4.

Yang Weimin (1992b) 'Answers to Comrade Dong Fan's Comments' (dui dong Fan tongzhi shangque de dafu), *The Economic Research* (jingji yanjiu), 7, 65–6.

Yang Wuyang (1989) *The Locational Principles – An Economic Analysis of Industrial, Urban, and Regional Locations* (quweilun yuanli: chanye, chengshi he quwei de jingji fenxi), Lanzhou: Gansu People's Press.

Yang Xingxian (1992) 'Resource Exploitation and Economic Development in the Greater China Economic Circle' (da zhonguo jingji quan de ziyuan yu jingji fazhan), in Youths Committee of CSNR (ed.), pp. 1–5.

Yang Shuzhen (1990) 'The Issues of China's Economic Regions' (zhongguo jingji quyu wenti), in Yang, Liu and Gao (eds), pp. 38–43.

Yang Shuzhen, Liu Zhenya and Gao Lianqing (eds) (1990) *Studies of Chinese Economic Regionalization* (zhongguo jingji quhua yanjiu), Beijing: China Zhanwang Press.

Yang, Dali (1990) 'Patterns of China's Regional Development Strategy', *China Quarterly*, 122, 230–57.

Young, J.C. and H.H. Ho (1993) 'China Moves Against Unfair Competition', *East Asian Executive Report*, September, pp. 9–13.

Youths Committee of China Society of Natural Resources (ed.) (1992) *The Cross-Taiwan Strait: Sustainable Development of the Issues of Resources and Environment*, Beijing: China Science and Technology Press.

Zhang Li (1982) 'A Review of the Discussions on Two Production Theories' (liangzhong shengchan lilun de taolun zhongshu), *Population Studies* (renkou yanjiu), 5, 12–14.

Zhang Ping (1994) 'The Peasant Income Distribution among Rural Areas' (nongchun jian de shouru fenpei), in Zhao and Griffin (eds), pp. 296–312.

Zhang Wenhuan (1990) 'Reform Well China's Administrative Division for the Continuous Peace and Stability of the Nation' (chong guojia changzhi jiu'an chufa, gaohao xingzheng qu hua de gaige), *Journal of East China Normal University*, 2, 1–9.

Zhao Renwei (1993) 'Three Features of the Distribution of Income during the Transition to Reform', in Zhao and Griffin (eds), pp. 74–94.

Zhao Renwei and Keith Griffin (eds) (1993) *The Household Income Distribution in China* (zhongguo de jumin shouru fenpei), Beijing: China Social Science Press.

Zheng Jingping (1996) 'How Large is China's Per Capita GDP in US Dollar?' (zhongguo de renjun GDP wei duoshao meiyuan), *Economic Highlights* (jingjixue xiaoxi bao), 193, 13 September, 1.

Zheng Peiquan (1992) *A Concise Modern History for Chinese Economy* (jiangming xiandai zhongguo shi), Beijing: Beijing Normal University Press.

Zheng Zhu-yuan (1988) 'A Framework of the Greater China Community' (da zhonghua gongtong ti shichang de gouxiang), *Economic Review*, 13 June.

Zhou Fang (1994) 'Measuring the Interregional Inequalities in Terms of a

Single Index and Multiple Indices' (zhuhe zhibiao he danyi zhibiao de diqu jian bu pingdengxing chedu), in Liu, Li and Hsueh (eds), pp. 193–200.

Zhou, Ba-jun (1989) 'The Chinese Community and Southeast China Free Trade Zone' (zhongguo ren gongtongti hua dongnan zhiyou maoyi qu), *Economic Review*, 6 November.

Zhou Jian'an (1992) 'To Establish the Greater China Economic Area between Hong Kong, Macau, Taiwan and Mainland China: A Basic Framework' (zhongguo dalu yu gang ao tai goujian da zhonghua jingji quan de jiben gouxiang), in the Youths Committee of CSNR (ed.), pp. 18–21.

Zhu Weifang (1990a) 'A Brief Introduction to China's Mineral Resources' (zhongguo kuangchan zhiyuan gaishu), in CISNR (ed.), pp. 627–36.

Zhu Wuxiang (1990b) 'A Preliminary Study of Economic Development in the Border-Region of Zhejiang, Fujian, and Jiangxi Provinces' (zhe min gan shengji bianjie diqu jingji fazhan cutan), unpublished MBA thesis, School of Economics and Management, Qinghua University, Beijing.

Index